******

A JOURNEY INTO THE CATHOLIC FAITH

*****

Father Francis Maple OFM Cap.

DEDICATION AND ACKNOWLEDGMENTS

To my parents, Lawrence and Isabel Maple, to whom I owe so very much, who were my first and best gift to me from God.

I would like to thank Paul Owen for his help editing this book. I am very grateful to Paul for giving me his time and support during the last 12 months on this work.

I would also like to acknowledge and thank my former secretary, Mary Halliwell, who supported me for several years in my work which has now culminated in this book.

This book would never have seen the light of day either without the technical expertise of Victor and Matthew Moubarak who very kindly assisted me in publishing the book.

CONTENTS

4.1 The Person of Jesus Christ

5. The Church

5.1 *The Sacraments*

5.1.1 *Introduction:*

(i) Introduction to the Sacraments

(ii) Do we need the Sacraments?

5.1.2 *The Sacrament of Baptism:*

(i) Do we need Baptism?

(ii) The ceremony of Baptism

5.1.3 *The Sacrament of Confirmation:*

(i) Why Jesus gave us Confirmation

(ii) How the Holy Spirit helps us

5.1.4 *The Sacrament of Reconciliation:*

(i) The benefits of going to Confession

(ii) Being sorry for our sins

(iii) Nuts and bolts

(iv) What do I say

5.1.5 *The Eucharist:*

(i) Our greatest treasure

5.1.6 *Holy Mass:*

(i) Setting the stage

(ii) We speak to God

(iii) God speaks to us

(iv) Offering and receiving

(v) We offer our gifts to God

(vi) Offering at the Mass

(vii) Preparation for Communion

(viii) Conclusion of the Mass

5.1.7 *The Sacrament of Marriage:*

(i) God created man and woman

(ii) Not good for man to be alone

(iii) Three things that last

(iv) For better or for worse

(v) Till death do us part

(vi) Contraception

5.1.8 *The Sacrament of the Anointing Of The Sick:*

(i) Anointing Of The Sick

(ii) A good life is the best preparation for the next life

5.1.9 *Holy Orders:*

(i) The servants of Christ

(ii) The Rite of Ordination

(iii) A day in the life of a Priest

(iv) The attractions of the Priesthood

FOREWORD

This book is a complete guide to the Catholic Faith. It is simple, concise and enlightening; in this sense it is Franciscan in nature and it appeals to the heart of the reader.

If the reader is looking to find out more about the origins of the faith, an understanding of the teachings of Jesus, the life of Our Blessed Mother Mary, the importance of the Sacraments, and how to live and die in God's grace, this book covers it all.

I can see an appeal in this book for anyone curious about Christian faith, those seeking to convert to Catholicism, and also practicing Catholics and other Christians. As a Catholic myself, I have found answers in this book both to questions about aspects of the Catholic faith, and, also about my own personal relationship with God.

Father Francis Maple, has made what might otherwise have been deep theological heavy reading into a very accessible handbook for the reader. At the same time, he has also managed to convey in his writings the divine mystery and beauty of the personal relationship which ultimately we each have with God.

There are hidden gems or golden nuggets in little phrases of succinct but profound explanation about faith sprinkled throughout this entire book. It makes it a true joy to the heart to read.

It has been truly gratifying to have had the opportunity to provide editorial support, both as a wordsmith and as a friend, to Father Francis for all his tremendous work on this book.

Paul Owen LLB, LLM

30 July 2024

ABOUT THE AUTHOR

Father Francis Maple entered the Capuchin Franciscan Order on 7 September 1955 and was ordained as a priest on 30 March 1963. He became known as the "Singing Friar" after producing many recordings of hymns and songs which he sang at concerts along with his acoustic guitar. He in fact recorded a total of 42 albums and was presented with a Golden Disc award by the music industry for his "Old Rugged Cross" album.

He has donated the royalties from his music and books over the years to charitable purposes, primarily to help the poor and starving in the world. He has raised in excess of £1m for charity through those means and was awarded the MBE in 1997 by Queen Elizabeth II in recognition of that achievement.

First and foremost, Fr Francis, through his ministry as a priest has always sought to encourage people in the deepening of their faith and growing ever closer to God through their personal relationship with Him. This book is intended to help the reader to do just that. It has been produced by Fr Francis to try and reach out to as many people as possible who are either interested in Christianity, looking to take up the Catholic faith, or practicing the faith already and seeking to deepen their relationship with God.

Fr Francis has produced a number of books on aspects of the Catholic faith, prayer and homilies. Some of his books are available on Amazon, or you can contact him directly either through the Contact Form on www.fatherfrancismaple.co.uk by email to brfrancis19@gmail.com or by writing to him at Father Francis Maple OFM Cap, The Franciscan Friary,15 Cuppin Street, Chester CH1 2BN. He says Mass at St. Francis Church, Grosvenor Street, Chester CH1 2BN and often at The Benedictine Abbey, 10 Curzon Park, Chester CH4 8AB throughout the week.
Paul Owen LLB, LLM
30 July 2024

Chapter 1 - Creation

Part 1.1

IN THE BEGINNING

We've all wondered at some time, "How did our world begin? How did life on earth develop? Do we have to take literally the Bible story about creation, or can we accept the theory of evolution?

Every good story begins, "Once upon a time..". Well, once upon a time a young man named Francis of Assisi was running through the woods, full of the joy of life. Then he stopped, and looking at the beauty of nature around him, he said, "Oh God, who are you? And who am I, a miserable worm!" He acknowledged that everything he saw and experienced in the world owed its existence to God.

An atheist, of course, would say that the universe came into being through a series of random events or accidents. In his theory there would be no room for any master plan. Everything "just happened". A Christian once took his atheist friend out for a meal at a newly-opened restaurant. The food was excellent, beautifully cooked and presented, and the two friends thoroughly enjoyed the meal. As they sipped their coffee afterwards, the atheist said, "That was a superb meal, who is the chef?" "There isn't one," replied his friend. "The whole thing just happened".

Nothing comes from nothing. Everything that exists must have had a cause and a beginning. When we think about the universe in which we live, and which we are only just starting to explore, we have to admit that Someone set the whole thing in motion. That Someone we call God. No-one can define or describe God, but what we can say of Him is that He is a Spirit. This means that He is a person who does not have a physical body, as we do. He has an intellect and a will, whereby He knows all things and loves all things. As the Creator of everything He had no beginning and will have no end. He is completely self-sufficient and is perfect in every way. He is not restricted to a time or a place, and He is unchanging. He is a creative force who is able to live within everything He has created.

Exactly how God brought about creation, we do not know; if we understood that we would be as wise as He is, and we would be gods, too. The first book of the Bible, Genesis, tells us that He completed the task in six days and rested on the seventh. We may accept this as literally true, or we may regard it as a metaphor explaining various stages of development. It may be that the writer of Genesis wanted to simplify the story of creation to make it easy to remember. He also wanted to teach his readers some very important lessons. At the time he was writing, some people were worshipping various created things such as the sun. He needed to prove to them that these things were God's creations, and only their Creator was to be worshipped. In telling us that God worked for six days he wanted to teach them the dignity of work and at the same time the importance of resting when that work is done.

It could be said that this was a poetic version of creation. If we prefer a more scientific description, we may choose to believe that life on this earth evolved and diversified over millions of years and is still evolving. This was the theory which Charles Darwin put forward in 1859, and at that time, it aroused fear and doubt amongst those people who had always accepted the simple Biblical version. Perhaps the earth came into existence in an instant, a "Big Bang". It doesn't matter which version of events we choose to accept, as long as we admit that the Prime Mover was God.

If God is the power within the universe, then He must be self-sufficient. He doesn't lack or need anything. Why, then, would He want to create the sun, the planets and our earth with all its varied species of plant and animal life and, above all, mankind? I think the answer must be that He couldn't help creating, just as, in a smaller way, an artist feels impelled to paint or sculpt. God is goodness and love, and all that love had to be shared and expressed in a joyful outpouring of activity.

There is a principle that says. "Goodness spreads itself." That means that you can't stifle goodness, nor limit it. God is goodness and He just had to spread Himself. We all know how it feels when we have received some good news which fills us with happiness. We must tell our loved ones and friends. Suppose you have been waiting for years to start a family and only now discovered that you are pregnant. Or you have been working hard for an exam and just been awarded first class honours. Can you keep such news to yourself? You are bursting with happiness and so you ring all your friends and family to share your good news with them. In a similar way God could not contain His goodness. He had to display Himself in more and more forms of life. Think about the immensity of the universe. When man walked on the moon for the first time, some thought that we had conquered space. But that was just the first tiny step that man had taken in discovering and conquering space. For beyond the galaxy of stars we can see there are thousands and thousands more. Or think of a common thing like grass. Did you know that there is not just one type of grass but over nine thousand different varieties? Even the great David Attenborough would have needed a few lifetimes to discover them all. I'm sure the writer of Genesis had the right idea when he said, "God saw all He had made, and indeed it was very good" (Gen. 1:31).

Let's consider some of the good things God made. His first creatures were those invisible beings we call Angels. Like God, they are spirits, and they can know and love and think. They live with God and worship Him. If they are invisible, how do we know that they exist? As we shall see later, the Bible is full of references to Angels and the work they do in the world. The name "Angel" means "messenger", and God created them as a means of communication between Himself and mankind. What good news it is to know that each one of us has a Guardian Angel.

The truth that we have a Guardian Angel is one of the loveliest of our Catholic faith. But perhaps parents do not talk to their children enough about it. Sadly, some people even doubt their existence, but we have the evidence in scripture and tradition. In the book of Exodus the Lord says, "I myself will send an angel before you to guard you as you go and to bring you to the place I have prepared for you" (Ex. 23:20); and the Psalmist wrote, "For He will command His Angels concerning you to guard you in all your ways; they will lift you up in their hands, so that you will not strike your foot against a stone. You will tread on the lion and the cobra; you will trample the great lion and the serpent." (Ps 91:11-13).

In the time of Jesus the Jews had a firm belief in the part Angels played in their daily lives. Every nation had its Angel. Every natural force, such as the wind, thunder, lightning and rain had its Angel. Each person had an Angel who informed and guided him or her. So when Jesus spoke about children having Guardian Angels this was nothing new.

Every single human being, Christian or non-Christian, whether in grace or in sin, remains during their entire life under the care of a Guardian Angel. And it is generally believed that each human being has his or her distinct Guardian Angel not assigned to anyone else. It is the words of Our Lord that point to this conclusion, "See that you never despise any of these little ones, for I tell you that their Angels in Heaven are continually in the presence of My Father in Heaven" (Mt. 18:10)

Angels come in many guises. When Saint Peter was imprisoned in Jerusalem the jail door was suddenly opened for him and he was led to freedom. Surely, that must have been his Guardian Angel? I think we have all had similar experiences in our lives. We have all been in difficulties, unable to see a way out and having almost given up hope, when someone suddenly arrives with just the help we need. We may even have said, 'Oh, you are an Angel!' So often when we feel desperate God sends that special messenger at the right moment.

It is comforting to remember that we have our own personal ally throughout life. We can hold conversations with our Guardian Angel, asking for his help at the beginning of each day or at the start of a journey. He can guide us through our daily problems and he can give us the strength to fight temptations and keep Satan at bay. We can beg for his guidance when we need counselling over important decisions we have to make. He can help us to prepare well for Holy Communion and Confession, and of course we thank him at the end of the day for being our constant companion.

You can be sure that our Guardian Angel helps us when we come to die. He is the one who conducts our soul to the Judgement Seat of God and will console us in Purgatory. They see in their charges souls of priceless value, since they have been redeemed by the blood of Christ.

We shall never know from how many dangers our Guardian Angels have saved us, nor how much of our salvation is actually due to them. Their work is a work of love. How can we ever be able to repay them for the love that they have shown us? Loving God and our neighbour is the only reward they desire.

So let us love our Guardian Angel with sincere affection, and try to be more aware of his presence in our lives. Let us often say the well-known prayer to our Guardian Angel:

Angel of God, my Guardian dear,

To whom God's love commits me here.

Ever this day be at my side

To light, to guard, to rule and guide.

After God made the Angels He created the visible universe, which includes the earth on which we live. There may be life on other planets; we don't know. Why did God create this earth and all the natural features to be found in it? As we've seen earlier, He just couldn't help spreading Himself in an abundance of life forms, and every one of them has a unique purpose.

Everything in nature has a vocation. Every insect, bird, tree, animal or plant is called to be itself. Simply by being itself each created thing gives glory to God, because it reflects some characteristic of its maker, just as children in some way resemble their parents. St. Francis understood this very well. He said, "Everything in nature speaks to me of God". The stars would speak to him of the vastness of God. The ebb and flow of the tide would signify the power of God. A mountain would suggest the splendour and permanence of God. A sturdy oak tree would be a sign of the patience of God. A dog would represent the fidelity of God. A rose spoke to him of the beauty of God. The opening of a tiny daisy reminded him of God's gift of another new day. The examples are infinite, as the characteristics of God are infinite. Infinity and omnipotence are the very essence of God and his presence in our lives and the universe.

At the same time, God was preparing the earth for the appearance of an even more complex creature: Man. All the splendours of nature were to provide us with delight, beauty, comfort, companionship and food. All God's creation was made for Man's use and enjoyment but we must care for it.

At last, Man appeared on earth. Was he moulded out of mud, as the Genesis story tells us? Or did he evolve from a branch of the ape family, until he finally emerged as a homo sapiens? Perhaps both stories are true in their own way. The important fact is that at some point God created in the first human beings immortal souls. This is what sets Man apart from the other animals. Man, like the Angels, was made in the likeness of God, having a spiritual dimension. Angels are purely spirit. Animals are purely material, but still enjoy the life God has given them. Man, being both, bridges both worlds.

Why did God make Man? What was so special about the human species? He must have foreseen that there would be men and women who would be deliberately evil, hurt others, and bring untold misery for themselves and others. Knowing all this, He brought us into being because He loved us as His sons and daughters. He made us so we could fulfil our potential and live in perfect harmony with Him.

Of course, God didn't simply press a button to start the world turning, and then sit back and ignore it. He is still at work, every moment sustaining the life of every man, woman, animal, insect and blade of grass. If He stopped thinking of His creation all that He had made would cease to exist. In the first place it was His love that created us and it is that same love that sustains us in existence.

Traditionally, we refer to the first true human beings as Adam and Eve. God lavished His most wonderful gifts on them, because as His beloved children they were to have a close and very special relationship with Him. He gave them intelligence, so they could know Him, and a will so they could love Him. He gave them integrity which meant there was a perfect balance of the spiritual and physical within them. They had that inner peace for which we all long. Living in complete innocence, they did not even know what sin or evil were. These horrors did not exist in the perfect home God had given them. They spent their days in complete harmony with nature, and they had all the food they needed. There was no discord, no sickness and no death. But our first parents were not robots; God paid them the complement of giving them freewill. Of course, He wanted them to maintain their friendship with Him, because in that friendship lay their happiness; but He would never force them to love Him. He wanted them to choose to love Him, as that is the essence of true love.

Adam and Eve were encouraged to explore and know their environment. The only restriction God placed on them was to limit their knowledge. This was for their own good. The harmful knowledge He was shielding them from was the knowledge of evil.

When God made our world it was perfect. In His goodness He could not make something imperfect or flawed. Even the human beings He created were perfect, enjoying complete happiness. So what went wrong?

Part 1.2

THE FALL AND REDEMPTION OF MAN

The first man and woman were Adam and Eve. The Bible tells us that on the sixth day God created man and called him Adam. God wished Adam to have a companion; so He caused Adam to fall into a deep sleep, and then took from his side a rib, out of which he formed Eve. Now God could have made Eve as He made Adam, by forming her body out of the clay of the earth and breathing into it a soul, but He made Eve out of Adam's rib to show that they were to be husband and wife, and to impress upon their minds the nature and sacredness of the love and union that should exist between them.

Adam and Eve were innocent and holy when they came from the hand of God. God placed them in Paradise, a beautiful garden, and gave them supremacy over all the other creatures. Adam gave all the animals their appropriate names and they were obedient to him. Even lions, tigers, and other animals that we now fear so much, came and played about him. Our first parents, in their state of original innocence, were the happy friends of God, without sorrow or suffering of any kind.

To prove their obedience God commanded Adam and Eve not to eat of a certain fruit which grew in the garden of Paradise. He told them (Gen.2) they could eat all the fruits in the garden except the fruit of one tree, which bore the knowledge of good and evil, and if they disobeyed Him by eating the fruit of that tree, they would surely die. God might have pointed out any tree, because it was simply a test of obedience. He gave them a very simple command, telling them that if you obey, you will not die. So having the gift of freewill they could take their choice, and either keep His command and be happy, or disobey Him and be miserable.

The chief blessings intended for Adam and Eve, had they remained faithful to God, were a constant state of happiness in this life and everlasting glory in the next.

Sadly, Adam and Eve did not remain faithful to God, but broke His commandment by eating the forbidden fruit. As it is told in the Bible (Gen.3), Eve went to the forbidden tree and was standing looking at it, when the devil came in the form of a serpent and tempted her. He told her to take some of the fruit and eat it. It does not appear that she went and tasted the fruit of all the other trees, but rather went directly to the forbidden tree first. Do we not sometimes imitate Eve's conduct? As soon as we know a certain thing is forbidden, we are more strongly tempted to try it.

Satan tempted her by saying, "You will not die! God knows in fact that on the day you eat it your eyes will be opened and you will be like gods, knowing good and evil." Eve listened to him, yielded to his wicked suggestions, and sinned. Eve not only took and ate the fruit herself, but persuaded Adam to do likewise. Most sinners imitate Eve in that respect. Not satisfied with offending God themselves, they lead others into sin.

Why should the devil tempt us? God created man to be in Heaven, but the fallen angels were jealous of man, and tempted him to sin so that he too should be kept out of Heaven and might never enjoy what they lost; just as envious people do not wish others to have what they cannot have themselves.

Adam and Eve on account of their sin lost innocence and holiness, were doomed to sickness and death. They were innocent and holy because they were friends of God and in a state of grace, but by their sin they lost His grace and friendship. The first evil which resulted, then, of Adam's sin was that he lost innocence and made his body a rebel against his soul. Then he was to suffer poverty, hunger, cold, sickness, death, and every kind of ill; but the worst consequence of all was that God closed Heaven against him and his posterity. All the people in the world could never induce God to open it again; for He closed it in accordance with His promise, and man was an exile and outcast from his heavenly home.

On account of the disobedience of our first parents we all share in their sin and punishment, whereas we should have shared in their happiness if they had remained faithful to God.

Does it not seem strange that we should suffer for the sin of our first parents, when we had nothing to do with it? No. It happens every day that children suffer for the faults of their parents and we do not wonder at it. Let us suppose a man's father leaves him a large fortune, with houses, land, and money, and that he and his children are happy in the enjoyment of their inheritance. The children are sent to the best schools, have everything they desire now, and bright hopes of happiness and prosperity in the future. But their hopes are vain. The father begins to drink or gamble, and soon the great fortune is squandered. House after house is sold and pound after pound spent, until absolute poverty comes, when not only does the father suffer through his stupidity but also the children do. What God gave Adam was to be ours also, and he squandered and misused it because he had freewill, which God could not take from him without changing his nature; for it is our freewill and intelligence that make us distinct from and superior to all other animals.

So Adam by breaking the command was left in sin; and as all his children sustain the same loss, and they too are all left in sin till they are baptised.

The sin which we inherit from our first parents is called Original Sin. This sin is called original because it comes down to us from our first parents, and we are brought into the world with its guilt on our souls. This corruption of our nature and other punishments remain in us after Original Sin is forgiven.

Our nature was corrupted by the sin of our first parents, which darkened our understanding, weakened our will, and left us with a strong inclination to evil.

Our "nature was corrupted" is what I have said of the body rebelling against the soul. Our "understanding was impaired." Adam knew much more without study than the most intelligent men could learn now with constant application. He had infused knowledge. Before his fall he saw things clearly and understood them well, but after his sin everything had to be learned by the slow process of study.

Then the "will was weakened." Before he fell he could easily resist temptation, for his will was strong. After Adam's sin his will became weak and less able to resist temptation; and as we are sharers in his misfortune, we find great difficulty at times in overcoming sinful inclinations. But no matter how violent the temptation or how prolonged and fierce the struggle against it, we can always be victorious if determined not to yield; for God gives us sufficient grace to resist every temptation; and if anyone should excuse his fall by saying he could not help sinning, he would be guilty of falsehood.

"A strong inclination" to do wrong subsists, unless we are always on our guard against it. Our Lord once cautioned His Apostles (Mt.26:41) to watch and pray lest they fall into temptation. We must be constantly on our guard for we are always prone to sin and temptation.

However it remains the case that we may merit by overcoming temptations; and also that we may be kept humble by remembering our former sinful and unhappy state.

Was anyone ever preserved from Original Sin? The Blessed Virgin Mary, through the merits of her divine Son, was preserved free from the guilt of Original Sin, and this privilege is called her "Immaculate Conception". We see explicitly this favour and grace of God for the Blessed Virgin Mary in Luke 1:28.

The Blessed Virgin was to be the Mother of the Son of God. Now it would not be proper for the Mother of God to be even for one moment the servant of the devil, or under his power. If the Blessed Virgin Mary had been in Original Sin, she would have been in the service of the devil. Whatever disgraces a mother disgraces her son also; so Our Lord would never permit His dear Mother to be subject to the devil, and consequently He, through His merits, saved her from Original Sin. She is the only one of the whole human race who enjoys this great privilege, and it is called her "Immaculate Conception," that is, she was conceived (brought into existence by her mother) without having any spot or stain of sin upon her soul, and hence without Original Sin. We acknowledge this every time we say the Hail Mary, by the words "Hail Mary full of grace…"

Our Lord came into the world to crush the power which the devil had exercised over men from the fall of Adam. This He did by meriting grace for them and giving them this spiritual help to withstand the devil in all his attacks upon them. As the Blessed Mother was never under the devil's power, next to God she has the greatest strength against the devil, and she will help us to resist him if we seek her aid. The devil himself knows her power and fears her, and if he sees her coming to our assistance he will quickly flee. Never fail, then, in time of temptation to call upon our Blessed Mother; she will hear and help us and pray to God for us. This is Our Mother who we can always turn to for help and for her to petition the Father in our time of need; the importance of this great power through Our Mother to overcome the temptations and deceits of the devil cannot be overstated.

You will often hear Christians speaking of Christ as "the Redeemer". What does this mean? The word redemption implies buying back, rescuing, reclaiming. Adam and Eve damaged their relationship with God through listening to Satan and falling for his attractive proposition. As a result they and their descendants lost their place in heaven and Satan gained a hold over them which he never had before. The whole of creation was damaged.

God our Father knew it was impossible for us to free ourselves from Satan's malevolent power by our own efforts. Even if the whole human race was to get down on their knees and tell God they were truly sorry for their sins that would not be enough to bring about their redemption. We have all succumbed to Satan through Original Sin and our own personal sins, and we are incapable of restoring the original harmony of man with God. Someone had to break the grasp of Satan, someone who was human like us but one over whom Satan had never had control. That could only be God, in the person of His Son, Jesus, whose name means 'Saviour'.

There are people who think of God as a stern judge who has to be appeased, but that is not the right way to look at redemption. Let's try to look at it from God's point of view. It is the point of view of a loving Father who does not want to lose any of his children. He saw that we were helpless, like people drowning, and He had to do whatever was necessary to save us, so He sent His Son to become one of us.

Have we appreciated how much our loving Father cares about us? What would you think of me if I told you that I had a tiny little ant that I loved. One day I said, "I'm going to have a special pair of spectacles made for you so that you can enjoy all the books I love to read and the television programmes I like to watch. I'm going to have a little box made for you so that you can be on the top of the dashboard of my car and enjoy seeing the countryside with me. I'll have a tiny guitar made for you so that you can accompany me at my concerts. And lastly, I'll have a red and white scarf knitted for you so that whenever I go to see Liverpool play I'll place you on the top of my hat and you can cheer Liverpool on to victory. I know what you are all thinking: Father Francis has gone mad!. How right you would be. Here's a grown up man spending so much time and energy over a tiny insect. Now, what about God? How has He treated us? He has taken each one of us into the palm of his hand and said, "I love you so much that I am going to become a man like you. I'm going to know what it is to have a headache, to feel the cold, to be hungry, to be insulted by others, just like you. And I'm going to die for you." Have you noticed, I wanted to raise that ant up to my level, but God, who is vastly superior to us has brought Himself down to our level. He couldn't have told us more poignantly how much he loves us.

We speak of Christ as our Redeemer, our Saviour, but from what does He save us? John the Baptist put it this way, "Look, there is the lamb of God that takes away the sin of the world." (Jn. 1:29). When we speak of sin, we mean Original Sin and all our own personal faults and wrongdoings.

Christ saves us from the power and subtleties of Satan. Satan is a very powerful force of evil in the world. He knows human nature so well, not only our strengths but our weaknesses. Satan knows how weak we are, it gives him confidence to deceive us and thereby make us give allegiance to him rather than to God. We can only overcome the irresistible power of Satan by the help of God.

Because Satan is the master of deception and falsehood he is able to make people think that sin and evil are actually good and attractive. Thus there are people who will deny that they are sinners because Satan has persuaded them that they are doing no wrong. When Jesus was approached by people who acknowledged they were sinners, like Mary Magdalene, He had words of peace and compassion for them. But for those who could not see that they were doing wrong He had sharp words hoping to make them realise that they were the ones who needed His help the most.

When we think of sin in this way we can see the enormity of it. How could we ever hope to overcome it by ourselves? Only God in the person of Jesus could accomplish that. This doesn't mean that we will never sin again. Jesus has taken away our sin, but not our propensity to sin. If He did He would have taken away our freewill. So we do sin, but we are not hopelessly trapped in our wrongdoing like drug addicts who cannot kick the habit.

Jesus doesn't save us from physical death; physical death is a consequence of sin. He saves us from spiritual death. Whenever we sin mortally, we kill the life and love of God in our souls. This is the death from which Christ saves us. But to restore our spiritual life, we need to ask God for forgiveness in the Sacrament of reconciliation (which we also call confession).

Part 1.3

A SAVIOUR IS BORN

So far in our story of redemption we have seen how humankind separated themselves from God's friendship. God took the initiative to restore the relationship by calling a woman named Mary to be the mother of our Redeemer.

Mary was a very ordinary young woman, but God had given her one very special grace and quality: unlike the rest of us, she was untouched by Original Sin. Her soul, from the moment of her conception, was spotless; immaculate. This did not mean that her freewill was taken from her and she could not sin. She still had her freewill. She could choose how to behave, but whenever she was tempted to sin she always chose to do God's will. God had given her this unique blessing and her cousin Elizabeth recognised it when she greeted Mary with the words "Of all women you are the most blessed, and blessed is the fruit of your womb..." (Lk. 1:42).

What would Mary's decision be? Gabriel knew that the salvation of the whole world depended on his mission. He could hardly contain his excitement. "Rejoice," he said to her, "so highly favoured! The Lord is with you." (Lk. 1:28). Mary had never thought of herself in such glowing terms. She was surprised to be visited by the Angel. I don't think she was afraid of the Angel but the greeting disturbed her. "Mary do not be afraid..." Gabriel continued, "you have won God's favour. Listen! You are to conceive and bear a son, and you must name him Jesus. He will be great and will be called Son of the Most High. The Lord God will give him the throne of his ancestor David...and his reign will have no end." (Lk. 1:29-33).

All this was very puzzling to Mary. She was a single young woman, engaged to be married to Joseph. She could understand how her Son could be of the line of David, since both she and Joseph were descendants of David. But how could her Son be the Son of the Most High? How could she be a mother when she was a virgin? She asked Gabriel, "But how can this come about?" (Lk. 1:34) Now Gabriel told her the wonderful news for which the world was waiting: the child Mary was to bear would be both God and man. His very words were, "The Holy Spirit will come upon you and the power of the Most High will cover you with its shadow. And so the child will be holy and will be called Son of God" (Lk. 1:35). In Gabriel telling Mary how the conception of this Baby was to come about, this was the first explicit reference to the Blessed Trinity as the Father, Son and Holy Spirit, being three Persons in one Godhead. Before her time all the great holy men and women, like Abraham, Sarah, Moses, and King David believed there was only one Person in God. Mary would conceive by the power of the Holy Spirit, the Third Person of the Blessed Trinity. The Most High would cover her with its shadow, the First Person, and her Son would be the Second Person. How fitting it is that Mary should be the first person to have this intimate detail of God's family revealed to her.

Now, not only Gabriel but the whole of heaven waited for Mary's answer. She was free to choose whether or not she would accept God's invitation, but because she loved Him so much there was only one answer she could give. "I am the handmaid of the Lord. Let what you have said be done to me." (Lk. 1:38). At this very moment, God became Man. God's Son, Jesus, began to live and grow in the womb of Mary. Suppose Mary had said "no" to God; there would have been no salvation for us, God's people. Everything hinged on her co-operation. Now as mother of Jesus, she bears the title Mother of God. This tells us how central she was to God's plan and what a debt of eternal gratitude we owe to her.

Imagine how Joseph must have felt when he discovered that Mary was to have a child. What was he to do? He began to ask himself, how had this come about? He thought he knew Mary and that no other man could have played a part in this. Yet how had it happened? He was bewildered. Above all he was so distraught and unhappy. How he loved Mary. There was no one else in the whole world like her. The thought of having to lose her was like the end of the world to him. But being an honest man he could hardly claim to be the father of her child when he was not. So, he decided the best thing to do, and the least pain to Mary, was to divorce her quietly. Once again, an Angel enters the story. This must have been in answer to Joseph's prayer, in a dream the Angel told him that no man had taken part in this conception. Mary had conceived through the power of God.

Shortly before Mary was due to give birth; she and Joseph were summoned by the Roman governor to register their names in a census which was obligatory. They had to return to their town of origin, and so they both travelled to Bethlehem. It was there that Jesus was born, in the City of David, just as the prophet had foretold.

The birth of Jesus was miraculous. Before, during and after His birth, Mary remained a virgin. Ronald Knox says, "Her childbearing cost her none of that pain which childbearing costs other women and left in her no traces of its happening". We can understand how she was a virgin before and after the birth of her son, but how did she remain a virgin while Jesus was being born? Just as the rays of the sun come through a pane of glass without breaking it, so too did the Son of Mary come from her womb without in any way taking away her virginity.

Our story began with Angels, and now once again they came on to the scene. Who were the first people to learn the good news of the Redeemer's birth? Not the religious authorities, nor Herod the king. It was to shepherds, who were mere poor working people on the fringe of society, that the Angels carried their message: "Today in the town of David a Saviour has been born to you; he is Christ the Lord." (Lk. 2:11). The promise God made to our first parents was now fulfilled.

Part 1.4

CHRIST OUR MEDIATOR

We have already seen how God's own Son, Jesus, was born into the world to be our redeemer but what do we mean by that? The word redemption implies buying back, rescuing or reclaiming.

As we have also already seen, Adam and Eve damaged their relationship with God through falling for Satan's attractive proposition. As a result they and their descendants lost their place in heaven and Satan gained a hold over them which he never had before. Now, who could put that right? How could men and women free themselves from Satan's malevolent power? It was impossible for man to do this by his own efforts. Simply because we have all succumbed to Satan through original sin, and our own personal sins, we are incapable of restoring the original harmony which existed between man and God. God as our creator had to make the first move towards our redemption. As our loving Father, He did not want to lose any of His children.

In everyday terms, suppose you bought a washing machine, complete with the maker's instructions. You decide not to follow the instructions, but to do things your own way. Eventually, of course, the machine breaks down. You try taking it to pieces, but you just make matters worse. In the end you have to admit that only one person can repair the machine, and that is the maker.

In consequence, the Maker's plan was then to send His Son to become a man like us. God knew we couldn't save ourselves, we needed a mediator. It is very much like if I offended the King and was later sorry for what I had done. It would be highly unlikely that I could apologise to him personally. I would have to do this through my local MP who would then take my apology to the Prime Minister who would offer it to the King on his next visit to them. I hope the King would forgive me and eventually I would hear that I had been forgiven. I know this isn't a perfect analogy but it does illustrate that we are unable to be restored to God's friendship through our own means.

Because Jesus was divine, He could have achieved our redemption in any way He chose. But it was His Father's will that He should experience human life in every aspect, even if it meant suffering and death. That meant that His whole life and death were freely offered to His Father. As a man, it was an act of love and obedience on behalf of the human race. As God, it was a demonstration of love for sinful mankind. The effect was to buy back the spiritual life we had lost and restore us to a loving relationship with God our Father. Alleluia! Only one who was innocent could redeem the guilty.

Was Jesus' death on the cross necessary for our redemption? We know that in the Garden of Gethsemane He prayed to be allowed to avoid that painful and humiliating death. Foreseeing the horror of Calvary, He cried out to His Father, "Let this cup pass me by" (Mt. 26:39). Yet He realised it was His Father's will that he should die for the sake of mankind, so He concluded, "Not my will but yours be done" (Lk. 22:42). At the Last Supper Jesus told His friends, "This is my blood, the blood of the covenant, which is to be poured out for many for the forgiveness of sins" (Mt. 26:28). He clearly understood that His death (and subsequent resurrection) would release human souls from Satan's power.

Do we appreciate to what lengths Jesus went to in becoming man and suffering for us and being our mediator. We can never thank him enough for this and may his death never be in vain.

Part 1.5

ARE YOU SAVED?

We have seen already how Christ saved us from sin and spiritual death. Now let us see how He continues to offer us salvation through the Mass. Christ is truly present at Mass, just as He was at Calvary. That is why, for Catholics, the Mass is of paramount importance always. It is the very heart of our faith, because we recognise that we continually need salvation, and it is only through the Mass that we can obtain it; but obtain it, yes we can, my dear friends in Christ.

We say Christ takes away the sins of the world, yet we are surrounded by sin; sins such as murder, greed, idolatry and so on. How can we say that we are redeemed, that the world has been freed from all sin? Although on Calvary Jesus loosened Satan's grip on us, Satan can still tempt us and try to frustrate Christ's work of salvation. Sin has been conquered but not our own propensity to sin. We still have our freewill and can choose whether or not to accept the gift of salvation Christ offers us. We can respond to Him with love, or reject His teaching.

The Mass is our weapon against Satan, because from the Mass comes the spiritual strength of the Sacraments. It's as if Christ has opened a spiritual bank account for us. In that account we have all that we need to live rich spiritual lives. The funds are unlimited and always available. Now it's up to us to draw on them. Occasionally we hear about people who live in such poverty that they look as if they haven't got two pennies to rub together. Then, when they die, we discover they have left half a million in the bank. We think how stupid they were in not using what they had to enjoy a better quality of life. We are like them if we don't draw on the spiritual bank account that Jesus has left us. He wants us to use the account, and to co-operate with Him in His work of redemption.

How do we gain access to the funds in the account? Christ gives us all the help we need through the Sacraments of His Church. At every stage of our lives, Christ is there to befriend us, and through the Sacraments we grow closer to Him. He explained this to His Apostles in a memorable image: "I am the vine, you are the branches...cut off from Me you can do nothing" (Jn. 15:5). That's how intimately we are linked to Him, and to each other.

Redemption, then, is an ongoing process in which we cooperate with Christ. We need Christ's saving help every single day of our lives. Some people claim that we can all be saved simply by believing in Jesus. No effort would be required on our part, and it wouldn't matter how we lived our lives. This is a major falsehood (and heresy), which is not to be underestimated. Of course belief in Christ is essential, but Christ also asks us to work in partnership with Him in order to gain salvation; the significance of this must not be lost on us. In other words, Jesus holds out salvation to us, but we have to stretch out our hands to accept it. Our faith must not be passive; it must be active in our relationship with Christ.

At the other extreme, there are those who say that we can earn our eternal salvation entirely by our own efforts. These people behave as though they don't need the Church and all the help that Christ has provided. They will tell you, "I say my prayers at home. I don't need to come to Mass and have the Sacraments." This is another falsehood and major heresy; this is man thinking he knows better than his Lord. How sad it is that they don't seem to realise or even in some cases reject the means that Christ has provided for their salvation with the Sacraments given to the faithful at the Mass.

A modern falsehood is to look upon God as a loving Father who would not allow anyone to go to hell. Such a premise is flawed as it fails fundamentally to understand the nature of God. Most certainly God wants all His children to go to heaven. He is most merciful. But they forget that another attribute of God is justice and truth and we will each face his judgment and have to account before him ourselves. Our sins have to be appeased by our actions. If we deliberately turn our back on God then we send ourselves to hell for eternity.

You will sometimes meet the type of Christian who will say to you, "Are you saved?" No-one can have the presumption to say, "I am saved." Whenever we feel particularly pleased with ourselves and confident in our own strength, that's just the moment that Satan drops a banana skin in our path. Every day of our lives we are challenged to seek good and avoid evil. But thanks to God's infinite love for us, we have Jesus fighting on our side. We can rely entirely on Him, by receiving Him and calling upon Him.

Part 1.6

FROM WHAT DOES CHRIST SAVE US?

We have read already about Christ as our Redeemer, our Saviour, but from what does He save us? First of all, He saves us from sin. John the Baptist put it this way, "Look, there is the lamb of God that takes away the sin of the world" (Jn.1:29). What is this "sin" of the world? Obviously it is Original Sin, which we inherited from our first parents, though we were not responsible for it. It also means our own personal sins, for which we are responsible.

It is even more than that. It is the force of evil at work in the world which is motivated by Satan. This force was like an avalanche that submerged Jesus. Because Satan is the master of deception and falsehood he is able to make people think that sin and evil are actually good. Thus there are people who will deny that they are sinners because Satan has persuaded them that they are doing no wrong.

Jesus saves us from the consequence of our sins. The consequence of sin is separation from God, which is spiritual death. What worse punishment can there be than to live in the total absence of God's love? It was that feeling of isolation and abandonment which Jesus experienced as He hung on the Cross. He, who was sinless, accepted the consequence of sin. That was His greatest suffering, far exceeding any physical pain. It made Him cry out, "My God, my God, why have you deserted me?" (Mt. 27:46). It was from that state of utter loneliness and Godlessness that Jesus rescued us.

Jesus also saves us from death. What do we mean by this? We have to say that there are two types of death, physical and spiritual death. Physical death is a consequence of sin, and Jesus doesn't save us from this because we all die. It must therefore be spiritual death from which Christ saves us. Whenever we sin mortally, we kill the life and love of God in our souls. This is the death from which Christ saves us. But to restore our spiritual life, in other words, the love and friendship of God, Jesus needs our cooperation. Jesus died and rose from the dead, and that completed His work, but He is still saving people today, and will go on saving them until the end of time.

When Christ died on Calvary, He died for all people throughout history. What about all those good people who died before Christ's time? How were they saved? Were their sins forgiven? We can look at the classic example of David who committed adultery with Bathsheba and murdered her husband. He repented and was forgiven in view of Christ's Sacrifice on the Cross. King David and all the other good people who had died before Christ came, had to wait until Christ had died and risen before they could enter heaven.

Christ released them from their long wait and enabled them to receive their heavenly reward.

Christ's Sacrifice was perfect. Why should it be repeated? Yet it is repeated every day in the Mass. Holy Mass is a Sacrifice and it is identical with Christ's Sacrifice on Calvary although He does not die again. Why should the Church say that it is obligatory for us to attend Sunday Mass? It is because of the importance of the words Christ said to His Apostles at the Last Supper: "Do this as a memorial of Me" (Lk. 22:19). He was thinking of all those billions of people who never had the good fortune of being present at Calvary. He died once and for all. His offering was sufficient, but He wanted to bring that offering to everyone in their time on earth. He knows that if we are not present at this offering there can be no salvation for us. He says through the action of the Priest at Mass, 'Father once again I offer Myself to you for all mankind, especially those people present at this Mass'. We are given the opportunity then of offering ourselves along with Him. It's not just our physical presence that is important, it's our sharing and commitment to what Christ is doing for us at that moment. This act of offering brings life and salvation to us; Alleluia praise the Lord!. But, if we don't attend Mass we are cutting off the lifeline between Christ and ourselves. The best image I can suggest to convey this by an image, is that of an astronaut walking in space and not having a lifeline to the spaceship. He will just drift into space and be lost for eternity. We need that lifeline with Christ through the Mass.

From the Reformation onward, this sacrificial offering was rejected. Protestants would meet together for prayer, Scripture reading and the sharing of a meal, but Christ's sacrifice was missing; how can the ultimate sacrifice of giving His life on the Cross be lost on us? It can't. This is the essential difference between the Catholic Mass and a non-Catholic service and recognition of what Calvary meant for the whole of mankind.

Chapter 2 – The Ten Commandments

Part 2.1

INTRODUCTION TO THE COMMANDMENTS

A rich young man in the Gospel came to Jesus and asked Him, "Master, what good deed must I do to possess eternal life?" (Mt. 19:16) Jesus replied in terms of the Ten Commandments, "You must not kill. You must not commit adultery. You must not bring false witness. Honour your father and your mother, and: you must love your neighbour as yourself" (Mt. 19:18). From the context we can infer that he would have given the same answer to anyone. To this, the young man replied that he had kept all these Commandments, but he felt the need to do more. Jesus saw something special in him and made a second reply, "If you wish to be perfect, go and sell what you own and give the money to the poor, and you will have treasure in heaven; then come follow me" (Mt. 19:21).

The second reply is directed to particular people, but the first tells us that it is the will of Jesus that everyone should obey the Ten Commandments. The tradition of the Church has conformed closely to the example of Jesus in this matter. From the earliest centuries the Church has taught all the faithful to observe the Ten Commandments.

Where do the Ten Commandments come from?

The story of Moses and the Ten Commandments is a dramatic one, much loved by film-makers. Thunder roars, lightning flashes and a loud trumpet sounds. Then, on top of the holy mountain of Sinai, in the midst of a dense cloud of smoke, God speaks to His prophet Moses. He outlines the instructions to be given to the Israelites, who wait at the foot of the mountain, trembling with fear. It's a wonderful scene, but perhaps not to be taken too literally in all its details. Nevertheless, we believe that Moses, as a prophet, was somehow inspired to convey to God's people a moral code by which they should live their lives. To this day, the Commandments are our guide to Christian living.

It would be a mistake though to think that they began with Moses. Rather they are built on that 'natural law' which existed from the time of Creation, and which is of the very nature of God Himself. Humankind can attain considerable knowledge of the natural law through reason, but it is certainly not merely the product of human reason. It was written in the human soul by God at Creation. The natural law is not a list of what to do and what not to do, but is made up of *principles* such as a need for truth, justice etc. in human behaviour.

Why then is there need for the Ten Commandments? Is there anyone more desirable and lovely than God? Of course not, and yet God has to command His children to love Him. It doesn't seem right. What parents command their children to love them? Good parents love them and guide their children and hope they will return their love. Yet in ten areas of human living we see God commanding His children to love Him. There must be a reason why this came about. This was because sin had obscured and distorted the light of the natural law in human consciences, as St. Augustine said, "God wrote on the tablets of the Law what men did not read in their hearts". When God created our first parents they lived in perfect harmony with Him, but once they had sinned, preferring their will to God's, their perception of good was distorted and clouded. Because God loved them and did not want to lose them He gave them guidelines to help them choose what is good and not evil. These guidelines have been called Ten Commandments. If we follow them we shall get the best from life.

I have heard people say, God in giving us the Ten Commandments is a spoilsport. So many of the Commandments are couched in negative terms, "Don't do this and don't do that". Also the very idea of "commandments" is rather unpopular nowadays. The sort of obedience "do as I say because I say it" which our grandparents would have accepted has probably gone forever. On the whole, we find obedience difficult; we don't take kindly to being told what to do. There seem to be so many restrictions regulating our lives, like school rules, parents rules, laws governing how we work, how we drive, where we live. Some people would say, "Do we really need another set of rules for our private lives? Surely, we are free people who have a right to please ourselves what we do!" The common perception is that God must be some kind of spoilsport, always saying "Thou shalt not...." But in this chapter I want to demonstrate that the Ten Commandments, far from being negative, are an essential guide to living in harmony with God and with other people.

The Commandments are in fact very practical. Human beings do not live in isolation, we live in a society. That means we have to find some balance between individual rights and privileges and the good of the community as a whole. If you are a driver, you are familiar with the many rules you are expected to observe as you travel around. "No Entry". "Give Way". "No overtaking". You must stop at red traffic lights, and you must not exceed the speed limits. Did someone devise the Highway Code out of spite, just to stop us enjoying driving? Of course not. The rules are essential for our safety. Just imagine what it would be like if everyone ignored those rules and followed their own selfish desires. Vehicles would crash, people would be injured, property would be damaged and there would be total chaos on the roads.

In the same way, God's instructions are for our benefit, not His. If we look at those "negative" commandments from another angle we can see how much better life could be for all of us. If no-one ever committed murder, we and our children could walk around safely and confidently. If no-one ever committed adultery or coveted his neighbour's wife then lives would not be blighted by jealousy and revenge. If theft was unknown we would not need to make our homes into fortresses and no-one would suffer the anguish of being robbed, mugged or burgled.

But it is not only on a practical level that the commandments are important. God is concerned primarily for our spiritual wellbeing. We can only be at peace within ourselves if we are at peace with Him, and so He must be the centre of our lives. He tells us that we must first and foremost recognise Him as our one true God. Setting our hearts on worldly things or falsehood of any kind will prove unsatisfying and dangerous. Again, we can only be at peace if we have a good relationship with others. How much more contented we would feel if we were not envious of other people's possessions or talents, if we refrained from spreading gossip about our neighbours. And how blessed are those people who maintain a loving and respectful relationship with their parents.

The Gospels show how Jesus both broadened and deepened the scope of the Ten Commandments in two particular ways.

Firstly, Jesus in His wisdom has combined the Ten Commandments into two. "You must love the Lord your God with all your heart, with all your soul and with all your mind" (Mt. 22:37). This is the greatest and the first commandment. The second resembles it: "You must love your neighbour as yourself. On these two commandments hang the whole Law and the Prophets also. (Mt. 22:39-40)" Jesus here in His first commandment combines the first three of the Ten Commandments placing great emphasis on the need to love and serve God. In His second commandment He combines the remaining seven. It is interesting to note that as the Apostles grew in His love He no longer said, "Love your neighbour as yourself," but "Love one another; just as I have loved you" (Jn. 13:34). He has loved us to the point of death, and we too should be prepared to aim at loving our neighbour equally and unstintingly.

Secondly, we are aware that the Decalogue confines itself to prohibitions about external acts (admittedly including that of speech) but Jesus points to where the origin of sin in us lies, to its roots. It is in our thoughts and feelings, "You have learnt how it was said: 'You must not commit adultery'. But I say this to you: if a man looks at a woman lustfully, he has already committed adultery with her in his heart" (Mt. 5:27-28). You don't even have to touch the other person before you sin against them. Sin begins in the mind with evil desires.

Since God created us He knows the best for us, and the best way of serving Him and others is through the Commandments he has given us.

Part 2.2 (i) – The First Commandment

LOVING GOD BY FAITH

In the last chapter I began to describe how God's Commandments fit into the story of the redemption of humankind. We saw how, from the first people, they had in their souls a light of understanding, placed there by God, by which they could know what they should and should not do. We also saw how sin obscured that light of conscience. God in His mercy then gave Israel the Ten Commandments, so that people would learn how to behave towards God and each other.

Throughout history there had been prophets who were inspired to remind people about God's Commandments. At last, came the greatest teacher of all, Jesus. His intention was not to abolish the ancient laws but to teach us a new approach to them. Many rules and interpretations had developed from that which had been handed down from the prophets. Jesus needed to teach the people what is at the heart of the Commandments. When someone asked Him, "Master, which is the greatest Commandment of the Law?" (Mt. 22:36). Jesus said, "You must love the Lord your God with all your heart, with all your soul, and with all your mind. This is the greatest and the first Commandment. The second resembles it: You must love your neighbour as yourself. On these two Commandments hang the whole Law, and the Prophets also." (Mt. 22:36-40). Jesus reduced them to two simple observances: love of God and love of neighbour. Most of the original Commandments are prohibitive, but Jesus goes to the heart of the matter and teaches us a positive way of living.

The first Commandment tells us, "You shall have no gods except me. You shall not make yourself a carved image or any likeness of anything in heaven or on earth beneath or in the waters under the earth; you shall not bow down to them or serve them." (Exodus 20:3-5). This Commandment describes how we should behave towards God. Nowadays we tend to assume that paganism is a thing of the distant past. No one in this modern age would think of carving an image of an animal or bird and then worshipping it. So how could we possibly break this Commandment? Unfortunately, false gods are still with us, though they may have changed in their appearance or materials.

If we acknowledge that God is our Father and Creator, then no created thing can be more important than Him, nor held in higher esteem than Him. A false god could be defined as anything which captures our imagination and pleasure to such an extent that it impedes our relationship with God. It is good to have a sport or a hobby we enjoy, but does it take over our lives to the extent that we do not have the time or energy to pray to God at least morning and evening? Some people make a god out of money. All their efforts are directed to getting more to hoard or to spend on their home, car or holidays. Some people would rather take it easy and browse the internet rather than go to Church to worship God. We each need to search our hearts to discern what is most important to us, for as Jesus says, "For where your treasure is, there will your heart be also." (Mt. 6:21)

So, how then can we love God? The Church teaches us that we love God by means of the three virtues of Faith, Hope and Charity.

The Penny Catechism defines Faith as "a supernatural gift of God which enables us to believe without doubting whatever God has revealed". Faith is essentially a gift, but a particular kind of gift. It is not the kind of gift that we can put away in a drawer to be used at a particular time, and which will not come to any harm. It is more like some very beautiful potted plant to which we need to give constant loving care. Our faith demands constant attention.

First of all we need to recognise that faith in God cannot be merely a product of our own thought. It is our spiritual connection with the Divine and not a man maid construct. Certainly reason can help us to come to the conclusion that there is a Supreme Spirit who is the First Mover and responsible for our world, but there is far more to know about God, and this we receive through the gift of faith.

How can we nourish this gift of faith? First by taking the trouble to know it. If we are interested in needlework, we perhaps buy the latest needlework book or look online to learn new stitches and look for new fabrics. The same is true of any other interests we may have. No one has to tell us to do this. We just do it. If we love our faith, I think we will make sure that we have a few basic reference books at our side, along with the Holy Bible. The first would be what we used to call the "Penny Catechism", which is a short compendium of our faith. We would then progress and want to learn more and so get the "Catechism of the Catholic Faith". This gives us so much food for thought that it would take us years to devour all that there is to read. I appreciate that this book is not easy to read but things like the lives of the saints can help us; they modelled their lives on Jesus and they can help us to do the same. Sermons and bishop's pastoral letters and Catholic papers and periodicals can also help us.

We nourish our faith too by practising it. Going regularly not only to Sunday Mass but also during the week when it is not obligatory. This is a sign that our faith is very special to us. Regular reception of Holy Communion and the Sacrament of Reconciliation gives us a close relationship with Christ and we become aware of the Divine help we receive. Religious practices, like morning and night prayers, Bible reading, fasting and almsgiving all help to keep our faith alive. Neglect of all these things can expose us to the danger of losing our faith.

There are two other matters we should be on our guard against. The first relates to the tolerance of evil. In our society we are surrounded by acceptance of pornography, of sexual perversions, and, above all, of blasphemy and the ridicule of the Christian religion. It is all too easy to go along with these things through a desire not to be different from other people. To do so endangers our faith. The second is to have an open mindedness in matters of religion, saying that "one religion is as good as another". This is not true. If it was, then why doesn't everyone become a Catholic? So many people can't, because they cannot accept the tenets of our faith. We believe that the Catholic Church is the one authentic presentation of Christianity, and however close other religions come to what the Church teaches, they cannot be the same.

Part 2.2 (ii) – The First Commandment

LOVING GOD BY HOPE AND CHARITY

Let's consider how we love God by hope and charity. Young children have tremendous belief in their parent's ability. There is nothing they can't do. Sometimes it can be very embarrassing for parents when they realise there are so many things they can't do. They have to admit that they get comfort from the fact that their children can put this absolute trust in their capabilities. If little children can show their love for their parents in this way, even more so should we show how much we worship God by the complete trust we place in Him. We believe that He is all wise, all powerful and all loving and there is nothing He cannot achieve for our good.

Hope is the supernatural gift of God, by which we firmly trust that God will give us eternal life and all the means necessary to obtain it, if we do what He requires of us. Why does hope have to be a supernatural gift of God? It is because we are incapable of getting to Heaven by our own efforts. But we trust that God who can do all things will give us all the help we need to get to Heaven. This trust in God's love and power dispels all our doubts and uncertainties.

When we make an act of hope we are claiming that God loves us so much that it is His ardent desire to bring us safely to Heaven. We know how sinful and weak we are, but we are confident that He does forgive us all our sins. But there is one condition. God expects cooperation on our part, namely, that we do our best. It just wouldn't be fair for God to do all He can for us while we just sit back idle. In other words I am saying that if I go to hell it will be entirely my own fault, not God's, the Church or anyone else. It would be because I wanted to lead my life my way and not God's way.

If we don't do our part and still expect God to take us to Heaven we are guilty of the sin of presumption, one of the sins against hope. If a person is troubled by strong temptations and knows that he should pray more fervently and receive the Sacraments more frequently, because these are the helps God has given him and yet he neglects them, he is guilty of presumption.

There is another sin against the virtue of hope and that is the sin of despair. It is the very opposite of presumption. Where presumption expects too much of God, despair expects too little. The person who claims that his sins are so great that even God can't forgive him is guilty of despair. Wasn't this the sin of Judas? Jesus died on the Cross for the sins of all the world. He would never have said to anyone, "I am dying for the sins of everyone, but not yours!"

If there is one thing that I find most hurtful it is when someone can't trust me. How must God feel when we don't trust Him, that He is incapable of forgiving all our sins, or that we don't need Him and we can get to Heaven on our own efforts?

We honour God by our faith in Him. We honour God by our hope in Him. But most of all we worship Him by our love for Him. We must love God above everybody and everything else for His own sake. The key words are "for His own sake". True love of God, is not motivated by what God has done for us, nor by what He is going to do for us. In true charity we love God. That love is solely because He is so good and lovable in Himself. If we genuinely love God there is nothing mercenary or self-seeking in our love. It is in charity that we love Him, giving ourselves to him with unconditional love.

Loving God resides primarily in our spiritual will and not in our emotions. I can feel unemotional towards God and yet have a very strong love for God. If I always desire to do all that He wants me to do, simply because He wants it, and I want to avoid all that He does not want me to do, simply because that is what He wants, then I do love Him, regardless of what I feel.

If we truly love God then it follows we will love all those whom He loves. That means that we love every person God has created and we will love our neighbour no matter whether he is lovable or not. We must never confuse liking and loving. Liking concerns feelings, whereas loving concerns our spiritual will. Are we to love the person who really harms us, for example, the person who kills my child, who sets fire to my home and business? The answer is yes. We may detest what they have done to us, but we must never stop loving them. We must love them to the extent that we want what is best for them. This is how God loves everyone. Consider all the terrible things we do to God and yet He can't stop loving us. This is how God wants us to love. He does not expect us to like everyone. Jesus certainly loved the Pharisees, but I don't think He liked the way they lived and treated others. I have never heard people say 'I like God' but I've heard many people say, 'I love God'.

Part 2.2 (iii) – The First Commandment

THE SINS AGAINST THE FIRST COMMANDMENT

We have described our faith as a delicate plant that has to be watered and tended with care if it is going to be strong. In our daily prayers we should make an act of faith, believing in God and all that He has revealed. But an act of faith is meaningless if it is not lived out in our lives. Such a life is saying, "There is no God and if there is, I don't care."

We should avoid the company of those who pose a threat to our faith. St. Paul tells us that bad company can corrupt even the noblest of minds (1 Corinthians 15:33).

We should also be careful of the books, newspapers and online media we read that may endanger our faith. If our faith is not strong they can be a means of leading us astray.

Sacrilege is a sin against the faith. It is a lack of reverence for things connected with God. It entails mistreating sacred persons, places or things. Making a bad Confession or receiving Holy Communion in the state of mortal sin is a sacrilege. Torturing people is wrong, but to torture a priest or nun consecrated to God is a sacrilege. Committing a murder in a Church is a sacrilege. It means desecrating a holy place and the Church would have to be blessed again. I trust we would not be likely to do any of these things, but we may fail to show reverence for religious articles and holy things which we personally use. Holy Water should be kept in a clean container and in a decent place. We should handle our Bible with reverence and give it a place of honour in our home. If we have soiled scapulars, broken rosaries and holy pictures we are disposing off they should not be thrown away with the rest of our rubbish but burned. Talking unnecessarily in Church, and I stress unnecessarily, and disturbing others who are trying to say their prayers is a sacrilege.

Do you believe that if you sit at table with twelve persons you will be unlucky? When talking about your health or your business do you touch wood for luck? Do you drive extra carefully when a black cat runs across your path? If the answer is "no" to all these questions then it means that you have not succumbed to any of these popular superstitions. Your faith and your reason are in firm control of your emotions. What makes superstition a sin is that it gives credit to some created things for powers that belong only to God. Everything good comes from God, and not from lucky charms like a horse shoe. Do we believe that seven years bad luck will come to us if we break a mirror? If bad comes to us, God permits it, He certainly doesn't will it, but God can make bad things work for our good.

Reading tea leaves in a cup and telling one another's fortunes with cards, if knowing that everyone present knows that it is a game of amusement, and no one would take it seriously, is not a sin. But it is a sin against the first commandment to put our trust in fortune tellers, horoscopes, ouija boards and spiritual mediums. If God wanted us to know the future He would have told us. In fact if some of us knew our future we might never cope with the truth. It shows a lack of trust in God's love and providence for us. If we want to know how to conduct our lives in the future we should talk to God about it in prayer.

Simony is defined as the buying and selling of spiritual things. This was the sin of Simon the magician, who wanted to buy the spiritual power he saw at work in the Apostles. When you give the priest some money for saying a Mass you are giving him a donation and requesting him to remember your intention in the Mass he says. In the early days of the Church this was his main source of income. The money or the gifts the person gave the priest for saying Mass for their intentions was supposed to be enough to feed him for the day. That itself is not Simony, as you are not buying spiritual power but offering charity to the Church for your faith and intentions.

There are some who are not of our faith who claim that we sin against God when we honour our Blessed Lady and the saints. We have our statues and pictures of saints because they are God's friends and they can help us. Those very same people who accuse us of idolatry also have photographs of their loved ones. This is to recall their presence to mind. In no way would we accuse them of worshipping those dear to them. In fact when we honour Our Lady and the saints, we are honouring God who made them what they are.

The atheist is one who denies that there is a God. It is a tragic situation to be in and often we feel sorry for such a person because their position may well be a result of honest but mistaken thought. For example, you hear of people who deny God's existence when they say, "How can there be a loving God when there is so much suffering in the world?" If your faith in God is not strong you could easily find yourself saying this. Why do other people say there is no God? Sometimes it is because of the sinful lives they are leading and do not want to be answerable to God as their Judge. The easiest way to get out of this situation is to eliminate the Judge. He doesn't exist! It is to these people that the words of the psalms apply, "The fool has said in his heart there is no God above" (Ps.13:1). So called 'believers' themselves can play some part in the growth of atheism. If the lives of 'believers' are cold and apparently devoid of the love of God and neighbour, not necessarily immoral, then they are bad advertisements for Christianity and do nothing to combat atheism in others.

The agnostic, unlike the atheist, refrains from denying God's existence. He either maintains that God exists but is incapable of revealing Himself, or he makes no judgements whether God exists or not. Agnosticism can sometimes include a search for truth, but it can equally be an unwillingness to think in any depth about religion or morality.

Having said all this we now see the importance of the daily making of an act of faith in God and all that He has revealed to us. In faith, hope and charity we must live, to then be gathered unto God when we die.

Part 2.3 (i) – The Second Commandment

THOU SHALL NOT TAKE THE NAME OF THE LORD THY GOD IN VAIN

A name stands for a person. A name is very intimate to a person. For example, if you ask a person his name in conversation, and he gives it to you, a more intimate bond has been established between the two of you. In revealing his name he has given you something of himself. Also, sometimes when someone unexpectedly remembers our name, it surprises, pleases and can even make us feel special.

We all like our personal name to be treated with respect, so it is easy to see that God's name should also be used carefully. The second commandment encourages us to show our love and respect for God by the correct use of His name.

When Moses asked God to reveal His identity he was simply told, "I Am who I Am" (Ex. 3:14). In fact, the Jewish people never spoke or wrote the name "God" because they considered it to be too holy to be used. Do we have that degree of reverence today?

In Psalm 8 we read, "How great is your name, O Lord, our God, through all the earth" That tells me how wonderful God's creation is and that the glory of creation praises His name. The sun, the planets, the earthly seasons all obey His laws and in this way give Him honour and praise. We human beings are also called to love and respect the Creator's name. Jesus teaches us how to do this in the prayer to our heavenly Father with the words "hallowed be Thy name". His very name is a prayer. St. Francis, for example, used the name of God as a prayer. One night he kept repeating the name of God and it told him that he had all he needed, so he wanted for nothing. His prayer was "My God and my all".

The use of a name can be a sign of friendship and intimacy. When we meet a stranger for the first time we don't know his name, but once we have exchanged names we have taken a step towards making friends. Our personal names are not only important to ourselves but also to God. That may seem strange, when we think of all the thousands of Michaels and Annes and Peters in the world, but when God wanted us to know how unique, how special each one of us is, He told His prophet Isaiah to express it in these words: "I have called you by your name" (Isa. 43:1).

When we think well of God, or speak well of Him, we keep this commandment. When we don't do this, we blaspheme. Some people blame God for disasters like famine or the death of innocent children. They think he ought to intervene and stop such events. These disasters are usually of human origin and the blame lies with dictators or terrorists. To accuse God is to abuse His name.

God can never do or support any evil. People who commit acts of violence and terror against others, while claiming that they are "doing God's will", are certainly breaking the second commandment. It is a wicked misuse of God's name.

There is another misuse of God's name which is so common and so casual that it almost goes unnoticed. I am referring to the use of God's name, or Jesus' name, as an exclamation or swear word. I recently turned on the television and heard a so-called comedian say "Christ" as an expletive three times in the space of a few seconds. If we use the Lord's name in this way we show a lack of reverence. We also give a bad example to non-Catholics and others, who will think that God means very little to us. This habit seems to be widespread, but it can certainly be overcome.

Sadly this commandment has no place in the lives of many people. They even go so far as to abbreviate Oh My God as "OMG". Have you ever thought about how French people use an expression "Mon Dieu", which means "My God", commonly which is a misuse of God's name.

Whenever we hear in conversation or in the media the Lord's name used irreverently, we could make immediate reparation by saying sorry to God on their behalf.

Of course, there is a difference between swearing and cursing. Swearing is the use of "bad" language, whether it is blasphemous or not. A curse is an attempt to call down evil and cause pain to someone. It would be blasphemous to ask God to do harm to one of His creatures. The other meaning of the word swearing is to take an oath in a court of law court. If we swear in God's name to give true evidence then we must do so. To tell a deliberate lie on oath would be perjury; it would show a contempt for the law, the truth, and God Himself.

Occasionally, some people feel inspired to take a vow, such as promising to give up drinking alcohol for a certain period of time. They believe that by making a formal vow before God they will be able to overcome their particular problem. I usually advise against making a vow, because if the person finds himself unable to keep it he will feel an even greater sense of failure, having broken his solemn word to God. A sincere desire to do your best, and a prayer for God's help day by day, is likely to be far more effective. Jesus says, "Do not swear at all, either by heaven, since that is God's throne; or by the earth...All you need to say is Yes if you mean yes, No if you mean no." (Mt. 5:36). In other words, an honest person's word is sufficient guarantee of his good intentions.

It's never too soon to teach children to have reverence for God. St. Paul says, All beings in the heavens, on earth and in the underworld, should bend the knee at the name of Jesus"

(Phil. 2:10). Do you teach your children to genuflect when they enter and leave their place in Church? Another good practice to show our love and reverence for the Holy Names of God and Jesus, is to bow our head. Do you encourage them to love the name of Jesus and His Holy Mother? With the help of their parents they will grow up to love God's name and delight in keeping this second commandment.

The Church seeing the importance of God's name begins all her prayers "In the name of the Father, and of the Son, and of the Holy Spirit". When we say this it is equivalent to saying "In the name of I AM." We are praying to the one God in whom there are three Persons, Father, Son and Holy Spirit. Notice they are given just one name, in the singular because there is only one God. The Church concludes all her prayers in the name of Jesus, "Through Christ Our Lord." Following the Church's example we should begin and end our day in this way.

In conclusion, let us make the name of Jesus a prayer. It's very sound is sweetness; we take him into our hearts and love him.

Part 2.4 (i) – The Third Commandment

REMEMBER THAT THOU KEEP HOLY THE SABBATH DAY

When we read the Genesis account of Creation, we find that God "blessed the seventh day and made it holy, because on that day He rested after all His work of creating." (Gen. 2:3) In the midst of all His activity God pauses to take stock of what He has done, takes a break, and prepares for the next task. This is perhaps a poetic description, but Jews and Christians have always believed that God intended one day of the week to be set apart as different from all the others. We Christians keep the sabbath on Sunday, in commemoration of Jesus' resurrection. Whether it is observed on Saturday or Sunday, it is a *sabbath* day (from the Hebrew "shabbath" meaning rest) and it is *holy* (meaning consecrated for a purpose).

The need for a holy day of rest was considered so important that it was enshrined in the Ten Commandments as a reminder to us. "Remember," we are told, "the sabbath day and keep it holy" (Exodus 20:8). Why is it so necessary? Is it, as some people suspect, a rule invented by the Church to keep us all in line? Jesus tells us that the "sabbath was made for man" (Mk. 2:27), demonstrating that the day of rest is actually God's gift to us. God wants us to set aside one day of the week in which we can rest from physical and mental work, relax and regain our strength. It is an opportunity to renew our spiritual strength, too, by spending some time in God's company. We have time for prayer and reflection, away from the distractions of our daily routine.

We need to make an effort to break that daily routine. This means that as far as possible we avoid working, shopping, or other day-to-day activities. People lead busy lives nowadays, but with careful organisation they can complete their chores before Sunday arrives. This "clears the decks", so to speak, so that we can make the best use of our leisure time. The Jews of Jesus' time had developed a complicated system of rules regarding sabbath observation. It had reached the ridiculous stage where picking ears of corn or helping a person in need would be regarded as "breaking the sabbath". Jesus, of course, favoured a common-sense approach. He did whatever was necessary, and still found ample time for God.

When trying to plan our holy sabbath we may find other distractions, too. Sunday is often the only day of the week when we have time for sport, hobbies, or visiting family and friends. It is good for us to do these things, and God wants us to enjoy them. He certainly doesn't want Sunday to be a gloomy day of self-denial! But we are losing the benefits of our sabbath if we fail to fit in some time for God as well. 'Don't forget me', He says; *"remember* the sabbath day and keep it holy" (Ex.20:8).

How do we keep our sabbath day holy? The first and best opportunity we have is to go to Mass. As part of a Christian community we share in the offering of Christ's sacrifice. We thank God for all the blessings of the previous week, we pray for each other and for the help we are going to need in the coming week. All this is so important to the spiritual life of each one of us that it is difficult to imagine any Catholic deliberately neglecting Sunday Mass. Yet there are many people who regard themselves as practising Catholics but only turn up one Sunday a month. Sadly, they are weakening their relationship with God and depriving themselves of the many blessings He wants to give them.

I've heard all sorts of excuses for non-attendance at Mass, ranging from "too busy" to "too tired", or, worse still, "I don't think I need to go". I always wonder whether these excuses represent a lack of organisation or a lack of appreciation of what God is offering. I'm sure that if people really understood the Mass they would be longing to go every Sunday. I would even add that we would not be content with just coming on Sunday, but as many times as we can during the week.

If Mass is an opportunity for holiness, then we need to have the right disposition to it. Do we love God in our hearts and really want to spend an hour with him? Or are we in Church merely from habit, present in body but not in mind and spirit? Our behaviour and dress in Church say a lot about our attitude to our faith. At one time, people would dress up in their "Sunday best", although there was quite possibly an element of vanity in that! Nowadays we are more relaxed and casual about the clothes we wear, but it seems to me to be inappropriate to turn up for Mass in scruffy jeans or skimpy tops and skirts. There are plenty of other opportunities to wear the latest casual fashions, but let's always reflect on showing respect for God and dress deferentially in his house.

Having made time for Mass, is there anything else we can do to keep our Sunday special? As well as enjoying reading a Sunday newspaper, consider picking up a Catholic paper, magazine or online Catholic media or apps. We can learn a lot from good Catholic publications and media online or in apps which can often strengthen our faith as well.

Finally, there are often extra opportunities for devotion on Sundays, for example Benediction, the Rosary during May and October, or Stations of the Cross during Lent. Yes, it requires a little extra effort, but it also means extra blessings from God. During the reformation, Catholics risked their lives and property to practise their faith. How lucky we are to have the freedom to keep our sabbath holy!

Part 2.5 (i) – The Fourth Commandment

HONOUR YOUR FATHER AND YOUR MOTHER

The fourth commandment exhorts us to honour our parents. Perhaps there is a similarity between our attitude to our earthly parents and our attitude to God, our Father in Heaven. Those of us who have been fortunate enough to grow up in happy homes may find it strange to be "commanded" to honour our parents; but sadly family life is not always completely harmonious. Let's look at what this commandment entails.

By honouring and respecting our parents we show our love for them. This loving relationship lasts for as long as they live, and beyond. When we are children, we depend entirely on our parents for food, clothes, a home, education and entertainment. In the same way we depend entirely on God for our spiritual wellbeing. Good parents, like our heavenly Father, have our best interests at heart, and so we trust them and try to obey their wishes. If we hurt or offend them, we need to restore our friendship with them as soon as possible.

As children become teenagers they grow in confidence and independence. Often they begin to challenge their parents' opinions and values. This is normal, but they need to maintain tolerance and respect for other people's points of view. It is sinful for youngsters to subject their parents to rudeness, contempt and defiance; as per the commandment: "Honour your father and your mother so that you may have a long life" (Ex. 20:12).

In adult life we often grow closer to our parents. We come to appreciate all they have done and sacrificed for us, and if we become mothers or fathers ourselves, we begin to realise what a challenging and rewarding vocation parenthood is. The Book of Ecclesiasticus tells us, "Whoever respects his father will be happy with children of his own." (Ecclus. 3:5). If we are on good terms with our parents we have laid the foundations for a good relationship with our children; and by our example our children will learn to love and respect us.

Even when we have homes and careers of our own we can show our parents that they are still an indispensable part of our lives. We honour them when we ask their advice, when we involve them in family activities, when we remember to call or phone, just to keep in touch. No matter how mature we are, our mothers still worry about us. "He who sets his mother at ease is showing obedience to the Lord" (Ecclus. 3:6) so it pleases God when we take the trouble to give mum comfort and reassurance.

When our parents become elderly and infirm, we enter into a new phase in our relationship. It's almost a reversal of roles, as the parent gradually grows more dependent on the child. This can be a very testing time for all concerned. On the one hand, the parent may resent the loss of independence and consequently seek to regain some control by being obstinate and demanding. On the other hand, the son or daughter who is trying to care for them may grow impatient and frustrated. It can be hard to "honour" a father or mother who is being downright difficult! But I think it helps if you remind yourself of all the good times, the happy memories, all the wonderful blessings your parents gave you in earlier life. Always pray for an increase in patience.

It is so sad to see families where the elderly parents are neglected, or sent to a "home" where they are never visited and almost forgotten by the children they love. We honour them by caring for their physical welfare and also by giving them some of our time. A day passes quickly for someone busy at work, but how it drags when you are housebound and lonely! We have a responsibility to our parents, and once again the author of Ecclesiasticus puts it into beautiful words: "Support your father in his old age, do not grieve him during his life. Even if his mind should fail, show him sympathy...for kindness to a father shall not be forgotten but will serve as reparation for your sins." (Ecclus. 3:12).

Parents deserve honour and respect, but they also have to earn it by the care, effort and example they give to their children. If the parents set good standards of behaviour, respect their children as individuals and give them love and attention, the children will we hope give them the honour due to them. But suppose you had a mother who was neglectful, a father who was too busy working or enjoying himself to spend time with his children? What if you had parents who deserted you or did you some harm? Can you honour them? Yes, we must always love, respect and honour our parents simply because they gave us life. God says, "Does a woman forget her baby...of her womb? Yet...I will never forget you." (Isa. 49:15). By this He is indicating that since He can never forsake us surely we should never forsake our mothers? Again His Son said, "Bless those who curse you, and pray for those who treat you badly" (Lk. 6:28). If we should treat our enemies in this way surely God would expect more from us when it comes to the way we treat unworthy parents, simply because of the bond between us. Should our parents disown us we must never shut the door on them for they may need us one day.

When our parents have departed this life we can continue to honour them by praying for the repose of their souls and having an anniversary Mass said for them.

I'd like to conclude with a delightful story which my father told me when I was a boy. There was once a king who had two sons. He said to them, I have the choice of choosing one of you to be my successor, I love you both so I have decided that whoever of you can go around the world the quickest will be my successor. Immediately the elder son said "goodbye dad, I'm going to fly round the world in my jet". The younger son just sat there, thought for a while and then walked round his father's throne twice and sat down. "Son when are you going to start going round the world" his father said. He said "Dad I've just been round the world twice. You are my world".

Part 2.6 (i) – The Fifth Commandment

THOU SHALL NOT KILL

We are making a start on the "prohibitive" Commandments, the ones which say "You shall *not*....". The first is the most serious and in many ways the most complicated: "You shall not kill" (Ex. 20:13). The message is simple enough; it is wrong to take the life of another human being. But modern technology and medical science raise many difficult issues which the Church is currently debating. For example, when is it permissible to engage in warfare? What action should doctors take when faced with a brain-damaged patient, or a severely handicapped baby? Should childless couples use in vitro fertilisation? These are questions for the moral theologians to consider, under the guidance of the Pope, but there are general guidelines on these matters.

On the subject of war, the Church tells us that we must do all in our power to avoid it. This would include the manufacture and sale of weapons. However, if a country is genuinely threatened, and all attempts at a peaceful resolution have failed, that country would be justified in defending itself.

The field of medical ethics is wide and complex, but I would just like to mention one or two situations which people often ask about. Childless couples sometimes wonder whether it is permissible to use IVF (in vitro fertilisation) to help them conceive. IVF is the fertilisation of an ovum outside the body, in a test tube. The sperm is produced through masturbation and the fertilised egg is implanted in the womb. The Church teaches that conception ought to take place through the marriage act of love and not in an artificial way. The second reason why the Church forbids IVF treatment is that it inevitably leads to loss of life. Large numbers of embryos are produced and the "spare" or weak ones are destroyed.

At the other extreme, there are those who do not want to have any more children and therefore consider sterilisation. The Church has always forbidden sterilisation for it regards it as the mutilation of one's body. Fertility is a gift of God and can only be controlled through abstinence.

Stem cell research is making huge advances at present, but what should the Catholic attitude be? It is wrong to take stem cells from an embryo because that would necessitate the death of the embryo, but it would be acceptable to use stem cells obtained in different circumstances. For example, in a newly-discovered process a paralysed woman had tissue taken from her nose and packed into her spine. She has now regained some movement and may one day walk again. This type of stem cell procedure could be very beneficial for a variety of conditions and does not involve the destruction of a life.

There have recently been debates about the treatment which should be given to premature babies, to the handicapped or the terminally ill. Each case would have to be considered in its own right, but in broad terms the Church suggests that it is not compulsory to administer "extraordinary" treatment to a patient. Of course, nourishment and fluids are necessities and do not fall into the category of "extraordinary".

Pope John Paul II spoke about a "culture of death" which seems to pervade modern society. He meant that there is in general a lack of respect for life and a disregard for Christian teaching in the defence of the vulnerable. All life is sacred, having been created by God. We therefore have a responsibility to take care of all living things in our environment. This would include the protection of forests from greedy exploitation; taking action to prevent the pollution of our air and water; a fair distribution of food throughout the world; defending animals from ill-treatment and scientific abuse.

We can be guilty of breaking this Commandment either directly or indirectly. Direct killing involves murder in all its forms, whether it is a violent act on an individual, the destruction of the unborn (abortion) or the elimination of the sick or elderly (euthanasia). Today many people think that euthanasia is a relief from people suffering serious illness, for example cancer, motor neuron disease etc, and that it is an act of mercy. We can appreciate how much they are suffering and that we try and alleviate their pain with the help of medications. But, they cannot see how a loving God would ever allow someone to suffer so acutely. They forget however the basic Christian principle that God alone has supreme authority over life; suffering is a part of life and should be accepted from the hand of God. Some saints go so far as to say that suffering is a gift from God to help us grow in this love and that it can be used for good, as in the case of our Lord Jesus Christ who suffered for the salvation of the world. Life and death are not our choice but God's.

The use of capital punishment has been abolished in many (but not all) countries. It is not morally justifiable to take a life as a punishment for murder. Even murderers must be allowed an opportunity to repent in God's good time.

We break the Commandment indirectly when our actions endanger life. This can result from selfishness or carelessness. A person who misuses drugs or alcohol will put their own health and even life at risk. Under the influence of drugs or drink they may cause harm to others as well, through loss of control. Again, we may become very angry with someone, but if we make no effort to control that anger it could flare up into violence.

Those of us who drive should be aware of our responsibility towards the lives and safety of others. Anyone who drives in a reckless and selfish manner is threatening human life. Jesus told His disciples that even angry thoughts and feelings, when uncontrolled, may be dangerous. This is a condition we now call "road rage".

We have no right to destroy a life, because it is God's gift. He alone may take back the gift, at a time of His choosing. There are, sadly, some people who find the stresses of life too much to bear; they may even be tempted to take their own lives. We must encourage each other to believe that life is worth living, no matter what trials may come. It is worth living because God, our loving Father, gives us our life and He has a purpose for us, even if we cannot see what that purpose is. To put it another way: for each of us, our life is a gift from God, it's precious to us and also to God as he loves every single one of us.

Part 2.6 (ii) – The Fifth Commandment

ABORTION

As we have seen, the Commandments forbid us to take life, because it is a gift from God. What about abortion, the destruction of a foetus? I would like to consider this form of termination of life, simply because it has become so common that it is no longer shocking. Some people would say abortion is not the taking of life but merely the prevention of birth. We Catholics, however, believe that a human being exists in the womb from the moment of his or her conception and therefore any deliberate intervention which results in the death of that human being is murder.

In this country, legal abortion is now practised on a huge scale. Literally thousands of lives are lost every year. Surely this is a situation with which no-one can be happy, neither the women who make the agonising decision nor the medical staff who have to carry out the grisly procedure. If everyone agrees that abortion is deplorable, what can be done about it? First we have to ask the question, "Why are there abortions?"

Some extreme pro-lifers would accuse people of being cruel, selfish, heartless and unnatural. This, I think, is not right. The vast majority of women who undergo abortions are desperate, frightened and lonely, and usually ill-advised. Some are rejected by their family, many are abandoned or abused. Some cannot face the anguish of adoption. Often there is financial hardship and tremendous pressure. Vulnerable and lacking the necessary support, they take the heart breaking decision to destroy their unborn child because this is the "remedy" offered to them and they are under pressure to believe they have no other option.

Today sex between young people, including teenagers, and sex generally outside of marriage has become a norm. This is one cause of abortions arising, due to unwanted pregnancies. If we look at this in the context of family life as Catholics we should recognise that sex is an expression of love; that love may result in conception; that new life comes from God. Sexual intercourse should therefore be confined to taking place within marriage, where there is nurturing of new life within the family. For a couple, giving of themselves to each other is a sacred thing of not a mere physical act, but one of union which may be blessed with the precious gift of a new life. That new life is to be protected; thou shall not kill, and who would then want to even consider abortion.

Many people will say that we cannot turn back the clock, society has changed so much. But it is not too late for Christian families to think about how they bring up their own children to understand love and what sex really is about. Only in this way can we begin to address the misuse of sex and the tragedy of abortion.

Part 2.7 (i) – The Sixth Commandment

THOU SHALL NOT COMMIT ADULTERY

In this chapter we are considering one of the major causes of marriage breakdown; adultery.

What exactly is adultery? It is a sexual relationship between a married person and a person who is not his or her marriage partner. That person may be single, or married to someone else. We know instinctively that it is wrong because of the pain and distress it causes. To commit adultery is to break the vows made before God at your wedding; vows which promised lifelong fidelity. It is to give someone else the privilege which is due only to your spouse. No wonder the cheated wife or husband feels angry, hurt, betrayed and humiliated. Sometimes there are children involved too, which makes matters even more complicated and tragic.

Such a betrayal strikes at the very roots of the marriage and does great damage. Is there any remedy? Jesus taught His disciples that marriage is for life. He also laid great emphasis on forgiveness. This is an enormous test of Christian love and faith, and it would be wrong to suggest that it is an easy decision. But I have known couples who, with help and counselling, have come through the crisis and rebuilt their relationship. It requires sincere remorse from the adulterous partner, and great generosity from the spouse. Sometimes the couple will declare a truce rather than cause their children the pain of a divorce.

In other cases the injured party feels that the damage is beyond repair. They can no longer trust or respect their erring partner and find it intolerable to continue with the marriage. Does the Church's teaching force them to stay together? No; they are allowed to separate and live apart. Before choosing this option, however, all the implications should be considered. If you separate from your wife or husband you are not divorced; you are still married, for as long as your partner lives. You must be prepared to live, in effect, a "single" life, because there can be no re-marriage or sexual relationship with a new partner. Marrying or living with a new partner would be adultery.

Jesus tried to explain this Commandment to His disciples and some of them were dismayed. They thought that marriage on those terms must be a very risky business! Of course, marriage *is* a risk. It is a journey into the unknown which a couple embark on together, trusting in each other and in God's guidance. As we have seen earlier, the risks can be minimised by preparation and courtship. It is vitally important to know each other's weaknesses (and be able to accept them) before making such an important commitment.

I am often surprised that Catholics fail to understand the meaning of this Commandment. When a marriage has broken down and one of the spouses meets someone else I have heard many Catholics say, "Isn't it wonderful that so-and-so has a new man/woman in her/his life! They deserves to be happy." How can that person be happy when they are committing adultery, breaking God's law? I sometimes wonder whether the Church is failing lay people by not stressing this Commandment sufficiently.

Re-marriage, in the adulterous sense, has become so prevalent in society generally that it is now widely considered to be acceptable. No wonder Catholics sometimes feel quite isolated and out of step when trying to defend the Church's teaching. If we try to find reasons for the increase in adultery we might come up with such factors as lack of commitment, self-indulgence and lack of control. These can lead to problems even before marriage.

Marriage is a union which both parties must work at it every day of their married lives so their love for each other is refreshed and never goes stale. Always putting the other one first is a sure way of making their love grow day by day. The greatest support for them is prayer, and better still praying together. Growing in love for each other every day will make the couple inseparable and most certainly protect the union of their marriage together.

Part 2.7 (ii) – The Sixth Commandment

MISUSING GOD'S GIFT OF OUR BODY

I have often remarked that Confession is the most unpopular Sacrament, but with a very heavy heart I'm beginning to wonder whether Matrimony now unfortunately holds that title! I seem to be conducting fewer weddings nowadays because more and more couples are simply living together. Most of those who do come to arrange a wedding have already been sharing a home for several years. They have usually had a Christian upbringing and education, yet they fail to see anything wrong in that. In a society which accepts pre-marital sex as the norm, it is difficult to promote Christian values and to live by them. Perhaps our consciences are becoming formed more by the standards we observe around us and less by the guidance God gives through His Church and scripture.

Those who are living together but do intend to get married have told me that in their hearts and minds they were married to each other the moment they had decided to share the same bed. They come to the Church for their "marriage" to be confirmed. This is misunderstanding the sacredness of marriage. Co-habitation does not have equal validity with marriage because it is not how God intended couples to live. If couples wish to be together, the Church provides guidance with marriage preparation, and when they are then ready to marry they make a covenant of vows to each other before God. Without the Sacrament there is no marriage, so co-habiting couples have none of the spiritual benefits which God confers through that Sacrament.

It is wrong to misuse any of the privileges of marriage, and that includes the habit of masturbation. Again the world would say it is not a sin. It is a natural tension that should be released, but this use of sex is a perversion of the union of marriage. It is a selfish act performed by one person rather than a loving act between two people. People in Confession who have difficulty in this matter ask me how to break this habit. I tell them that they are using their body as a plaything and in God's eyes they have not grown up. So when they are tempted to sin in this way to say to themselves, "Grow up". Their own pride plus their use of Confession and Holy Communion can slowly make it a sin of the past.

Sexual activity outside marriage is nothing new. St. Paul called it fornication and he saw plenty of it going on in the pagan society of his time. The fact that "everyone was doing it" did not make it right, and he urged Christ's followers to strive for a better and holier way of living. If our bodies are temples of the Holy Spirit, we should try to respect them and maintain some control over them. So, why exactly is fornication wrong? As with all the Commandments, God's rules are for our wellbeing and happiness. It is sometimes argued that when two people are attracted to each other it will make them happy to have a sexual relationship. They are considered to be doing no harm to anyone, and in fact it would be harmful to repress their natural feelings. But God knows that we cannot find real happiness by experimenting with multiple sexual partners. There is a unique bond between a husband and wife which is achieved through a genuine and complete commitment to each other, within the Sacrament of Matrimony. We cheat ourselves and our spouse if we have already given away to others the intimate gift which we want to offer to our husband or wife.

It is said that young people need to get to know each other well before embarking on marriage. This is very true, but it does not justify living together. The intimacy of marriage is the fulfilment of the "getting-to-know-you" process, not part of it.

The danger is that sexual attraction may become confused with love. In practical terms, living together does not ensure a successful marriage. In an age where everything has to be "instant", whether it's coffee or communications, we're unwilling to wait for what we want. But sometimes waiting is the better course, and never more so than when it comes to marriage. If you and your partner have practised patience, respect and self-control before marriage, you are much more likely to cope together with the ups and downs of married life.

As we have already seen, there is nothing new about the sin of fornication; but it seems there is almost intolerable pressure on young people today to conform to the prevailing secular standards of behaviour. I can see the difficulties. Young people want to be accepted by their peer groups and no-one wants to stand out from the crowd as some kind of old-fashioned oddity. How is it possible for a young man or woman to resist temptation and to hold on to those values which they know in their hearts to be the right ones? You need courage, strength and faith because you will probably be ridiculed, but you can rely on spiritual help to strengthen you particularly through prayer. Keep up your practice of regular prayer, keep going to Mass and the Sacraments of the Eucharist and Reconciliation. If you are doing these things you are far less likely to fall into temptation. Don't be afraid to say "No". Value yourself; you deserve better than a "trial marriage".

Parents often speak to me in some anxiety when their sons or daughters are living with a partner outside marriage. They disapprove, but at the same time they don't want to alienate their children. It can be a difficult situation, but I think parents have to maintain an open-door policy where their children are concerned. You can make it very clear to them that you disapprove of their behaviour, but at the same time you have to assure them that you still love them and always will. If the Church from the pulpit and in newsletters, the schools in their Catholic education and parents in the spiritual upbringing of their children set the right Christian standards of marriage then parents must not blame themselves.

Individual Catholics are not likely to turn the tide of social behaviour, but I do think that we can make a difference. We must continue to cherish our marriages and families and hand on God's guidance to our children. This can be our greatest witness to the world.

If you really want to give your marriage the best footing you possibly can for it to be sustainable with God's blessing, speak to your Priest and undergo marriage preparation, not cohabitation.

Part 2.8 (i) – The Seventh Commandment

THOU SHALT NOT STEAL

Most civilised societies recognise that owning property is a basic human right. Therefore theft (like murder and slander) is universally regarded as a crime punishable by law. Yet ever since Eve took the fruit from the tree, people have been helping themselves to things which do not belong to them. From the powerful nation which invades a smaller one, to the office worker who pilfers a few envelopes, there's a lot of stealing which goes on. To list every possible variation on this theme would be tedious, so I would like to consider just a few examples and motives, with some thoughts on how to avoid breaking this Commandment.

Taking away another person's money or property, damaging property by vandalism, and borrowing money with no intention of paying it back are all obvious examples of stealing. But what about the less obvious ones? We have a duty to deal fairly with our families, our employers and the society in which we live. If you are the breadwinner in your family you may feel that you are entitled to spend your earnings in any way you wish. You've worked hard and you deserve a bit of recreation, but not to the detriment of your family. If your children are being deprived of what they need because you are spending too much on gambling or expensive hobbies, then you are stealing from them.

In the workplace, theft has become so widespread that many people have ceased to regard it as wrong. If you help yourself to a few postage stamps, a handy bit of timber, a few electrical fittings, what does it matter? It's not actual cash but legitimate perks? Well no, it's still stealing and repeated petty theft can amount to a serious crime. Just imagine what it costs a company if everyone was doing it; the total cost per year might be enough to create more jobs!

At the present time, shoplifting is so rife that it's become a way of life for some people. While in some cases this may be out of desperation, it's still not the right thing to do; God will always send someone to give you charity for what you need.

What about our duty to our neighbour? If you borrow tools without asking permission from your neighbour, even with the intention of giving them back, it is theft. We also have responsibilities towards the community. No-one enjoys paying taxes, but they are necessary in order to finance the services we take for granted. If you are deliberately evading tax or taking unfair advantage of loopholes in the system, or making a fraudulent claim for state benefits, you are stealing from the state's resources which are used for the welfare of others.

Why do people steal? In most cases they are motivated by greed or envy. Some are impelled by genuine need. There are many who, over a period of time, fall into a habit of petty theft. If you recognise that this is your weakness, there are several things you can do to break the bad habit. First, try to put yourself in the place of the person from whom you are stealing. Treat them as you would like them to treat you. Second, pray for the strength to overcome temptation. Third, avoid situations which are likely to lead you into trouble. If you find it hard to resist stealing from the parts warehouse at work, make sure you don't go in there alone.

If parents taught their children to respect their own property, very likely children would grow up to respect other people's goods and property. I remember an occasion when my sister was having some building work done at her house. Her four year old son was watching and when he saw the builder about to put a heavy spanner down on a polished table he cried, "Mummy wouldn't like you to do that!" Children who learn to value family possessions are not likely to damage or steal what belongs to others.

If you do break the Commandment, the first steps to take are to go to Confession and also restore the stolen goods to the person you took them from. You should explain the circumstances and the details of the theft; don't be like the man who told the priest he had stolen a rope, but didn't mention the fact that there was a donkey on the end of the rope too! The priest will be able to give you advice. Obviously, the theft of a few pounds on a sudden impulse is less serious than a pre-meditated bank robbery. As far as possible though, you must make an attempt to restore what you have stolen. This can be done anonymously. You must also repay any profits that accrue from what you have stolen. For example, if a farmer steals a cow in calf, he must not only return the cow but the calf that has been born as well. If you can't pay the full amount immediately, pay what you can at the moment and then pay the rest in instalments, without of course impoverishing your family.

This Commandment is just as much about respect and love for other's as the other Commandments are too. We must obey it out of love for our neighbour whom God loves and expects us to as well.

Part 2.9 (i) – The Eighth Commandment

YOU SHALL NOT BEAR FALSE WITNESS AGAINST YOUR NEIGHBOUR

William Shakespeare wrote in Othello "Who steals my purse steals trash...But he that filches from me my good name robs me of that which...makes me poor". Stealing someone's money is reprehensible enough, but not as damaging as stealing or besmirching someone's good name. The honour attached to a good name is far more valuable than material possessions. Furthermore, you may be able to repay a theft of money or goods but it is far more difficult to restore a ruined reputation.

A good name is so highly prized that it has often been the subject of litigation. If a famous person finds that someone has made untrue and damaging statements about him, verbally or in writing, he may well take legal proceedings against them. The celebrity may be awarded thousands of pounds in compensation, but the money isn't important. He wants to set the record straight, making the offender retract the allegations. Otherwise the world might believe the lies and the celebrity would lose all respect, and possibly his livelihood, too.

In the same way, someone who deliberately gives a false statement in a law court may well cause great harm. An innocent person might be convicted and punished, while the guilty party escapes justice. It will then be extremely difficult for the convicted person to prove his innocence and regain his good name. This is a very serious matter, all the more so when the witness has sworn an oath before God to tell the truth.

Reputations can be damaged in less dramatic but equally harmful ways. The damage is done in homes, at work, in pubs and clubs, in local shops and streets. The weapon used is gossip. We like to admire and respect the people we live and work with, yet there seems to be something in human nature that enjoys hearing scandalous news. Once a titbit of gossip has been shared, the story takes on a life of its own, being embroidered and exaggerated with every re-telling. We seem to be eager to believe the gossip, never doubting that the lurid details are true. After all, we say, 'there is no smoke without fire'.

The victim of the gossip can do very little to redress the balance. You know that your neighbours are accusing you of wicked behaviour, but how can you prove it isn't true? That is the real damage done by gossip. Eventually it will all blow over and someone else will become the focus of attention, but the memories linger. You will always be aware that certain people around you no longer respect or trust you, and that is very painful. Your reputation is in ruins and it may take years to rebuild it.

Children can sometimes suffer from false accusations, with far-reaching consequences. A bit of childish mischief, or being seen with a "rough" group, may gain the child the unfair reputation of being a trouble-maker. Later on, such prejudice may drive them to live up to their bad reputation.

False witness against our neighbour is, in fact, a lie. It is certainly the devil's work, for he is the father of lies. It is very easy to be tempted to break this Commandment because we all love a good story. The story is all the more enjoyable if it concerns someone who has perhaps been a little too proud or too full of their own importance. We may sometimes feel that they deserve to be "taken down a peg or two". But nothing justifies spreading malicious lies. We need to be very discreet and careful in our conversation. If we pass on gossip we are just as guilty as the person who originated it.

Of course, one way of avoiding becoming the subject of gossip is to avoid giving any grounds for it. If you put yourself in a compromising situation, if you act in a secretive manner, if your behaviour is sometimes inappropriate, then people are going to suspect that something unseemly is going on. Suspicion leads to comment and so the gossip begins.

Bearing false witness is a sin because it causes pain and injustice, fear and isolation. Our personal reputation is important to each of us because it is on this that we are judged by other people. Ultimately, of course, God will be the judge; He knows the truth about us, the good and the bad. We should really leave it all in His hands. Meanwhile, if we hear a juicy piece of gossip we should refrain from commenting on it or passing it on.

Like theft this Commandment demands that we make restitution for defrauding a person of their good name. This can be very hard. A story is told of a woman who told a saint in Confession that she had ruined the name of her neighbour. The saint told her to go to the market, buy a chicken, pluck out its feathers as she made her way back to Church and then go back and collect all the feathers. "Impossible", she said, "It's so windy", "And neither will you ever be able to restore the reputation of your neighbour!" was the reply. This is very true but nevertheless you must try to restore your neighbour's good name in so far as you can. You will have to apologise to the person concerned and tell all the people you gossiped to that either what you said was a lie or it should not have been related.

Mary, Our Mother, must have often met women as she drew water from the well, as she went to the market, and there she would have met other women. There may have been times when gossip arose, but one thing we can be certain about is that Mary, being free from sin, would know how to change such talk into more charitable conversation. Let Our Lady be our model.

Part 2.10 (i) – The Ninth and Tenth Commandments

THOU SHALT NOT COVET THY NEIGHBOUR'S GOODS

THOU SHALT NOT COVET THY NEIGHBOUR'S WIFE

These two Commandments seem at first sight to be quite different from the others because they concern our minds and thoughts rather than our behaviour. In the "I confess" at the beginning of the Mass we confess that we have sinned "in our thoughts and in our words", so we recognize that it is possible to sin by wrong-thinking as well as wrongdoing. The danger is that the sinful thought, if it is encouraged, may lead on to an even more sinful act. Covetousness is one of those dangerous thoughts.

The goods mentioned in the Commandment in the bible are house, ox and donkey. Nowadays, greatly encouraged by advertising campaigns, we are more likely to envy a car, an expensive watch or a smartphone. Covetousness goes beyond admiring our neighbour's goods; we want to possess them for ourselves, and such envy could lead on to the sin of theft. Certainly, it is destructive of our contentment with life. Many people are unhappy, because they are constantly striving to "keep up with the Joneses". Envy can have a corrosive effect on a marriage when a one spouse is continually reproaching the other for them not having a bigger house, better car or more expensive holiday, just like "other people" have. That sort of greed and criticism courses damage to the relationship.

People have a right to their property and no-one has a right to covet their goods. Obviously, if some people have a superabundance of goods they should not be selfish and miserly. We all have a responsibility to help the needy, for what God has given us is to be shared. We have no need to envy the wealthy if we learn to be content with what we have. Jesus said, "How happy are the poor in spirit" (Mt. 5:3) and it is indeed a blessing to be free from envy. One who took this beatitude to heart was St. Francis. One whole night he prayed over and over again this prayer, "My God and my all." He was so sure that if He possessed God he had all he needed. He had learned to rely entirely on the providence of God. He was convinced that just as God looks after the birds and beasts in the field He would also look after him. So when we see people who have more than us let us pray not be envious of others but be content with what we have.

When in our minds we are covetous, we are guilty of the sin of theft. In fact, we have not stolen anything, but the sin has been in our mind. However, there is no restitution to be made for it (because we have not actually stolen it) but we must acknowledge it and make a Confession to God to help us not to commit that kind of sin again.

Perhaps we could try to be a little more grateful to God for His goodness, thanking Him and praising Him for His daily gifts to us.

In the final Commandment, what is God telling us when He says, "You shall not covet your neighbour's wife" (Ex. 20:17). It is natural to admire an attractive woman and you should be glad that your neighbour has such a lovely lady for his wife, but if you covet her then it becomes a very serious matter.

Jesus told His disciples that if they merely looked at a woman lustfully they would be committing adultery in their heart. (Mt. 5:28). Just as coveting someone's material possessions could lead to the sin of theft, so coveting another man's wife could lead to the sin of adultery. A marriage destroyed, children hurt, a family divided, all because a covetous thought was allowed to develop into an action.

Covetous thoughts come to us unbidden. Sometimes they are attacks from Satan and we must try to stifle them before they can lead us further into trouble. As soon as we are aware of them we should tell Satan to get back into hell. Each time we say "No" we become stronger. At times we may feel that Satan's suggestions are almost irresistible, but God will not allow us to be tempted beyond what we can endure. He will always show us an escape route. (1Cor. 10:13).

How wise God is to warn us about our covetous thoughts. These two Commandments, like all the others, are given to us for our benefit. God knows that if we are living in a constant state of envy, anxious about success and social status, we are not happy. We are not at peace. If we are yearning for someone else's wife (or husband) we are not at peace. Jesus says, "My own peace I give you, a peace the world cannot give." (Jn.14:27) True peace is not to be found in the corruptible goods of this world. We find peace when we are content with what we have, and when we are trying to do what pleases God.

If ever we are tempted in this matter we can call to mind the gifts of fortitude and purity we received from the Holy Spirit when we received the Sacrament of Confirmation. We have great friends to help us in our Blessed Mother Mary. She is the model of purity. We can pray to St. Joseph who showed great respect to Mary, his wife. We can also of course pray to our Guardian Angel who is always by our side praying we will do only what pleases God.

Part 2.11 (i) – The Beatitudes

WHY DID JESUS GIVE US THE BEATTITUDES

The Ten Commandments in the Old Testament were given by God to Moses to tell us how we are to conduct our lives and lead lives of practical holiness. In the New Testament in Matthew 5:3-12 and Luke 6:20-23 we find the accounts of the Beatitudes which Jesus preached to a large crowd who had gathered before Him.

I look upon the Beatitudes as a short autobiography of Jesus. In telling us them He is giving us a description of His life and showing us how we can be like Him. In the Beatitudes Jesus is listing the values in life which will lead us to salvation and the joys of Heaven. The Beatitudes are a key component of Christian teachings, and they offer guidance on how to live a blessed life. In them people see the nature of Gods and His plan for how we should live.

The Ten Commandments were intended to direct the community to meet the needs of each individual in a loving and responsible manner. The Beatitudes are more challenging. They show us how Jesus lived and how we are to follow Him. Each Beatitude is an almost direct contradiction of society's typical way of life. In the last Beatitude, Jesus even points out that a serious effort to develop these traits is bound to create opposition.

If we want to live for God we must be ready to say and to do what seems strange to the world. We must be willing to give when others take, to love when others hate, and to help when others abuse. We must be prepared to give up our own rights in order to serve others. In this way we will be blessed and receive everything that God has stored up for us. In the Beatitudes we can't just pick one and leave the rest. They must be taken as a whole.

Each Beatitude tells how to be blessed. "Blessed" means more than happiness. It implies the fortunate and enviable state of those who are in God's kingdom.

In the Kingdom of Heaven, wealth and power and authority are unimportant. Kingdom people seek different blessings and benefits, and they have different attitudes. Are our attitudes a carbon copy of the world's selfishness, pride and lust for power, or do they reflect the humility and self-sacrifice of Jesus, our King?

Let's look briefly at each Beatitude and see what we can learn from them.

Blessed are the poor in spirit for theirs is the Kingdom of Heaven

"Poor in spirit" means that we are entirely dependent on God. We rely entirely on Him for our very next breathe and our very next heartbeat. In comparison to God we are nothing. It tells us of the importance of humility in our lives. Humility is the understanding that all your blessings originate from the love of God. Humility brings openness and inner peace, enabling one to do the will of God. Those who humble themselves are able to admit our fragile nature, repent, and permit the love of God to guide us to reformation. By being humble we gain the gift of wisdom from God to give us that very guidance.

Blessed are those who mourn, for they will be comforted

We mourn for our sins and intend to be sorry for them, and try not to commit them again and follow God's righteousness. The reward for this is we will be comforted by the grace of God.

We mourn with other people too for their loss, especially of loved ones. By doing this we are sharing the comfort that God gives us with them.

Blessed are the meek, for they will inherit the earth

A meek person manifests self-control. We are encouraged to follow God's way, not oppose but be faithful to him. Submission to the will of God can be difficult and tiresome, but it will bring peace and tranquillity in this world and the next. It is another way of saying we shall inherit the land, which is Heaven. Whenever we find God's will hard to accept, remember that God's will is our peace.

Blessed are those who hunger and thirst for righteousness, for they will be filled

To hunger and thirst for righteousness is to possess an active spiritual longing: "My soul is thirsting for God, the God of my life; when can I enter and see the face of God?" (Ps. 41:3). This desire is not passive; it is a fervent seeking. The servant who hungers and thirsts for righteousness is the same as the one who seeks God's kingdom and His righteousness before and above everything else (Mt. 6:33). That person is blessed because he or she experiences a satisfied heart. That person can say, "It is well with my soul."

Righteousness speaks of right relationship with God and with other people. The idea of right relationships with others forms the link in the chain to the next section of the Beatitudes. While right standing with God is His gift of salvation given through faith in Jesus Christ to those who believe in Him (Rom. 3:22).

Luke's rendering of the fourth Beatitude holds only the notion of hunger: "Happy are you who are hungry now: for you will shall be satisfied" (Lk. 6:21). But Matthew's report intensifies the desire for righteousness with the addition of thirst. Those who thirst for righteousness receive the water Jesus offered to the woman at the well: "But anyone who drinks the water that I shall give will never be thirsty again: the water that I shall give will turn into a spring inside him welling up to eternal life" (Jn. 4:14). The term filled or satisfied in the Beatitude means that the pangs of hunger and thirst will disappear. The verb is passive, indicating that God Himself will fulfil our intense desire for right relationship with Him. Salvation is His gift. We can't earn it (Eph. 2:8).

Blessed are the merciful, for they will be shown mercy

Jesus tells us, "Be compassionate as your Father is compassionate" (Lk. 6:36). How often we offend God and He is always merciful to us. Jesus told Peter not to forgive just seven times, but seventy times seven. In other words, we have to keep offering mercy like our heavenly Father. St. James tells us that there will be no judgement for the one who is merciful (Jas. 2:13). Love, empathy, and mercy towards a family member or neighbour will bring peace to your relationships. The reward for being merciful is that we will be shown mercy.

Blessed are the pure in heart, for they will see God

To be pure of heart means to be free of all selfish purposes and self-seeking motives. Jesus never did His will but the will of His Father. He sacrificed His own life for the salvation of mankind. It also means being free from lust and the sins of the flesh. The reward will be that we shall see God.

Blessed are the peacemakers, for they will be called children of God

Peacemakers not only manifest peaceful lives but also work to share peace and friendship with others and to cultivate peace between God and man. However, we cannot give others what we do not possess and must strive to achieve peace within ourselves. The reward for peacemakers is that they will be called the children of God.

Blessed are those who are persecuted because of righteousness, for theirs is the kingdom of heaven

The biblical passage continues: "Happy are you when people abuse you and persecute you and speak all kinds of calumny against you on My account. Rejoice and be glad, for your reward will be great in Heaven; this is how they persecuted the prophets before you" (Mt. 5:11-12). Jesus said many times that those who follow Him will be persecuted. "If they persecuted Me, they will persecute you too" (Jn. 15:20). This Beatitude is important because even if we are wrongfully persecuted for belief or devotion to God, we shall be blessed eternally in the Kingdom of Heaven.

Chapter 3 – Our Mother Mary

Part 3.1

THE MOTHER OF JESUS AND OUR MOTHER

Mary was born into a humble home in an unremarkable town. There are very few recorded facts about her life. Yet, as she herself foretold, all generations call her blessed and millions of people love and honour her throughout the world. Why do we hold the Blessed Virgin Mary in such high esteem? Because of the role she played in our salvation.

Whenever we think about God's great love for us we have to marvel at the plans He made. We were to be saved by one of our own kind and so Jesus must enter the world in human form. He would be a man like us in all things "though He is without sin" (Heb. 4:15) and so, like us, He would be born of a woman. Scripture (Lk. 1:29-31) tells us that the woman was Mary and that God chose her and called her for this vital task.

The Old Testament prophesies the coming of a Saviour and hints at how His coming will be accomplished. The offspring of a woman will crush the head of the serpent (Satan). (Gen. 3:14-15). The prophet Isaiah says a young woman will give birth to a son who will bring peace to the world. The Jews lived in constant expectation of a Messiah and many a young Jewish girl must have wondered if she would be the honoured mother. But when God created Mary of Nazareth He gave her a unique privilege: her soul was free from those effects of original sin which damage every other human soul. This privilege we call the Immaculate Conception and it made Mary worthy to receive the Son of God. We could say that this predisposed Mary to be generous and co-operative with God's plan. Like everyone else, she had freewill, and when the angel visited her with God's request she could have said No.

St. Bernard speaks of the whole world holding its breath, waiting for her answer. But her whole inclination was to love God and to do what He needed her to do. So Love was conceived in Mary's womb and born as the human child, Jesus.

Mary scarcely understood how the plan was to work, but of course God provided the help she would need. He encouraged Joseph to overcome his initial anxieties and accept Mary as his wife, and to bring up Jesus as his foster-child. It is the tradition of the Church that Mary and Joseph had a platonic marriage, by mutual consent. Mary remained a virgin before, during and after Jesus' birth.

In addition to practical support, Mary was given spiritual help. Her cousin Elizabeth acknowledged this when she greeted her with the words, "Of all women you are the most blessed" (Lk. 1:42) Mary had received at her conception all the graces she needed for the life she was to lead. We are all offered grace to help us in our spiritual life, but we don't always use those opportunities; Mary, however, was so aware of God's presence that she was able to take full advantage of His grace.

One of the highlights of Mary's life was giving birth to her beloved Son. Those nine months she carried her baby, we can only imagine what their relationship must have been; how she longed to hold him in her arms, nurture Him and care for Him. Although the surroundings in which she gave birth to her Son were far from palatial, it did not detract from the bliss she had in loving Him. Jesus left Heaven but he found Heaven with his mother Mary.

After the birth of Jesus, Mary and Joseph had the ordeal of living in exile as refugees in a foreign country, Egypt. Her stay away from her homeland must not have been easy at all. The journey to Egypt and then back was an ordeal in itself. How Mary and Joseph must have longed to set up home for their little family back in Nazareth, and for Joseph to establish his business as a carpenter to provide for them.

If someone were to write a biography of Mary based on the New Testament it would not be full of exciting action or clever conversation. The Gospels show us a very ordinary woman who had ordinary concerns and preoccupations. She had little to say but thought very deeply. Like many of us, she was often perplexed by life's events. Even the behaviour of her Son was mysterious to her. Many parents will identify with Mary's reaction when the twelve-year-old Jesus went missing for three days and was subsequently found chatting to the elders in the Temple. "Why have you done this to us? See how worried your father and I have been" (Lk. 2:48). But Mary simply got on with the careful upbringing of her Son. She meditated and wondered, but at no time did she doubt God's wisdom.

Mary's faith and trust in Jesus were absolute; so much so, that it was she who launched Him into His public ministry. During the wedding at Cana when the wine had run out, it was Mary who whispered to the servants, "Do whatever He tells you." (Jn. 2:5) Jesus felt that the time was not yet right, but His mother believed that He had the power to help and so, for her sake, He performed His first miracle. The wedding party was saved and, we are told, many people became believers. We should never doubt the power of Mary's intercession.

When the time came for Jesus to begin His public ministry, it must have been a wrench to see her Son leaving their home. Mary accepted this because He was doing His Father's will, but insofar as she could with other women she followed Him and cared for Him and His Apostles.

The devotion and respect we give to Mary are not the same as worship; worship belongs only to God. We honour her solely because of her relationship to Jesus. She gave birth to God's Son and is therefore rightly called the Mother of God. She remained a virgin out of respect for the Son she had borne and she is honoured for her purity. Tradition tells us that when her earthly life ended she was assumed bodily and spiritually into heaven. The Saviour would not permit His holy mother's body to suffer corruption. We don't know how Mary's physical life ended, and whether she actually died or not, but we do believe that she has been assumed into heaven.

Mary is an intercessor on our behalf because of the close and unique bond between her and her divine Son. I would now like to go on to consider what Mary means to you and me in our daily lives.

When Jesus was dying, only a few friends remained at the foot of the cross. Among them were Mary, His Mother, his Mother's sister, Mary of Clopas, Mary Magdalene and St John. It must have been the lowest point of Mary's life when she saw her darling Son nailed to His cross and dying in agony. Her heart must have been broken and inconsolable.

John has been described as "the disciple Jesus loved" (Jn.13:23), the one for whom Jesus had a special affection. Some people may wonder why John was not chosen as the first Pope instead of Peter, but Jesus had a different mission for John. Looking down at the people dearest to Him, He said to Mary, "This is your son," and to John, "This is your mother". From that moment John "made a place for her in his home." (Jn. 19: 26-27).

These two people needed each other. John could give Mary the security and companionship she needed for the rest of her life. She in turn would treat John as a son, loving and caring for him as she had for Jesus. It is wonderful to think of Jesus making provision for them in this way. But the Church has seen in this incident a wider significance. John represents the whole human race, given to Mary to love as her own children. We, too, embrace Mary as our mother and give her the love and respect she deserves.

When Jesus was dying on the cross, Mary couldn't wait for Him to breath his last and end His sufferings. She was the only one who expected Him to rise again, and although no mention is made in the Gospels that Jesus appeared to her, surely His first visit would have been to His mother. We can only imagine what an ecstatic meeting that must have been; they had both done the Father's will perfectly.

When Jesus ascended into Heaven, Mary must have shed a tear to know that she had to wait before she could be united with Him again. Those years would have seemed like an eternity, but she knew there was still work for her to do guiding the early Church. Having been assumed into Heaven, Mary has not forgotten us. We are brothers and sisters of her Son and we are her children, and like any loving parent she is praying and longing for each one of us to be united with her Son and herself for all eternity.

Do we "make a place" for Mary in our lives? In most Catholic homes you will see a statue or picture of Our Blessed Lady as a reminder of her constant care for us. But a picture is not enough, she must have a place in our hearts as well and we should pray to her regularly. The least we can do is to remember her in our morning and evening prayers. It would please Jesus if we recited her rosary every day, or at least a decade of the rosary if time is limited. If possible we should try to attend Mass on Mary's feast days, the Immaculate Conception, her birthday the Annunciation and the Visitation. If there are May and October devotions to Mary in your local church, this is another opportunity to show Mary how much we love her.

We hear of Mary appearing in various places throughout the world. The Church is very cautious in granting approval of these apparitions. For example, Medjugorje has been a popular place of pilgrimage for many years, but the Church has not yet accepted the claims made by the seers. Other apparitions such as Lourdes and Fatima have been given the Church's approval. At both these places Mary's message is that we should say the rosary daily, praying for peace in the world and the conversion of sinners. God could have sent any saint or even an angel to give us this message, but it was because of Mary's love and concern for us that she wanted to come in person. This surely enhances the importance of the message.

There are some people who claim that Mary is a barrier to ecumenism and Christian unity. How wrong they are! When Pope Pius XII proclaimed the doctrine of the Assumption some critics thought this would be a stumbling block for non-Catholics. Yet it is from that time that the churches began to draw closer to each other. Old suspicions and hostilities started to break down and Christians of all denominations learned to have more respect for each other.

Again, some people will object to the statement that Jesus is the only mediator between God and man, and also that Mary's help is unnecessary. But it was Mary who brought Jesus into the world. She was and still is a channel of God's grace and she has many good things to give us if we ask her. Her closeness to Jesus makes her a powerful intercessor on our behalf.

One of Mary's titles is 'Spouse of the Holy Spirit'. The Holy Spirit chose Mary above all women to be His bride and by His power she would conceive Jesus, God's Son. Words cannot describe the union and the love Mary had for the Holy Spirit. The Holy Spirit must have been constantly in Mary's thoughts as she carried Him in her heart. Is it true to say that for us the Holy Spirit is the forgotten Person of the Blessed Trinity in our lives? All of us have the title 'temple of the Holy Spirit'. If this is so then we can go to no better person than Mary and ask her to give us a love for the Holy Spirit. He wants us to accept all the graces He wishes to shower on us and thereby be His fitting temples.

When I was training to be a Capuchin friar we were taught not only to bow our head at the name of Jesus but to a lesser degree when we say the name of Mary. I have never forgotten this practice and it has helped my devotion to our Blessed Lady. Perhaps you may find this helpful.

Jesus ascended into Heaven to plead our cause before His Father. I'm sure you would agree with me that when Mary was assumed into Heaven she too joined her Son to plead our cause.

O Mary, conceived without sin, pray for us who have recourse to thee. Amen.

Chapter 4 – Jesus Christ

Part 4.1

THE PERSON OF JESUS CHRIST

There are two words that people use to describe the 'wow factor'. They are 'awesome' and 'amazing'. Those words though actually describe the unconditional love God has for His children. God knows how people treat Him, but never gives up on us. God the Father knowing how we would treat His Son, nailing Him to a cross, never deterred from sending Him into our world. Why should this be? It is because it has always been the will of the God the Father, God the Son and God the Holy Spirit, that is God, Three Persons in One God, to be loved perfectly by all of His creatures. Most people think that God's Son became Man to save us from our sins and take us to Heaven. That is true, for that is what is stressed when we talk about the Incarnation, God becoming Man. But there is more to it than that. What should be stressed is the fact that God from the very beginning, always, wanted to be loved perfectly by all of His creatures. Jesus expressed this thought perfectly when He said, "God loved the world so much that He gave His only Son, so that everyone who believes in Him...may have eternal life" (Jn. 3:16).

The whole plan of Our Lord's life and the whole manner of His death are designed to show forth His love for His Father, and His love for us, His brothers and sisters. Through love He became man for us, through love He lived and worked for us, through love He suffered for us, and through love He died for us. With St. Paul each one of us can say, "The Son of God...loved me and...sacrificed Himself for my sake." (Gal.2:20) The whole plan of our spiritual life should be a loving union and intimate partnership with Jesus in which we return to Him love for love.

It goes without saying that Jesus' first love was His Father. What other explanation can we give to Him stealing Himself from His disciples to spend whole nights in prayer after a busy and hectic days and with the prospect of more to follow? He was torn between spending time with His Father, getting to know His will and sharing Himself with people. In spending time with His Father He teaches us the importance of spending time with God in prayer; this is a hugely important teaching to us for our daily lives. We too will want to spend time with God because we love Him, and will want to know His will for us. When it came to teaching us how to formulate our prayers He couldn't have given use a more compact and comprehensive prayer than the "Our Father" which teaches us to get our priorities correct in life, the honouring of God's name, desiring the coming of His Kingdom and the doing of His will. Then He teaches us to pray for our basic needs, our daily bread, forgiveness and help in time of temptation and deliverance from evil.

After His love for His Father, His Mother had a very special place in His heart. It was because of her "yes" that He was able to become man and achieve all that His Father wished Him to do. Since Jesus had no earthly father He took every part of His humanity from His mother Mary. He was always happy in her presence. Jesus left Heaven, but He found Heaven in His mother Mary. Words just can't describe the bliss of their presence together during those thirty years they spent in Nazareth. So little is said of His foster father Joseph, but Jesus must have had a very warm and special relationship with him since he was the person chosen by His Father to take His place on earth.

There was no greater teacher than Jesus. Others may lean heavily on greater authorities than themselves when they taught, but Jesus depended on no other authority than His own. Others would bolster up their teaching with the words, "You have heard it said..." Jesus did not need others. He could say, "But I tell you.,." When He taught He had the art of condensing whole chunks of knowledge in a nutshell. The teachers at the time of Jesus would multiply knowledge into hundreds of rules and regulations, but Jesus could sum up the Law in two short sentences. "Love the Lord your God with all your heart...Love your neighbour as yourself." (Mt. 23:37-40). He was the greatest teller of short stories. Is there any greater story than the Prodigal Son? He had the art of teaching through parables which were home loving stories with heavenly meanings. One of the interesting things about the parables of Jesus is that most of the time we can find ourselves somewhere in the story. Almost subconsciously, you find yourself thinking, 'Hey, this story is about me." His teaching was relevant. His parables display His evident love of nature. Perhaps the most revolutionary thing He ever taught was that He lived in everyone no matter who they were. In loving them you are loving Him.

He never grew tired of preaching forgiveness, because He knew there was to be no forgiveness for us if we did not forgive. He knew it was the hardest thing for us to do and He stressed it so much because He just didn't want to lose one of us. He gave us the example of forgiveness for when His enemies had nailed Him to a cross He forgave them, "Father, forgive them; for they do not know what they are doing." (Lk. 23:34).

He proved He possessed love at its greatest depth when He died for us. "A man can have no greater love than to lay down his life for His friends." (Jn. 15:13).

He taught us how to treat our enemies by praying for them. In fact loving our enemies was to be the hallmark of His followers. "By this love you have for one another, everyone will know that you are my disciples." (Jn. 13:35). He taught us that we are to be different from those in the world who did not believe in God. If we are nice and good to those who are nice and good to us, we are not doing anything exceptional. Even pagans who have never heard of Christ do that. We are not to be overcome by evil, but overcome evil with good. That is how a Christian behaves.

No one ever taught so beautifully by His life, the true meaning and exercise of authority, as did Jesus. For Him authority was service. "The greatest among you must be your servant." (Mt. 23:11). He was the greatest, and yet He was at everyone's beck and call. He washed the feet of His Apostles when they failed to understand what He was saying. "If I, then, the Lord and Master, have washed your feet, you should wash each other's." (Jn. 13:14).

He taught us how to handle worry. Simply by not putting trust in our resources, but in the providence of God. One person with a firm faith in God is stronger than all the adversity that life can bring. He told us where to look and on whom to depend when we are in trouble. Very simply the message is, "Do not let your hearts be troubled. Trust in God still, and trust in Me." (Jn.14:1) "And know that I am with you always; yes, to the end of time." (Mt. 28:20).

If you want to lead a full life only Jesus has the answer and the means to provide it. His very words are, "I have come so that you may have life and have it to the full." (Jn. 10:10). Fullness of life was not to be found in affluence for He accumulated nothing of this world's possessions. He was not scornful of money or those who had it. He knew that riches could get such a hold on a person that it was hard for them to get to Heaven. They would rely more on their own resources than on God. When He died all He left behind were a seamless robe, a pair of sandals, and the most beautiful, creative life that the world has ever seen.

His love for children was evident. Towards the end of His life at a time of personal stress, when most of us become impatient and have little or no time for children, Jesus wanted children to be round Him. He gathered them in His arms and blessed them. His love for children was something more than sentimental affection. It was a conscious commitment. He cared for them. "It is to such as these." He said, "that the Kingdom of God belongs" (Lk. 18:16).

He would perform miracles whenever He saw the slightest glimmer of faith. This was so not only for His Mother Mary at Cana when He saved a wedding reception from disaster, but also for the blind man who could plead with Him with the words, "I do have faith. Help the little faith I have." (Mk. 9:24). Little in our hands is much in the hands of Jesus. From a few fish and loaves of bread He fed 5,000 people.

The sick were His special friends. They flocked to Him from everywhere and He always had time for them. He even gave them a special sacrament.

Insincerity and hypocrisy He could not stand, and Jesus who some call "gentle Jesus" could be forthright and strong in there denunciation. But He never lost faith in people. He knew the minds of people better than we ever will. He was well aware of the deceitfulness and wickedness of the human heart, but He never stopped believing in people. The conversion of Zachaeus says to you and me "Do not lose faith in people." Also this is shown in His treatment of Judas, "Are you betraying the Son of Man with a kiss." (Lk. 22:48). Even at the eleventh hour Jesus was giving Judas a chance to change his ways. His look of love at Peter after he had denied Him three times was enough to melt Peter into bitter tears of sorrow. Jesus always saw the saint in the sinner.

He knew that following Him would bring division and conflict in a household. Is it possible to imagine Jesus dividing a household? It can be safely said that He has done more to sanctify and stabilise family life than anyone who ever lived. So what does He mean when He speaks of dividing people and setting one against another? Firstly, He believed that God loved all people, not just Jews, and He was not willing to compromise that. And secondly, He believed that people were important, and that they should not be cheated and abused, not even in the name of religion. He believed that with all of His heart, and He wasn't willing to compromise it. It was primarily these two non-negotiable convictions that brought Him into conflict with corrupt authority and eventually brought Him to the cross. Had He been willing to compromise on these issues, He would never have been crucified; but neutrality just wasn't His way.

Jesus could be described as the bravest man who ever existed, because being God He knew every detail of the mental and physical suffering He was to endure and yet despite this knowledge He could live a serene and peaceful life as though He never knew a glimmer of what was to happen to Him.

I have always admired what could be considered the shortest and most popular biography written about Jesus Christ. It is called the "One Solitary Life."

It begins, "He was born in an obscure village, the child of a peasant woman. He grew up in another village. He worked in carpenter shop until He was 30. Then for three years He was an itinerant preacher. He never wrote a book. He never held office. He never owned a home. He never travelled more than 200 miles from the place where He was born. He never did any of the things that usually accompany greatness. He had no credentials but Himself".

"Although He walked the land of Palestine curing the sick, giving sight to the blind, healing the lame, and raising people from the dead, the top established religious leaders turned against Him."

"When He needed His friends most, they ran away from Him. He was turned over to His enemies. He went through the mockery of a trial. He was spat upon, flogged and ridiculed. He was nailed to a cross between two thieves. While He was dying, the executioners gambled for the only piece of property He had on earth and that was His robe. When He was dying

He prayed for His enemies. When He was dead He was laid in a borrowed grave through the pity of a friend."

"Two thousand years have come and gone and today this man is the central figure of the human race."

"All the armies that every marched, and all the navies that were ever built, and all the parliaments that ever sat, and all the kings that ever reigned, put together, have not affected the lives of men on this earth as has that one solitary life."

Without a doubt Jesus is the greatest Person in history:
He had no servant…yet they called Him Master.
He had no degree…yet they called Him Teacher.
He had no medicines…yet they called Him Healer.
He won no military battles…yet He conquered the world.
He committed no crime…yet they crucified Him.
He was buried in a tomb…yet He lives today.
His name is Jesus.

Yes, with St. Paul each one of us can say, "The Son of God…loved me and…sacrificed Himself for my sake" (Gal. 2:20). The whole plan of our spiritual life should be a loving union and intimate partnership with Jesus in which we return to Him love for love.

Chapter 5 – The Church

Part 5.1 – The Sacraments

Part 5.1.1 (i) - Introduction

INTRODUCTION TO THE SACRAMENTS

The best definition for a Sacrament is the one given to us by what used to be called the Penny Catechism. A Sacrament is an outward sign of inward grace, ordained by Jesus Christ, by which grace is given to the soul. It has all of these three elements, namely the outward sign, the inward grace and instituted by Jesus Christ.

Another way of defining the Sacraments is the one given by Sr. Eustochium Lee in her CTS booklet on Baptism. She says a Sacrament is "a visible sign of the invisible saving action of God". The visible sign is something tangible, for example, water or bread; the saving action of God, being something spiritual, cannot be seen.

Christ's death and resurrection achieved our salvation and the Sacraments of the Church are the means by which we can gain the benefits of that salvation. Christ Himself used the image of the vine; "I am the vine, you are the branches" (Jn. 15:5). Just as the life-supporting sap flows through the vine, feeding every branch, so Christ's life flows through His Body, the Church, to give every person the spiritual help he or she needs. It was Christ's wish that grace should be available to the world through the Church. This is why He founded the Church, to be a source of salvation to the world. As Catholics, therefore, we are immensely privileged to be able to receive the Sacraments and, in the case of the clergy, to administer the Sacraments to the faithful.

At every important stage of our lives there is a Sacrament to help us. When we are born there is the Sacrament of Baptism, which washes away original sin. When we reach the age of reason, knowing right from wrong there is the Sacrament of Reconciliation (Confession), whereby God forgives us our sins. On our spiritual journey to heaven Jesus accompanies us and provides us with food in the Holy Eucharist. As we approach adulthood we make a commitment to Christ, and so we are strengthened for this by the Sacrament of Confirmation. If we have a vocation to the priesthood, Jesus provides us with the Sacrament of Holy Orders which gives the spiritual power to perform all of the priestly functions. To those who have a vocation for marriage, Jesus gives the Sacrament of Matrimony which strengthens the bond between partners. Finally, when we are seriously ill or dying Jesus gives us the Sacrament of the Sick to comfort and encourage us.

The Sacraments are described as Sacraments of the living or of the dead. When we speak of life and death in this way we refer to the spiritual life, or the life of grace. Some Sacraments can only be received when we are in a state of grace, that is to say spiritually alive and healthy. The Sacraments of the living are the Holy Eucharist, Confirmation, Holy Orders, Matrimony and Sacrament of the Sick. If we have sinned then the grace in our souls is extinct and we have lost God's friendship, so we need to be spiritually resuscitated and reunited with God. That is what is meant by mortal sin. The Sacraments which restore our spiritual life are Baptism and Reconciliation. These two Sacraments are referred to as the Sacraments of the dead, because they are to restore our souls from sin and to the friendship of God.

Some people wonder about the efficacy of the Sacraments. Does it depend on the state of the priest's soul, or the soul of the person receiving the Sacrament? In every case it depends on the disposition of the recipient only, not the priest's soul. For example, when a couple are preparing for marriage they must first go to Confession if they are in a state of mortal sin. If they don't, the Sacrament of Matrimony will not work until they have been to Confession. So if they were to get married today in a state of mortal sin, but only go to Confession a year later, they would only receive the grace of the Sacrament from the moment they have been forgiven. Similarly, if someone receives Holy Communion in a state of mortal sin, he receives Christ's Body and Blood but it does his soul no good. He should have first received the Sacrament of Reconciliation. Without being reconciled with the Lord they would be committing a sacrilege, that is to say a grave lack of respect for the Sacrament.

When it comes to the Sacrament of the Sick, what about a person who is unconscious and close to death? Perhaps they are not in a state of grace at that moment, but in such a case we rely on the wisdom and mercy of God. The Sacrament of the Sick also gives the person absolution from their sins, which is one of the reasons why when someone is dying we must get a priest to come and give them the Sacrament.

And what about the disposition of the priest administering the Sacraments? He may be a very holy priest, or he may unfortunately be a great sinner, but you can be quite sure that the Mass is validly said and the Sacraments will always have their full effect, no matter how casual or lacking in holiness a priest may appear to be. No sin committed by the priest can reduce the power of the Sacraments. Here again, God's wisdom and mercy override human weakness. The priest has the authority, but the power comes from God; he is God's instrument in administering the Sacraments.

Three of the Sacraments confer a character or mark on our soul and can only be received once. They are Baptism, Confirmation and Holy Orders. These marks remain on a soul for all eternity. For example, if a priest went to hell everyone would know he was a priest because he has the priestly mark on his soul. It can never be erased. Once you are baptised you become a Christian and you will always be a Christian, and so this Sacrament cannot be repeated. The same is true of Confirmation. Once you are an adult Christian you will remain an adult Christian. Just like you can't have two twenty first birthdays.

The Sacraments, then, bring us spiritual life, strength and guidance. They give us a sharing in the life of Christ. We should make full use of them.

Part 5.1.1 (ii) - Introduction

DO WE NEED SACRAMENTS?

The seven Sacraments which the Church administers were established by Jesus Himself as a means of giving us grace. It might be helpful to start by examining what 'grace' is and why we need it. We need grace to help us know and love God better and to live the life He wants for us. Eternal life, the life of salvation, begins here on earth and it is grace which nourishes that life.

Grace is a difficult word to define, but the best explanation I've come across so far is the one given by Fr. Leo Trese. He starts by saying that grace is: 'a gift from God'. Everything we have, our power of speech, sight, hearing, our skills and abilities, life itself is a gift from God. But these are natural gifts, part of human nature, but grace is something more than this.

There are gifts which are above human nature and therefore supernatural. These are gifts to which we are not automatically entitled as human beings. Grace is included in this category, so we can say that grace is 'a supernatural gift from God'. Let me give an example of a supernatural gift. Miracles are supernatural gifts from God, but they are not grace. Peter and John cured a lame man who sat begging daily at the Beautiful Gate of the Temple. This miracle was made possible by a supernatural gift of God by which they were able to heal the lame man, but it was not grace. These gifts operate externally, they are visible and tangible, whereas grace is an interior, invisible gift which operates in the soul. Now we can say that grace is: 'an interior supernatural gift of God'.

Again, not all interior supernatural gifts can be called grace. The power of prophecy, the power of a priest to change bread and wine into Christ's Body and Blood, these are interior supernatural gifts, but they are given for the benefit of others. Grace is given for the benefit of the individual. So we can now add to our definition by saying that grace is: 'an interior supernatural gift of God for our own salvation'.

We don't, in fact, deserve this gift. We can't earn it and we have no right to it. Grace was given to Adam, but he lost it for himself and for us, his descendants. It was Christ who regained what Adam had lost. By His death and resurrection He earned for us what we could not earn for ourselves, the gift of grace. Now we have Fr. Trese's complete definition of grace: 'Grace is an interior supernatural gift of God, bestowed on us through the merits of Jesus Christ, for our salvation'.

Theologians will tell you that there are two kinds of grace, sanctifying grace and actual grace. Sanctifying grace is that which makes us holy. ("Sanctifying" comes from the Latin words *sanctus facere*, to make holy.) We receive this kind of grace for the first time through the Sacrament of Baptism and later through the other Sacraments. Grace is as essential for our souls as food and drink are for our bodies. God intends, of course, that we should remain holy, but we sin and lose that precious grace. How can we get it back? This is where actual grace is needed. We have to repent of our sin and come back to God, but it is God Himself who prompts us to take that step.

We can think of actual grace as the little nudges in the right direction which God gives us on a daily basis. I think we are all quite familiar with this experience. He may put into our mind the idea that we should visit a sick person, phone someone who is lonely, try to heal a rift with someone we've quarrelled with, do a kind act for a neighbour. Those ideas, those promptings, are actual graces. When we feel strongly tempted to do something wrong, or to give in to despair, God will give us the strength to overcome the problem. That is actual grace at work.

Actual grace is a fleeting opportunity. We can resist it or refuse to take advantage of it, and then the opportunity is lost. If we use actual grace, then it can build up our store of sanctifying grace in our soul. God's generosity is truly amazing!

We have now defined what grace is. Next we shall look at each of the Sacraments themselves.

Part 5.1.2 (i) - The Sacrament of Baptism

DO WE NEED BAPTISM

Jesus was once visited secretly by a Pharisee called Nicodemus. He was a leader of the Jewish community, but he was interested in the teaching of Jesus and recognised Him as having come from God. He wanted to know more about Him. Jesus told Nicodemus, "Unless a man is born from above, he cannot see the kingdom of God" (Jn. 3:3). Nicodemus misunderstood Him and wondered how a man could be born again from his mother's womb. But Jesus was referring to a spiritual birth through baptism. "Unless a man is born through water and the Spirit, he cannot enter the kingdom of God" (Jn. 3:5). In these words Jesus is indicating the necessity of baptism.

Baptism is the first of the three Sacraments of Initiation. The Church regards Baptism as the beginning of new spiritual life, Confirmation as a strengthening of that life, and the Eucharist as the nourishment every disciple of Christ needs. Baptism is such an important Sacrament, that none of the other Sacraments of the Church will have any effect if we haven't first been baptised. So important is it, that we normally baptise children soon after they are born. We want them to receive the benefits of this Sacrament from the earliest possible moment. If a baby is in danger of death, Baptism can be performed by any layperson if no priest is available.

Jesus could have chosen any method He liked as a means of initiation. Why water? There was a tradition among the Jews of ritual cleansing, so it seems natural that Jesus developed this idea for the benefit of His followers. Baptism is from the Greek word for bathing. The water symbolises the washing away of sin. In a baptism it is important that the water flows on the forehead of the child or adult. If someone simply dips his thumb in holy water, and makes the sign of the cross on a child's forehead, and says the words, "I baptise you in the name of the Father and of the Son and of the Holy Spirit" it is not a valid Baptism. The water must flow on the child's forehead.

So what are the benefits of Baptism? The burden of Original Sin, inherited from Adam, is removed. In the case of an adult, actual sin is also forgiven. The soul now becomes alive and is filled with God's sanctifying grace. At the same time it receives a permanent mark or character. This means that although we may commit sin, thereby losing sanctifying grace, we can still regain the grace we have lost through the Sacrament of Reconciliation. Had we not been baptised, confession would be to no avail and our soul would remain spiritually dead. At this point I make a very important point: If anyone Catholic or non-Catholic offends God seriously, but if they tell God they are truly sorry for having offended Him and assure Him that they will try their best not to sin again, their sin is forgiven. But there is an obligation for Catholics to confess that sin in confession.

Another name for baptism is christening, because it is through this Sacrament that we are made into Christians. The Three Persons of the Blessed Trinity, Father, Son and Holy Spirit come to live in us. We become members of God's family, the

Church, and so for the rest of our lives we are part of a mutually supportive community. As with any family, we learn to love, help and comfort each other and to share our experiences.

We cannot reach heaven without Baptism. Jesus made that plain to His friend Nicodemus. But what about unbaptised babies who have died, where do they go? We did not know where they went, and we had referred to them as going to a place called Limbo. Limbo was believed to be the border place between Heaven and Hell where those souls who died without being baptised, though not condemned to punishment, were deprived of eternal happiness with God in Heaven. But with a deeper understanding of God's love, we know that He will always have a place for them.

So far I have been referring to the Baptism of water, which is the usual method, but the Church also tells us that there is a baptism of desire and a baptism of blood. It might happen that someone had the intention of becoming Christian, and was perhaps receiving instruction, but died before the baptismal ceremony could take place. Nevertheless, the desire for baptism was there, along with love of God, and this is sufficient to remove Original Sin. Similarly, a person living in a country where Christians are persecuted may suffer execution before being able to fulfil his wish to be baptised. He would be, in effect, a martyr and this is known as a baptism of blood.

If Jesus says that Baptism is necessary for salvation, what about all the Jews, Muslims and pagans who will never be baptised? We can't assume that they will be condemned, because the final judgment belongs only to God. Also if through no fault of one's own a person knows nothing of the teachings of Christ or His Church, but led a good and honest live they too may obtain eternal salvation. God would not punish them for not knowing the truth. But it is still the responsibility of all Christians to tell others about Christ, and to teach them that there is a means of salvation for them through Baptism.

This, in fact, was Jesus' last instruction to His disciples. "Go out to the whole world; proclaim the Good News to all creation. He who believes and is baptised will be saved" (Mk. 16:15). This is part of our vocation as Christians.

Part 5.1.2 (ii) – The Sacrament of Baptism

THE CEREMONY OF BAPTISM

We have noted already that Baptism is the most important event in the life of a Christian. Most of us were baptised as babies, so we remember nothing about it. Even those of us who have children and have attended baptisms may be unaware of the significance of the baptismal ceremony. So today, let's follow an imaginary family as they present their baby to God.

Anne and John have a three week old baby boy, whom they have called Matthew. They know how necessary it is to give their child a Christian name. Little Matthew will have a patron saint in heaven to befriend him and help him throughout his life. The godparents have also been chosen with care: one godfather and one godmother, who of course must be practising Catholics and over the age of fourteen. Anne and John have chosen their friends Peter and Pauline. Not only are they very good friends, they are also very good Catholics who will take their responsibilities seriously. Godparents undertake to see that the godchild is brought up in the Catholic faith if the parents should die. That's why they need to be practising Catholics.

The priest begins by asking the parents what they want for Matthew. They reply, "Baptism". Then the priest explains what this entails. The child must be trained in the practice of the faith, which means bringing him to church every Sunday, teaching him right from wrong and teaching him his prayers. He asks them whether they understand what they are undertaking and calls on the godparents to help with this task.

The ceremony begins at the door of the church as the priest traces the sign of the cross on Matthew's forehead. Now he is branded as a Christian. (Note: It is a good idea for parents to make the sign of the cross on their child's forehead every night, reminding them of their baptism.)

Anne and John have chosen suitable readings for the service and then the priest in his homily encourages the parents and godparents in their duties. Special bidding prayers are said for Matthew, then the priest calls on the saints to pray for the family with their prayers. Of course, he includes St. Matthew and the patron saint of the parish church.

Then follows the prayer of exorcism. This sounds a bit scary, but really it is a prayer that the devil will never harm Matthew and that the Holy Spirit will keep him safe. Now Matthew is anointed with the oil of catechumens on his chest. This recalls a practice in the early church. If you were a catechumen (that's to say a person under instruction) you had to undergo a two-year preparation for baptism. After one year you would be anointed, to mark the first step on your journey, and that anointing has been incorporated into Baptism.

Now we move to the font. The water has usually been blessed at the Easter Vigil; if not, it is blessed now and a prayer said over it. Anne and John make a profession of faith on behalf of Matthew, and along with the godparents they renew their own baptismal vows. Everyone joins in, renouncing Satan and sin and re-affirming their Catholic faith in the words of the Creed.

Once again the priest questions Anne and John, making sure that they really want their baby to be baptised in the Catholic faith. Then we reach the central moment of Baptism, when God in a mysterious way gives new life to Matthew. The priest pours water over Matthew's head three times, saying "Matthew, I baptise you in the name of the + Father and of the + Son and of the + Holy Spirit." This action represents the cleansing of Matthew's soul, the washing away of Original Sin.

This is the new birth "by water and the Holy Spirit" which Jesus described to Nicodemus. Now the priest anoints Matthew with chrism, an oil blessed for this purpose. Anointing is a very ancient ceremony, used in Old Testament times in the coronation of kings, in the ordination of priests and in the appointment of prophets. It signified a person who was specially consecrated for an important task. Matthew now shares in the priesthood of Christ, he is a prince in God's kingdom and has been given the power to proclaim Christ to the world.

Anne's mother now wraps her little grandson in a white christening robe. The white garment symbolises the purity of Matthew's soul, which we hope will never be stained by sin. The priest takes a candle and lights it from the paschal candle. He hands the lighted candle to John and says, "Receive the light of Christ". While he holds the candle the priest prays for Anne and John and for the godparents, that they will encourage Matthew to walk in the light and that they will keep alive for him the flame of faith.

The priest touches Matthew's ears and mouth with his thumb. This is a reminder of the healing power of Jesus, when He made the deaf and dumb man hear and speak. It's also a prayer that Matthew may soon hear the word of Christ and also bear witness to it.

The family and friends now process to the high altar. This is because Matthew is entitled, when he is old enough, to receive the Eucharist from the altar. Everyone recites the Our Father, the prayer which unites all God's family. While Anne holds Matthew in her arms, the priest blesses her and gives thanks to God for the safe delivery of her child. Then John holds his little son while the priest prays that he and Anne, will be the first and best teachers of the faith for their child. The ceremony concludes with a prayer for everyone present and a blessing.

After the baptism the priest gives a certificate of baptism to the parents, which should be framed and kept in the child's bedroom.

On the anniversary of the child's baptism, it would be beneficial to all, to have a small party where the parents and godparents renew their baptismal vows together while also relighting the candle used at the child's baptism.

Part 5.1.3 (i) – The Sacrament of Confirmation

WHY JESUS GAVE US THE SACRAMENT OF CONFIRMATION

Confirmation is the second Sacrament of Initiation. Like Baptism, it is a Sacrament through which we receive the Holy Spirit. Let's look at why Jesus gave us this Sacrament and what it means for us in our everyday lives.

I have to say straightaway that you will not find the word Confirmation in the New Testament. This Sacrament was originally referred to as the laying-on of hands, because this was how it was administered. In Acts 8:17 we read that Peter and John "laid hands on" the Samaritans "and they received the Holy Spirit". When Jesus was preparing to leave His Apostles and ascend to heaven He promised that the Holy Spirit would come to them as a guide, comforter and teacher. "The advocate, the Holy Spirit, whom the Father will send in My name, will teach you everything and remind you of all I have said to you." (Jn. 14:26). Jesus told the Apostles, "You will receive power when the Holy Spirit comes on you, and then you will be my witnesses" (Acts 1:8).

As we have already received the Holy Spirit in Baptism, why do we need another Sacrament? Confirmation is sometimes described as a Sacrament of Christian maturity. It marks the stage of adulthood in our faith. Our spiritual development can be compared with our physical growing-up. A small baby needs food, but it is food specially adapted to its stage of development and it doesn't have much choice in the matter. As the child grows bigger it needs different nourishment to maintain growth and health until, at the appropriate time, it is able to cope with "grown-up" food. Similarly, when a baby is baptised it receives the Holy Spirit in a passive way. Later, the child chooses to be confirmed, making their own personal commitment to follow Christ. It is then that the Holy Spirit comes to them with that power which Jesus spoke of, giving them an understanding and spiritual insight which they couldn't have taken in when they were a baby.

The Apostles of Jesus had to undergo a similar process of initiation. At the Last Supper Jesus made them His priests. On Easter Day they had their first recorded encounter with the Holy Spirit when Jesus appeared to them in the upper room saying, "Peace be with you...Receive the Holy Spirit." (Jn. 20:21-23). They needed the power of the Holy Spirit in order to forgive sins. Later, at Pentecost, they received new powers from the Holy Spirit. They were given the skills and gifts they would need to build up the early Church and hand on the faith to their successors. For them, this was their sacrament of Confirmation.

Confirmation is usually administered by a Bishop, though a priest may be authorised to perform the ceremony, for example at the reception of a convert. The Sacrament is administered by the laying of hands on the person to be confirmed, anointing them with chrism, which is blessed oil, with the words, "Be sealed with the gift of the Holy Spirit". The sign of the cross is made on the forehead. The oil is olive oil which was traditionally a source of strength. It was also used for illumination, and it softens and soothes. It is therefore a very fitting symbol of the effects of Confirmation, which strengthens us against spiritual enemies, gives light to our understanding and comforts and calms us. Mixed with the olive oil is a sweet-smelling balsam. This suggests that once we are confirmed our lives should be a sweet and pleasing offering to God. When we are confirmed we can choose another saint as our patron. Along with our baptismal patron, he or she will help us to be faithful witnesses of Christ.

Just as we have godparents at our baptism, so at confirmation we have a sponsor. Like the godparents, the sponsor is a member of our spiritual family and does their best to guide us in our faith.

Jesus wants His followers to be witnesses, to make a difference to the world. He knew that we could never do that by ourselves, we could only do it with the help of His Holy Spirit. In fact, He told the disciples that He must ascend to heaven to activate the Holy Spirit: "Unless I go, the Advocate will not come to you" (Jn. 16:7). It's rather like the relationship between the sun, the moon and the stars. While the sun is shining, the moon and stars are more or less invisible, but when the sun has set they come out and shine brightly with reflected light. Jesus is the sun, and while He was on earth His followers were insignificant; but once He ascended to heaven they began to shed His light on the world. Now, our Confirmation enables us to shed Christ's light into our own surroundings. We can only do it though with the help of the Holy Spirit. When Jesus was on earth He could only influence those people who heard Him preach. But now that He has ascended into heaven we are meant to be His witnesses. His presence is now multiplied by the many people who have been confirmed by His Holy Spirit. Whenever anywhere in the world there is a confirmed Christian, there is Christ at work through the Holy Spirit.

Part 5.1.3 (ii) – The Sacrament of Confirmation

HOW THE HOLY SPIRIT HELPS US IN OUR DAILY LIVES

When Jesus ascended to heaven He promised to send His Holy Spirit to be our guide and comforter. How does the Holy Spirit help us in our daily lives? He continues God's creative work in the world, acting through us by means of His gifts. According to the prophet Isaiah (Isaiah 11:2) there are seven gifts of the Spirit: Wisdom, Understanding, Knowledge, Counsel, Fortitude, Piety and Fear of the Lord. Let's see what these mean in practice.

Remember Jesus' explanation of the purpose of the Holy Spirit: "The Holy Spirit...will...remind you of all I have said to you". (Jn. 14:26). So, with Wisdom, Understanding and Knowledge the Holy Spirit helps us to think like Jesus. When we read the words of Jesus in the Gospels the Spirit helps us to learn the lesson Jesus is teaching us and to see ways of putting it into practice in our lives. With Counsel, Fortitude and Fear of the Lord He helps us to act like Jesus. Fortitude gives us the strength to bear all kinds of problems and difficulties. It helps us to resist temptation and to make the right decisions. Piety is the gift whereby we act as sons and daughters of the Lord. The gift of Fear of the Lord encourages us in our prayer life and fills us with love and respect for God.

Of course, not everyone will receive the same gifts, nor to the same degree. St Paul observed that "there is a variety of gifts, but always the same Spirit". (1 Cor. 12:4). Not everyone will have the same level of Wisdom, or Fortitude. One person may be very knowledgeable about scripture and adept at interpreting it for others, but find that in times of adversity they have very little Fortitude. Another person may lack Wisdom but may be able to pray with great devotion.

St. Paul (Gal. 5:22) lists what he calls the fruits of the Holy Spirit. There are twelve of them and they are: Charity, Joy, Peace, Patience, Kindness, Goodness, Forbearance, Meekness, Faith, Modesty, Continency and Chastity. We don't need to remember this list and in fact some of these fruits can be grouped together. Patience, Meekness and Kindness form a group. Modesty, Continency and Chastity go together. Charity and Goodness are almost the same thing. Joy and Peace can be linked together.

We call them the fruits of the Holy Spirit because they are really the result of using the gifts we've just considered. By activating the gifts we reap the fruits. For example, if we call on our reserves of Fortitude, which the Holy Spirit has given us, we should find that we become more patient, tolerant and able to cope.

How do we activate the gifts the Holy Spirit has given us? We can't leave them to lie dormant, otherwise we shall not experience the benefits. We have to co-operate with the Holy Spirit, asking Him to awaken in us the gifts we need. Think of a gas cooker. You want to boil a kettle or heat a pan of soup. If you place your pan on the pilot light you'll wait forever for it to heat up. You have to press the appropriate knob in order to ignite the gas and produce the heat you need. Similarly, it's no good waiting for the Holy Spirit to work wonders all by Himself; we have to ask for His help and act on His advice. When you wake up each morning and think about the day ahead, ask the Holy Spirit to revive in you the gifts you are going to need.

Another way of looking at the fruits of the Holy Spirit is to use them as a guide in examining our conscience. Have I been a joyful person today? Have I been charitable and modest? If I am not experiencing these fruits, and sharing them with other people, then perhaps I am not using the Holy Spirit's gifts as I should. I need to ask Him for a little more Wisdom, or Piety, or respect for the Lord.

People sometimes wonder how we can recognise the Holy Spirit at work. When individuals claim to be acting under the power of the Holy Spirit, is it authentic? Jesus said, "You will be able to tell them by their fruits" (Mt. 8:16). So if someone claims to be filled with the Holy Spirit but in fact they do not lead good holy lives you could question their claim; that's fairly obvious. But there are many strange phenomena which are attributed to the Holy Spirit and which need to be examined rather critically. I'm sure you will agree that the Holy Spirit has two important characteristics: He always acts for a purpose and He is always outward-looking. An action which brings spiritual benefit to another person, such as healing or counselling, may be regarded as the work of the Holy Spirit. In the early Church when God wanted to spread the Good News he gave the Apostles the power of speaking in tongues. This enabled others to hear the Good News in their own language.

When we think of the Holy Spirit or pray to Him, how do we feel? When someone mentions the name of your best friend, whom you haven't seen for many years, how do you respond? Your face lights up and you are eager to know how this person met them. Is there any better friend than the Holy Spirit, who is the spirit of love? Every time we think of Him or pray to Him He is waiting to fill us with his love.

The gifts we receive on the day of our Confirmation are not short-term benefits. They remain within us for a lifetime; gifts of spiritual strength on which we can always draw in time of weakness or perplexity. Perhaps we should be like Solomon and pray especially for the gift of Wisdom; then we would understand how to use all the other gifts!

Part 5.1.4 (i) – The Sacrament of Reconciliation

THE BENEFITS OF GOING TO CONFESSION

We all need forgiveness and God wants us to be forgiven through the Sacrament of Confession (or also known as the Sacrament of Reconciliation). We know this because Jesus Himself has told us. On the evening of the first Easter Sunday, when He had died for our sins, He came and stood among His disciples. His words to them were, "For those whose sins you forgive, they are forgiven; for those whose sins you retain, they are retained." (Jn. 20:23). With this instruction He gave to His Church the power to absolve the sins of those who repent and confess. You may ask how the priest receives this power to forgive sins. The Bishops are the direct successors of the apostles. I, as a priest, received the power to forgive sins from the Archbishop of Southwark. He received this power from another Bishop and he from another Bishop and so on until we can get back to an apostle who received this power from Jesus Himself.

The benefits we derive from this Sacrament are enormous. It puts us right with God. When we sin we damage our friendship with God. If we do something which damages a human friendship, we can only restore that friendship when we have told the one we love that we are sorry. In the same way we should be eager to make peace with God, our best Friend.

Peace is perhaps one of the greatest gifts we receive from the Sacrament of Confession. As a confessor I have experienced this peace from both sides of the confessional. Like you, I have sinned and wanted that guilt to be removed from my life. This has been achieved by a sincere confession. I have also heard many confessions where people have sighed with relief at having such a huge weight lifted from their shoulders. They have said, "Now I know what it is to be at peace, and what a wonderful feeling it is". We as Catholics have absolute confidence that when we are sorry for our sins and we hear the words of absolution our sins are forgiven. How many people of other faiths would love to have this same certainty.

Let's remember that the Sacrament of Reconciliation is intended to be healing, not punitive. This means that we should not think of God as a stern judge but as a conscientious doctor who is there to heal our wounds. If we are sick in body we go to a doctor who will diagnose the cause of the problem and recommend a treatment for the ailment. Likewise, if we have sinned we are spiritually sick and we need to bring our problem to God. Through His priest He can help us on the road to recovery.

One thing I think many of us are not very conscious of is the fact that we are all members of the Body of Christ. He is the head and we are the members. Whenever we sin we damage the Body of Christ. As St. Paul told the Corinthians, "If one part is hurt, all parts are hurt with it." (1Cor. 12:26). When we go to Confession and confess our own personal sins we help to repair that damage. We need the forgiveness of each other. This is why at the beginning of every Mass we confess our sins not only to God but to our 'brothers and sisters'. I think if we realised this truth and we really loved the Church we would do our best not to let its members down and damage the health of the whole body. Isn't the same true of any family who love each other? They do their best not to damage but enhance the health and reputation of each member of the family. So every time we make a sincere confession we are helping to heal the Body of Christ (His Church).

The commandment of the Church is that we are to make our Easter Duty of going to Confession and receiving Holy Communion between Ash Wednesday and Trinity Sunday. This is the Church's way of making sure that we are observing at least that minimum respect to God. But if we have committed mortal sin we must also go to Confession as soon as possible. The Church says if we constantly commit venial sins we are likely to fall victim to a mortal sin. Therefore we should go and make a Confession of our venial sins; this is one of the reasons why the Church encourages us to go frequently to Confession, at least once a month.

Another reason why it is good for us to go to Confession frequently is that we get to know ourselves better; how weak we are and how easily we can fall into sin. As we become more conscious of our own faults we should grow more understanding and tolerant of other people's faults. This is a good habit to develop.

Confession is not only for the forgiveness of sins, it is also a store house of grace. From this store we can draw strength to help us in times of temptation. Not one of us can be certain what lies ahead in the future and so we must be prepared for whatever we have to face. You never know what trap Satan is laying for you.

What a wonderful gift Jesus has given us in the Sacrament of Reconciliation. If we fail to go to Confession Satan must be having a field day. How happy we make him when he knows that Catholics do not use this power available to them. We make life so easy for him. In the Sacrament Jesus has given us the most powerful weapon to crush Satan, so let's make good use of it.

Part 5.1.4 (ii) – The Sacrament of Reconciliation

BEING SORRY FOR OUR SINS

When you actually come to Confession you must have at least one sin to confess. That might sound obvious, but you'd be surprised there are some who say, "I haven't done anything, Father. I've got no sins to confess." I gently suggest to them, "Could you perhaps say your prayers a little better?" "Oh no, I always say my prayers, Father." "Have you been unkind to anyone?" "Oh no, I never hurt anyone." Sometimes no matter how much gentle probing I do to draw out one sin, I get no success. In other words, why have they come? If there is no sin, there is nothing to absolve. I would like to note the words of St. John, "If we say we have no sin, we are liars and the truth is not in us". If we do find that we have no sin to confess since our last confession, we can always mention a sin of our past life and renew our sorrow for it.

A person sometimes comes into the confessional and doesn't say anything. I've tried twenty questions sometimes to draw them out and there's been nothing but silence. Then they get up and walk out. My guess is that it's a young person whose parents have said, "I'm taking you to Confession," and they've said to themselves, "We'll see!"

If we have given so much importance to the examination of conscience we have to give even more importance to our act of sorrow. We may be excellent at delving inside ourselves and fluent at confessing our sins, but all this effort will be fruitless if we are not actually sorry.

There are different degrees of sorrow. There is what is known as attrition. This is sorrow motivated by fear; fear that we may go to hell for all eternity. This really is not sorrow though as we are only thinking of our own skin and having very little concern about displeasing God. But God in His kindness is prepared to forgive us even on our selfish terms.

What God really wants from us is a sorrow that is not motivated by fear but love, love of Him. This is known as contrition. This sorrow is expressed so beautifully in the long act of contrition, "because by our sins we have crucified our loving Saviour Jesus Christ and offended God's infinite goodness." That is true and unselfish sorrow which is pleasing to God. That is the kind of sorrow for which we should always be striving.

Proof of our sorrow is our intention that we are going to try not to commit the same sin again. You may have noticed that one act of contrition contains these words, "I will not sin again." Can you really say that? I can't. I know the person who wrote that act of contrition was giving us the ideal, but because we are human we are always going to fall short of the ideal and so I like to say instead, "I shall try not to sin again." God knows how weak we are and how prone we are to repeat our sins, but He just asks us to keep on trying to do better. That's what we call a firm purpose of amendment.

It is this firm purpose of amendment and the intention to avoid the occasions of sin that indicates the genuineness of our sorrow. Someone may ask, "How do I know that I've got a firm purpose of amendment when I have a chronic problem to deal with - a difficult relative who lives with me. I find that whenever I go to Confession I have to say that I get angry with them. They are always putting me down and they have irritating habits. Almost every day they cause me to lose my patience with them. Now where's the firm purpose of amendment?" In circumstances like this all you can do is your best. When you come out of the confessional your relative is not going to run away, worse luck, but all God expects of you is to try and do your best and cope with the problem. Your effort to cope is your firm purpose of amendment. As for the occasion of sin, this is something you can't always avoid. In the meantime, God knows how difficult it is for you and how hard you're trying, and He makes allowances.

Part 5.1.4 (iii) – The Sacrament of Reconciliation

NUTS AND BOLTS

Do you have worries and queries about going to Confession, about what to say and how to say it? Perhaps you haven't been to Confession for a long time and you've forgotten what to do. Or perhaps you're a convert and you're not sure if you're going about it in the right way; you perhaps feel it must be much easier for cradle Catholics. I would like to tackle what I like to call the 'nuts and bolts' of Confession, to help us to dismantle those obstacles and build a framework for a really good Confession.

You probably don't discuss Confession much with other people, after all, it's a very personal matter. You may therefore wonder whether anyone else feels the same way as you do. Let me assure you straightaway that you are not alone and you certainly should not feel isolated or worried about it at all.

Let me address a few of the common queries people have. Will the priest know me? Won't it be terribly embarrassing to tell him what I've done? And there may be one or two who ask themselves, "suppose the priest later mentions to me or someone else the things I've told him?" My reply to that is, if you go to the same priest every month and if he knows you, it is highly probable that he will recognise your voice. However, this shouldn't put you off for there may be benefits in the priest knowing you. If he's aware of your background he'll be able to understand your position and so be better able to advise and help you. For example, a teenager confesses he is not a regular churchgoer. The priest knows that he comes from a home where these is no example of Mass attendance.

Immediately the priest appreciates the boy's difficulties and says, "Well done for the efforts you are making with so little example," and then goes on to encourage him to persevere with coming to Church every Sunday. So the priest's knowledge of your circumstances can enable him to help you. There are many people who like the continuity of going to confession with the same priest because they feel he knows them and has some understanding of their life.

There is no need to be afraid that a priest will reveal what you have told him in Confession, because he is bound to absolute secrecy and confidentiality. As for remembering your sins, I can tell you God gives the priest a bad memory and what you tell him in Confession; it goes in one ear and out of the other by the time the Confession is over. A priest hears so many confessions that it is impossible to remember everyone's sins. He trains himself to shut out of his mind what he's told in Confession and doesn't dwell on it. Remember, in the confessional you are confessing your sins to God and the priest is acting as God's instrument in giving you absolution. The priest is there to help you to unburden yourself and make a good Confession so you are reconciled again with God and His love. The priest is not interested in dwelling on the detail afterwards; all of that has now come and gone.

Some feel that they would like to discuss personal problems with the priest and ask for his advice, but is Confession the right time and place? Will he think I'm a nuisance? I would like to assure you that you are definitely not wasting the priest's time. In fact he would be only too pleased to think that he could help you. And don't worry about the time element.

It is possible that you may worry about your sins and feel that the priest may speak to you sharply or get angry with you. Remember how Our Lord treated the Good Thief. All he said was, "Jesus, remember me when you come into Your Kingdom." (Lk. 23:42). Jesus never got angry, nor did He reprimand him for his past life. Rather, He said to him "I promise you today you will be with Me in paradise." (Lk.

A JOURNEY INTO THE CATHOLIC FAITH

23:43). Just one appeal for love was enough to blot out a lifetime of sin. The priest is there to guide and help you so that you make a good Confession to God.

People sometimes say, "I can't possibly remember every sin I've committed since my last Confession." Don't worry, it isn't necessary to mention every sin, only serious sins. What is a serious sin? To commit a serious sin three conditions must be present at the same time. First, it must be of a serious nature. One example I can give is missing Mass on Sunday or on Holy Days of Obligation. Second, you must actually know yourself that it's a serious offence to God. And third, you must have done it deliberately. If you genuinely forget to mention a sin it will be forgiven along with all the other sins you've confessed, but you must mention it at your very next Confession.

We have noted earlier about preparing for Confession by examining our conscience. When should we begin this procedure, when we actually arrive at Church? No, we need to give ourselves as much time as possible. If you are intending to go to Confession, you can begin thinking it over a day or two in advance. Start by asking the Holy Spirit to help you to make a good Confession. Call upon the help of Our Blessed Lady, your guardian angel and your patron saint. From that moment, start to review how you have failed God, others and yourself and what you are going to say in Confession. In this way, you will be well prepared to mention your failings. Then the time spent in Church before Confession can be used in trying to be really sorry and asking the Holy Spirit in prayer for the help you need not to commit these sins again.

Part 5.1.4 (iv) – The Sacrament of Reconciliation

WHAT DO I SAY?

When you are ready to make your Confession you can choose whether to use the confessional box or to speak to the priest face to face. If you are hard of hearing or have some impediment I would strongly suggest that you make your confession face to face, so that the priest can help you as much as possible. If a deaf person does decide to use the confessional box, do tell the priest that you are deaf or hard of hearing.

Taking the right approach is important to make sure you make a good Confession. Remember, the priest is on your side, but if you feel nervous or uncomfortable just say, "Hello, Father."; immediately then the priest thinks, "ah, a nice friendly person." and you'll find him even more friendly. Then you can go on to say, "Bless me Father, for I have sinned," and tell him how long it has been since your last Confession.

Perhaps it has been a very long time, say twenty years, and you don't know how to begin. Well, don't worry. Just tell the priest how long it has been, and say, "Father, will you please help me." You'll be surprised how easy the priest will make it for you. He will ask the right questions. Be sure that he will be delighted that you have come back to the Lord and that he was the one chosen to hear your Confession.

If a penitent doesn't make himself or herself clear, a priest may have to ask questions. If someone merely says, "I missed Mass, Father," and the priest asks, "did you miss Mass deliberately?" very often the penitent says, "I couldn't go, Father, I had the flu" or "I was in hospital." If that's the case it is not a sin and there's no need to mention it therefore. Again, if someone merely says, "I stole some money", the priest has to ask what you stole. You could have taken 50p or robbed a bank, but there's a world of difference between the two. The priest has to ask questions also if you merely state that you were "impure". You can be impure in thought, word or act. The act could be with yourself, or with another. The other person could be single, or married, or in vows.

You have to tell the full truth. Should anyone deliberately conceal a serious sin because they are ashamed or embarrassed, they have not made a good Confession; in fact, they have committed another sin, the sin of sacrilege, which is the desecration of a holy thing. Never be afraid of saying anything to the priest. He's heard it all before and he will think more highly of you for being to truthful to God.

After you have enumerated all your sins, end with these words, "For these and for all the sins of my past life and for the ones I cannot remember, I ask God's pardon and from you, please Father, penance and absolution".

Then, you can now listen to the advice the priest has to give you. He may suggest certain changes you could make to avoid committing those sins again. He will also give you encouragement and guidance. For example, you may have confessed half a dozen sins which need tackling. You want to improve, but you can't deal with all these sins at once. The priest may ask you to work on just one of them, and you'll be surprised to find that gradually you then improve in every area.

Now it's time for the priest to give you your penance, which usually takes the form of a prayer. Why is a penance necessary? If you have committed a sin, large or small, it means that you have done some kind of harm to another person. You have told God that you are sorry, but you still have to try in some way to put right the damage you have done. You may feel that the penance the priest has given you hardly makes up for the wrong you have done. In that case you may like to repeat your penance daily until your next Confession. This also lessens the time we may have to spend in purgatory.

Before the priest gives you absolution he will probably discuss with you the way in which you can try to make up for your sins. If you have stolen money or possessions he will tell you that you must do your best to return the stolen goods or repay the money, without harming your family or losing your good name. If you have gossiped about someone you may never know the harm you have done. Your tale may have gone from one to another, being embroidered on the way. You must try your best to restore that person's good name. But what about those offences for which there is no obvious remedy? What if you have had an adulterous relationship which has broken up a family? Suppose you have had an abortion? You can't turn the clock back, but you can still make amends by other means. Prayers, almsgiving, or charitable work could be offered as reparation for your sin. Your priest will discuss with you the most appropriate action.

When you hear the words of absolution, be consciously happy and think of your heavenly Father putting His arms round you and saying, "All is forgiven." There are some people who, even having received absolution, cannot forgive themselves. When they feel this way, they distrust God. If God has forgiven you, you must forgive yourself and put your faith in Him.

If God forgives us, we must also be ready to forgive others. Isn't it true that when we go to Confession we expect God to forgive us? We would be astounded if the priest were to say, "There is no forgiveness for you." Yet how forgiving are we to one another? Definitely not as magnanimous as God. But we must remember that God only forgives us insofar as we are willing to forgive others. Isn't that what we pray for when we say, "Forgive us our trespasses as we forgive those who trespass against us"?

People sometimes ask, "How often should I go to Confession?" We have it on no better authority than Saint Pope John Paul II himself who recommended that we should go once a month. Why not look upon our monthly Confessions as twelve meetings a year with our heavenly Father? Those of us who have bank accounts like a monthly statement from the bank. Why don't we take our spiritual life just as seriously and give God a monthly statement? Even though, thank God, we may have no serious sins to confess, nevertheless the advantages we receive are enormous. Sins are forgiven, grace is received helping us to sin less in the future, God is praised, right order is restored, restitution is made, we also receive help against future temptations and we are keeping ourselves on track for a place in heaven. Knowing all this, shouldn't we be looking forward to monthly Confession?

There is a lot more attention in society generally these days on our own wellbeing. When we go to Confession we are being given the opportunity to unburden ourselves of our sins and the guilt in our own minds. At the end of a good Confession being reconciled to God and our neighbour brings inner peace and harmony to our souls. This gives us wellbeing for our spirit, mind and body.
Let us thank Jesus for giving us this beautiful Sacrament in helping us restore our friendship with Him.

Part 5.1.5 (i) – The Eucharist

OUR GREATEST TREASURE

If Jesus began His Public Ministry with the words, "My flesh is real food and my blood is real drink', I would be the first to say, this is nonsense. Instead He began His Ministry by gradually unfolding who He was. St. John tells us that His first miracle was to change water into wine at a wedding feast at the request of His mother who wanted to save the embarrassment of the bride and groom. Then He showed His love for the sick and handicapped by giving sight to the blind, hearing to the deaf and healing lepers. He even raised a twelve year old girl from the dead. He fed a multitude of 5,000 on a few barley loaves and fish. He calmed a raging storm and walked on the water. Was there anything He couldn't do? When the people had seen all these wonders if He'd said, "My flesh is real food and my blood is real drink', I would be among those who would say, I can't understand this, but there must be something in it?. If He can perform all these miracles and show what power He has over water, by walking on it, and by changing it into wine, why is it impossible for His flesh to be real food and His blood real drink?

Jesus was to keep that promise of giving us His Body and Blood to be the food of our souls at the Last Supper He had with His apostles. He took bread into His hands and said the words, "Take it and eat...This is my Body". When He took the cup of wine and said, "Drink all of you...for this is my Blood" (Mt. 26:26-27). When He added, "Do this as a memorial of Me" (Lk. 22:19), He wanted His followers to continue perpetuating His presence in the Church He had founded.

Jesus could have remained with His apostles and His Church in another way. When visiting Bethlehem, He could have told His apostles to build a basilica to commemorate His birthplace. When passing the Sea of Galilee He could have told them to erect a plaque to say that He and Peter had walked on this water. He loved preaching in the synagogue at Capernaum, He could have wanted that synagogue to be persevered forever. As the centuries rolled by His followers could have pointed out these places associated with Jesus, their Founder. Instead He did something better which no other founder of a religion has ever done, He left His very self to be the Food of our souls.

Our closeness to Jesus depends upon our faith. I remember once being asked by someone who was not a Catholic, "How do you Catholics regard Holy Communion?" I told him that in what looks like a wafer of bread and wine is the true presence of our Founder, Jesus Christ, who is God. He said, "Do all Catholics really believe that?" I said, "Of course, we do". He said, "If I believed that, I would never get off my knees in Church. I would never leave His presence". It is true, the stronger our faith in the Eucharistic presence of Jesus, the more fervent would be our adoration and love of Jesus.

Holy Communion not only unites us with Jesus, but with all His followers who receive Him. The reception of Holy Communion should be like a golden thread uniting us all to one another. In fact, if we are at enmity with another person Jesus would first want us to patch up our differences with each other before we approach Him. Receiving Him in Holy Communion demands that we should be on loving terms with our neighbour. He said, "If you are bringing your offering to the altar and there remember that your brother has something against you, leave your offering there before the altar, go and be reconciled with your brother first, and then come back and present your offering" (Mt. 5:23).

Whenever we eat any food that food eventually becomes a part of us. But when we eat the flesh of Jesus and drink His blood we are meant to become more like Him.

To receive Our Lord worthily in Holy Communion we must be in a state of grace, that is, we must be friends with Jesus. We must be free from mortal sin. We must also take no food or drink (except water) for one hour before Communion. The sick may take medicine without time limit and the housebound do not need to fast.

It is sad, but it must be said that there are some Catholics who feel they have the right to go Communion every time they go to Mass. Of course, none of us is worthy to receive the Lord. Every time we approach the table of the Lord we must always ask ourselves, 'Am I in a state of grace and prepared to receive the Lord?' Some Catholics unfortunately only go to Mass when they feel like going, which could be once every three or four weeks or more infrequent still like at Christmas only. I know that some say, what's the point of attending Mass if you feel you are going to get nothing from it, but then when they do go to Mass they go to Holy Communion. Isn't that like suiting themselves, rather than suiting the One who laid down His life for them? It is a serious commandment of the Church that we attend Mass every Sunday. There is no question of whether we feel like going or not. We have to think along the lines of the Church. If we have missed Mass deliberately we must first go to Confession and be sorry for that sin. Only then can we receive the Lord in Holy Communion. There are others who never go regularly to Mass. They only attend Church at Easter and Christmas, baptisms, marriages and funerals, and yet go to Holy Communion whenever they attend Mass. They never go to Confession. They are wrong to receive Holy Communion and they are committing a sacrilege. It was St. Paul who wrote, "The person who eats and drinks without recognising the Body is eating and drinking his own condemnation" (1 Cor. 11:29). How happy Jesus would be if those sheep who are lost returned to His home every week because they love Him and want to receive Him as food for their souls so that one day they may be united with Him in Heaven.

Holy Communion is our greatest treasure on earth. My own father taught me to believe that one Holy Communion is worth more than the entire wealth of the world. If we looked upon every Communion as our last one on this earth, we would surely make it the best.

Part 5.1.5 (ii) – The Eucharist

FIVE DIGIT THANKSGIVING AT HOLY COMMUMNION

Satan is most active in Church the moment we have received Holy Communion. Have you noticed that as soon as you go back to your place after Holy Communion your mind is full of distractions? When you do get down to the serious business of making a fervent thanksgiving your mind is carried away with a 101 thoughts about what you have to do that day.

This is where we have to take very strict control of ourselves. We must take the necessary precaution of keeping our eyes shut to cut out all visual distractions. That is a very important practical point that has to be observed if we are to make a fervent thanksgiving. Now the stage is set for a loving conversation with Jesus who longs for you to open up your heart and tell Him how much you love Him.

Look upon every Holy Communion as a foretaste of heaven. What is heaven? Heaven is nothing else than the possession of God, and that is precisely what you have every time you come to Holy Communion. Make your heaven begin here on earth. The times we spend with Jesus after Holy Communion is so short and so make this thanksgiving continue during the day. Also look upon every thanksgiving as the last one you are going to make on earth, and you will try to make it your best one.

May I suggest a form of thanksgiving? As soon as you have received Jesus in Holy Communion say, "Heavenly Father, thank you for giving me your Son. I love You, Jesus (Jesus once told a saint that those were the words He loves hearing and so few say them to Him). Jesus, thank You for all You have done for me, for becoming a man, for the example of Your life, all You have taught us, dying of the Cross for us and particularly at this moment for giving me Yourself in the Holy Eucharist. Holy Spirit, be my best Friend. Help me to love the Father, the Son and You with all my heart. Mary, my Mother, (Jesus was happiest on this earth when He was in your company) help me to love and give joy to Jesus as you did."

Whenever you mention Our Lady's name we have to couple it with that of her husband, Joseph. He loved Jesus very much and we can ask him to help us. You can ask the help of your patron saints to help you make fervent Holy Communions as they must have done. Ask your Guardian Angel to stand guard at the entrance of your mind and keep Satan away from flooding your mind with distractions.

The greatest compliment we can pay to Jesus is to say the 'Our Father,' the very prayer He put on our lips. Then recite the 'Glory be to the Father,' because wherever Jesus is there is the Father and the Holy Spirit. Finally, we can recite the second half of the 'Hail Mary,' remembering the two moments of time we single out, 'now and at the hour of our death.' We want Mary to be with us right now and at the greatest moment of our life - the moment of our death. We want her to take our hand and place it in the hand of our Heavenly Father.

Now we can use the five digits of our left hand to remind us to pray for all we should pray for.

The thumb is the digit nearest to us. This reminds us to pray for those nearest and dearest to us, Mum, Dad, brothers and sisters, aunts and uncles and all grandparents going right back to Adam. I mention them because we are what we are today because of what they gave us. Aren't you going to look forward to meeting your great, great, great grandfather and grandmother and say, "I prayed for you? Thank you for all you gave me?" The thumb can also remind us to pray for all our friends. We can whisper their names to Jesus.

Now we come to the index finger. This reminds us to pray for those who so often in love have pointed this finger at us as they have directed us on our journey to heaven; priests and nuns, who have influenced our lives, teachers and all those who have helped us through example and their writings.

The next finger happens to be the highest finger on our hand and this reminds us to pray for those highest in Church and State. The Holy Father, the Pope - what responsibility he has to face! Cardinals, bishops, priests and deacons and for an increase in vocations. Then mention the Royal Family, the Prime Minister and the leaders of the other parties and the rulers of all the other countries. On this finger I also like to pray for all those people in the entertainment and sporting world who have added happiness in my life.

Then we come to the ring finger. This is why I have chosen the left hand. We can pray for all married couples, especially if our prayers today can avert the breakup of at least one marriage. This finger too happens to the weakest finger on our hand and the one we use least, and so it can remind us to pray for the helpless - the Holy Souls in purgatory; prisoners all over the world and the starving; doctors and nurses and all those who work for the sick and handicapped.

Finally, we come to our little finger. This reminds us not to forget to pray for ourselves. We can ask God for three things:

1. An abundance of His Holy Spirit, especially with His gift of wisdom, because God has said, "I will never refuse my Spirit to the one who asks for It."

2. The gift of prayer and perseverance in prayer. That is another way of saying I always want to be in love with you.

3. The grace of final perseverance, pleading with Jesus to make sure that I get to heaven.

Briefly we can pray for our enemies; the hardest sinner in the world; the peace that Jesus bequeathed our world and the unity for which He prayed, and for the Jewish people to accept Jesus as their saviour.

Now we can thank Jesus for His four gifts, for creating us, for our parents, His first and best gift to us, our Catholic faith and finally our Guardian Angel.

This five digit form of thanksgiving can help you to cut out distractions. You will find that there is just no time to get distracted. With practice it doesn't take a long time.

Part 5.1.6 (i) – Holy Mass

SETTING THE STAGE

I want to begin by saying that when we come to Mass we are not merely spectators, waiting to be entertained by the priest's performance. Some young people claim that the Mass is boring. They enjoy a school Mass where they play guitars and sing or dance, but when they come to Church there is none of that and so they lose interest. This is because they often, but through no fault of their own, do not realise what is going on during Mass. The prayers and symbolism may in fact mean nothing to them.

Everything we use during Mass has a purpose or a symbolism. The candles are a reminder of Mass being said in the dark Catacombs. At one time, the vessels had to be of precious metal, silver or gold, and the inside which held the body and blood of the Lord had to be lined with gold.
Nowadays the Church has relaxed that ruling and other materials can be used.

You will notice that the priest wears different coloured vestments according to the season or feast. For feasts of Our Lord and Our Lady, the priest wears white vestments, but for very important feasts such as Christmas and Easter some churches have gold vestments. White is also used for feasts of virgins and confessors, but for martyrs and the feast of Pentecost we wear red. Purple is the colour for the seasons of Advent and Lent, and for funerals. Throughout the Sundays and ferials of the year, green vestments are used. Finally, on the middle Sundays of Advent and Lent, rose vestments are allowed.

We all have our own personal ways of joining in the Mass. There may still be one or two people who say the Rosary during Mass, but this is really not appropriate. We need to concentrate on what is actually happening. There was once a lady who could not read or write and when she came to Mass she just brought three coloured cards with her. When Mass began she would look at the first card, which was black, to remind her of her sinfulness. At the consecration she would look at her next card, which was red, reminding her that the Blood of Christ had saved her. Finally, at communion she looked at her white card for now she was united to the Lord and everyone. That was how she prayed the Mass, and she did it well.

I would like to go through the Mass step by step, suggesting a prayer and a thought to match every action. It is so easy to become distracted during Mass, and suddenly find that Mass is over and we haven't consciously given anything to it or received anything from it. I, as the priest, am the chief celebrant, but it is your sacrifice as well and I need you to offer it with me.

When you come to Mass, try to come early, at least three to five minutes before Mass begins. This is not chatting time, but preparation time. Any job that is worth doing needs good preparation, whether it's cooking, dressmaking or writing an essay. Without that preparation you can't produce your best work. You want to offer your best to God at Mass, and so you are going to prepare well. If you come early for Mass, that is your opportunity to spend some time with the Lord.

People often say how sad it is that the Church is closed during the day. Unfortunately there is a general lack of reverence and respect for all things, not just holy things. If our Churches were left open all day they would be vulnerable to vandalism, desecration and theft. Priests have experienced this time and time again in their Churches, and so they have had to be locked when there are no services taking place. If religious minded people frequented our Churches then perhaps there would be no need to lock them during the day. This is so in the Hidden Gem in Manchester where people are dropping in all day to pray, but even then the priest has to alarm the sanctuary where the Blessed Sacrament is exposed.

If you come early for Mass, that is your opportunity to spend some time with the Lord. Your mind may be full of little worries and problems, or a list of things you have to do today, but for the next hour you are going to put them on one side and concentrate on the Lord. Isn't this the most important hour of the week?

If we are careless about being on time for Mass, we are showing disrespect for the Lord. How many of us would be late for an appointment with a doctor, a dentist or a solicitor? Who is more important to us, these people, or the Lord?   In the same way, we are cheating ourselves if we are late for our appointment with the Lord.

Part 5.1.6 (ii) – Holy Mass

WE SPEAK TO GOD

We are now going to look at the shared prayer of the priest and people, which constitutes the Mass itself.

Mass begins and the priest goes to the altar and kisses it. He does this because the altar contains a stone enclosing relics of martyrs. This is a remnant of the early days of the Church, when Mass was often said in the Catacombs on the gravestones of Christians who had died for the faith. As the priest kisses the altar, he gives thanks for the heroism of the martyrs and ask them to help us pray the Mass.

Now we all make the sign of the cross. We should make it reverently and proudly. It reminds us of two things: that Jesus died on the cross for us and that the three Persons of the Blessed Trinity live within us. Whenever we make the sign of the cross we should use the three fingers of our right hand, not just one finger, to remind ourselves of the three Persons of the Blessed Trinity who live within us. The priest then greets everyone with words like these, "The Lord be with you." He is not just saying, "Hi!" or "Good morning". He is wishing the Lord to be with you. Is there any greater thing he could desire for you? And so you return the compliment by saying, "And also with you."

The Entrance Antiphon is important because it sets the theme for the Mass. For example, on Easter Sunday it is, "The Lord has indeed risen, Alleluia." For the feast of SS. Peter and Paul it is, "These men, conquering all human frailty, shed their blood and helped the Church to grow." You will find that every sentence in the Mass has a purpose. This Antiphon leads into the Penitential Rite, in which we admit that we are sinners. We are like the tax collector in the parable, who stood at the back of the temple and beat his breast, saying, "God, be merciful to me, a sinner" (Lk. 18:13-14).

Two main forms of Penitential Rite are commonly used. We may say the Kyrie, in which we ask Christ's mercy three times. The Kyrie is taken from Greek meaning Christ have mercy. Notice that we address the three acts of sorrow to Christ and not to each Person of the Blessed Trinity. Or we may say the "I confess", in which we not only confess to Almighty God but to our neighbour. This reminds us that when we sin we don't only hurt ourselves but all our brothers and sisters who make up the Body of Christ. As St. Paul tells us in his First Letter to the Corinthians, Chapter 12, Christ is the Head and we are His members. We then go on to ask the help of Our Lady, the angels and saints, and our neighbour. The Penitential Rite is not only a plea for forgiveness but also a joyful acknowledgment of the saving presence of the Risen Christ in our midst.

On Sundays and feast days we say the prayer, "Glory to God in the highest." These opening words were first sung by the angels to announce to the shepherds the birth of their Saviour. This wasn't just a second-rate choir singing, it was part of the heavenly choir of angels and it must have thrilled the shepherds. You may remember that I said refer to the word ACTS to help us remember how we pray: Adoration, Contrition, Thanksgiving and Supplication. These four themes run through the Mass, like the themes of a symphony, and they are all contained in the Gloria. Now we worship God, then we give Him thanks, now we praise Him for His glory and then we ask Him to receive our prayers. Notice how each part of this prayer is addressed in turn to each person of the Blessed Trinity. We give glory to God the Father. We acknowledge Jesus as His Son. We recognise that the Holy Spirit is equal to both the Father and the Son. So when we say the Gloria we think of that thrilling song of the angels who sang at Jesus' birth, and we remember the four themes of the Mass.

Then the priest says, "Let us pray". He is calling us to attention, because he is going to collect together all our prayers and offer them with the official prayer of the Church. That is why this prayer is called the Collect. This is the time to collect our thoughts together, in case they are starting to stray. Every Collect has four parts. It is addressed to God. An attribute of God is mentioned. The petition is stated. The prayer ends, "Through Christ Our Lord." An example would be, "God, who are merciful to sinners, forgive us our sins. We ask this through Christ our Lord." Try to recognise these four points, and in particular make the petition your own. This prayer, like all our prayers, is made in the name of Jesus because this is how He taught us to pray.

Part 5.1.6 (iii) – Holy Mass

GOD SPEAKS TO US

Up to this point in the Mass, we have been speaking to God. Now we come to the Liturgy of the Word, where God speaks to us. We sit down, but that doesn't mean we go to sleep or let our minds wander. We have to give our full attention to what God has to say to us in the Scriptures. In fact we need elephant's ears so that nothing goes past them. If you are a reader in Church, you have a great responsibility. You must read clearly, slowly and fluently so that the Word of God will be heard and understood. I know that there are some experts in the liturgy who will tell you to listen to the reader for this is God speaking to you and not to follow the reading in a book. I find there are times when I don't hear all the reader is saying and so miss the meaning of the reading. So to make sure that I don't miss any of the reading I sometimes prefer to follow the script from a book.

As you listen to the readings, ask yourself, "What does God want to say to me today?" This is an important question and

not always an easy one to answer. I think we would all agree that some of the scripture passages are very difficult to understand. We can't immediately grasp the meaning of the text, much less see its relevance to our own lives. This is where preparation can be helpful. If you have your own missal, or if your parish has mass books available in Church, spend a little time before Mass reading through the three texts which have been chosen for this particular Sunday. Try to see a connection between them. You will find that the first and third readings have a connection. The second reading is often taken form the letters of St. Paul and there is much richness there to meditate on. Pray to the Holy Spirit to help you understand the personal message God wants to give you today through His Word. At first, the readings may say nothing to you, but when you hear them again during the Mass you may find new insight into their meaning.
Remember, the message is personal to you; other people will find different ideas to ponder on.

In the Old Testament passage, God may be speaking through one of His prophets, like the prophet Jonah who warned the people of Nineveh to repent. Some prophets told stories of courage and faithfulness, some reminded people of God's unfailing love. The reader ends with, "The Word of the Lord," to which we respond, "Thanks be to God." Let's make sure that our thanks are heartfelt, for the message of life which God gives us. The Psalm is usually an echo of the first reading and is on the same topic. The Psalm also represents one of those four themes I mentioned, for in the Psalm we may be praising God, expressing our sorrow, thanking Him for His goodness, or asking Him to help us with our problems.

The second reading is taken from the letters or writings of the Apostles. In the early days of the Church, when Christianity was spreading far beyond Israel, Apostles like Paul and Peter would send advice and encouragement to the new converts. That advice is just as relevant to us today. We can pray to the Holy Spirit to help us understand and put into effect the words we are hearing. They are His words.

We now stand to proclaim the Gospel, and we begin by singing the Alleluia. This word means Praise to God - or Yippee!! The Gospel is always read by the priest or deacon, because these are the words of Jesus Himself. The priest at Mass is meant to take the place of Jesus. At High Mass, you will see the Lectionary carried aloft by the priest between two acolytes who carry candles. To show reverence for the Gospel, the priest incenses the Missal. When the Mass was said in Latin the altar server would carry the book from one side of the altar to the other. This symbolised passing from the old covenant to the new covenant. The Word of God had been preached to the Jews and is now being preached to the whole world. Since that symbolism is no longer being practised, when you see the priest going to read the Gospel, keep this idea of old and new covenant in your mind.

The priest prepares himself by saying silently, "May I humbly and worthily proclaim your Gospel." Perhaps you could make this your preparation, too. The priest introduces the Gospel and makes a sign of the cross with His thumb on the Lectionary. The priest and people then make three signs of the cross, on the forehead, lips and heart. As we do, we silently say this prayer, "May the Lord be in my mind, and on my lips, and in my heart."

As we listen to the Gospel, we use our imagination to enter into the story. We are aware that it is Jesus speaking to His Apostles, to a sinner, to a leper or to the Pharisees, and we must picture ourselves in that crowd. In this way we make the Gospel come alive for us. The priest concludes with the words, "The Gospel of the Lord," and the people answer, "Praise to you, Lord Jesus Christ." The priest kisses the Lectionary and says these words, "By the words of the Gospel may our sins be blotted out." Make this prayer your own.

There then follows the priest's homily, in which he tries to explain the meaning of the texts or make some observation on the Gospel message.

As you sit down to hear the homily, remember to say a prayer for the priest, who is about to unfold the word of God to you. He, too, prays that the Holy Spirit will guide him so that he can find helpful words for his congregation. May I make a few observations from a priest's point of view? A little encouragement goes a long way, and if the priest can see you giving him your attention, 'the come on, sock it to us look', it will help him to give you his best. Please try not to yawn audibly! If you must look at your watch, do it surreptitiously. It's lovely to see families coming to Church, but should you have babies who want to compete with the priest, don't be afraid to take your child out to the Church porch where you can amuse them. Everyone will understand that you don't want to disturb the priest while he's preaching, and they will appreciate your unselfishness. Children are often inquisitive and like to ask questions about what is going on around them. Again, don't be afraid to take them to the back of the Church and quietly answer their questions. Just as the priest is instructing the congregation, you are instructing your child. Sometimes there are toddlers who are allowed to run freely around the church, distracting everyone. I would never want to offend a parent but I am just making a plea on behalf of the people and the priest as a whole so they can be undistracted from the message they have come to concentrate on.

After the homily we stand to profess our faith in the words of the Creed. This prayer is so familiar that we can easily rattle it off and give no attention to what we are saying. We need to say it thoughtfully. When we say the Creed privately we say, "Credo - I believe", but at Mass it's "We believe." This is because the Creed is a joint declaration of what Catholics believe. It binds us together in faith. And so as we begin this great prayer we think of the millions of fellow Catholics who are reciting it today with us all over the world. We remember the people who helped to hand on the faith to us, and the martyrs who bravely died defending these same truths that we profess.

Think carefully about the words as you say the Creed, and try to keep one thought in your mind at each stage. "We believe in one God..." Everything around us, the things we can see and even the things we can't see, was made by God. What created thing are you most grateful for? Is it a person you love? A child? A favourite place? A beautiful landscape? Focus on that one idea.

"We believe in one Lord, Jesus Christ...." This is the central part of our Creed and it is the complete life story of Jesus condensed into a few lines. Think of those words, "for our salvation". Everything Jesus did, all that He suffered and achieved was for that end, our salvation. How He must love us, and how faithfully we should be loving Him as we recite what He has done for us.

"We believe in the Holy Spirit, the Lord, the giver of life....." The Father and the Son have sent us their Spirit to be our Companion throughout life, comforting us in times of sorrow, guiding us in knowledge of our faith, strengthening us when we feel disheartened, firing us with enthusiasm; in a word, to be our best friend. How do you treat a best friend? You're always in touch and share so much together. Think of the Holy Spirit like that. He's always with you and you can talk to Him and trust Him, so make sure you never neglect Him.

"We believe in one holy, Catholic and apostolic Church....." The Spirit works through the Church, and we end the Creed by professing our loyalty to her. The Church is our home, where we live as one family. It is a place where we can feel loved, accepted and at ease, a place where we can bring our friends. We have the security of knowing that the Church has the power to guide us in all truth and will never mislead us. The idea to focus on is "home" and all that means to you.

In the early days of the Church, the first part of the Mass, up to and including the homily, used to be called the Mass of Catechumens. At one time, when converts were being instructed in the faith, they would be required to leave the

Church at this point. The second part, the Mass of the Faithful, was only for those who had been baptised and received into the Church. It is this second part which will form the subject of next part of this chapter.

Part 5.1.6 (iv) – Holy Mass

OFFERING AND RECEIVING

The Mass is a representation of the perfect sacrifice offered by Jesus. Now we shall look at the ways in which everyone in the Church, priests and laity join together to offer the Mass.

Priests are ordained to offer Mass, in fact it is their chief duty; but lay people have a role to play in offering the sacrifice. They, too, are sharers in the priesthood of Christ. St. Peter addressed everyone in the Church with these words, "You are...a royal priesthood, a consecrated nation, a people set part." (1 Pet. 2:9) He included everyone, not just ordained ministers. Every Christian receives this power at their Baptism. This is expressed when the priest anoints the Christian with the oil of chrism. A priest is anointed at his ordination to the priesthood. So, too therefore, every baptised person is anointed to share in the priestly role of Christ.

What do we offer to God our Father at the Mass? We offer His Son, Jesus, and we offer ourselves as well. We acknowledge that we owe our very existence to God, and so we place before Him everything that we have, everything that we are, everything that we do. We give Him our work, our leisure, our thoughts and hopes, our fears and anxieties and our pain. We thank God for the good things He has given us: the beauty of our world, the security of home, the love of family and friends, the companionship of pets, the pleasure of hobbies. Remembering the times when we have done wrong, we admit our pride and bring Him our sorrow for all our failings. We bring Him our prayers of request, asking Him for His help, comfort and guidance, not only for ourselves but for all the people for whom we pray. You might find it helpful to remember these offerings by thinking of the word ACTS – adoration, contrition, thanksgiving and supplication.

When God has accepted our offerings He transforms them and gives them back to us in a different form. Our sorrow is changed into forgiveness. Our pain is changed into peace. Our thanksgiving is changed into joy. But above all the bread and wine are changed into Christ's body and blood. When we receive Christ in Holy Communion we ourselves are changed and become more like Him.

Receiving Holy Communion is the completion of our sacrifice. What would you think if you came to Mass and you noticed that the priest never received Holy Communion? He offered the bread and wine and the Risen Lord to the Father, but he refrained from Holy Communion. I'm sure you would say, "He's a very strange priest." Have you ever thought that, since you share in the priesthood of Christ, you would be a very strange priest if you did not receive Communion? We should always try to complete our sacrifice by receiving Christ in Holy Communion because this is the gift our heavenly Father wants to give us.

Nevertheless, receiving Holy Communion should not be a matter of thoughtlessly following the crowd. Knowing that Communion is holy, we have to make sure that we are properly prepared to receive it. St. Paul warns us, "Anyone who eats the bread or drinks the cup of the Lord unworthily...is eating and drinking his own condemnation." (1 Cor. 11:27-29) In certain circumstances, then, it would be wrong to receive Communion. For example, we show our respect for Our Lord by fasting for a short time before receiving Him. You cannot receive Holy Communion if you have not abstained from food for an hour beforehand; this rule does not, of course, apply to the sick, who may need regular nourishment or medicine.

We will be all the more eager to receive Jesus in Holy Communion if we remember that when Jesus gave us the Holy Eucharist He said, "I have longed to have this passover with you" (Lk. 22:15). How ardent was His desire to be with us! We should long to be with Him in Holy Communion.

We must not receive Communion whilst in a state of mortal sin. That sin is an obstacle which we must remove by confessing it in the Sacrament of Reconciliation. I know of people who will tell you that they don't go to Mass every Sunday but receive Communion whenever they do go to Mass. They don't seem to realise that in so doing they are committing a further sin. They must first go to Confession and tell the Lord that they have deliberately missed Sunday Mass before they can receive Holy Communion.

To participate fully in the Mass we should make sure that we are able to share in Holy Communion. When we have received Holy Communion we need to remember to pray reverently to God the Father thanking him for sending Christ the Son of God to be the Saviour of the world. While other prayers we may individually wish to say at this time are important, they should come after first and foremost acknowledging to God His gift to us by having sent His only Son to be sacrificed for our sins and those of the whole world.

Through Mass and Communion we receive that wonderful pardon and reconciliation which Christ won for us on Calvary. We form a bond with Christ and with every other member of the Catholic Church, those who belong to our parish, those who live in other parts of the world, those who have died and are in Purgatory, and those who are now in Heaven. These are the reasons why Catholics love the Mass so much and will often try to attend Mass on weekdays as well as Sundays. It is part of our heritage, for our ancestors also loved the Mass and made it an important part of their lives right up to the time of the Reformation. Many of them would face death rather than abandon the Catholic faith.

Part 5.1.6 (v) – Holy Mass

WE OFFER OUR GIFTS TO GOD

We have considered the Creed, that triumphant declaration of our Catholic faith. Now, we come to something for which parish priests are noted. I'm sure you've heard the story about the plane that was in trouble. They knew there was a Catholic priest on board, so they asked him to do something religious, so he said, "Let's have a collection". This is what follows the Creed.

On Sundays and holy days we have an offertory collection. Nowadays we give cash, but in the early Church people presented the priest with the produce of their land. This was to keep the priest fed for the coming week. Whatever was surplus to the priest's needs was shared among the poor and widows.

People sometimes ask, "How much should I put on in the collection basket?" If you were a Mormon you would be expected to pay one tenth of your income. Aren't you glad you are not a Mormon? Cardinal Hulme suggested as a guideline that if people work 40 hours a week they ought to give one hour's wage to God. When I was a parish priest I'd be very happy if my parishioners gave 1% of what they earned. So, if you receive £500 a week, you give £5. In some places you can't even get a cup of coffee for £5. In 1976 I knew a woman who lived on Social Security. I think she received about £30 a week. As soon as she received her money she would put aside £1 for the Church, which was a lot of money for her. She told me she never wanted for anything. God always looked after her and she said it was because she put Him first!

Preparation of the Altar and Gifts begins with the priests words, "Blessed are you, Lord God of all creation..." The collection, along with offerings of bread and wine, is brought up to the altar to be received by the priest. These gifts of bread and wine represent our work. God provides the raw materials of wheat and grapes and we make them into bread and wine. These were the staple diet of the people of Our Lord's time and that is why He chose them as the elements which would be changed into His Body and Blood. In offering bread and wine, "which earth has given and human hands have made," we are actually giving back to God what He has given to us. It's rather like a parent receiving birthday presents from their children. The parent provides their pocket money, and with that money they buy the presents to give to their parent.

When the priest raises the paten on which the host lies and offers it to God, he is really offering himself and us. This is your opportunity to offer your whole self to the Lord: your work, your pleasures, your family, your loved ones, your joys, your anxieties, your sufferings. Give Him your thanks for all the good things He has given you and your sorrow for your sins. Think of yourself placing all these things on the paten along with the bread and being accepted by our heavenly Father.

The priest pours wine into the chalice and then adds to it a drop of water. The wine represents the Lord and the water ourselves. The prayer you can say is the one the priest says at this moment, "By the mystery of this water and wine may we come to share in the divinity of Christ who humbled Himself to share in our humanity." We think of Jesus becoming one of us and us becoming more like Him.

As the priest offers up the wine, you can think of this wine which is going to be changed into Christ's Precious Blood, shed on the cross for us. At this point we can make an act of gratitude for Christ's generosity. The priest concludes the offering of the bread and wine with the words, "Lord God, we ask you to receive us and be pleased with the sacrifice we offer you with humble and contrite hearts." We can make this prayer our own. Then the priest washes his fingers in a little water, asking the Lord to cleanse him from sin. This washing is a symbol of the washing of the priest's hands in the early Church. After receiving the produce of goods from the land, fruit, vegetables, meat etc. given to him by the people, his hands needed washing. Think of Jesus washing away all your sins and making you acceptable to our Father in heaven.

The bread and wine are offered separately, because that is what Jesus did at the Last Supper. His actions foreshadowed His death, when His body would be broken on the cross and His blood would be shed.

In the prayer over the Gifts the priest invites you to pray that God will accept this sacrifice which we are making together. The response that you give sums up what the Mass is all about: "it is for the praise and glory of God's name, for our own good and for the good of the whole Church". The Offertory is completed with a final prayer. We have offered the bread and wine, we have offered ourselves. The priest has made sure that we are ready to present our offering. Now, we join with the priest in saying to God, "Father accept these gifts."

Part 5.1.6 (vi) – Holy Mass

CHRIST WITH US

In our study of the Mass we have arrived at the Eucharistic Prayer. The priest calls you to attention with the words, "The Lord be with you" and he reminds you to cheer up! Whatever troubles you may have, put them on one side and lift up your hearts to the Lord! The word Eucharist means "thanksgiving", and at this moment you can think of all the good things which have happened to you, all the blessings which God has given you, and say a sincere "thank you" to Him. We have so much to be joyful and thankful for, and how right it is to give God our thanks and praise. In a person gives you a gift, the first thing you do is you thank them; how hurt the person who gave you the gift would be if you didn't thanked them for it. Imagine then how God feels if we do not thank Him regularly for all the gifts

He gives us in our daily lives. The theme of the Preface, which the priest now recites is to give thanks and praise to God.

As we say, "Holy, holy, holy" we think of the angels and saints in heaven who are worshipping God with these words. Their whole attention is focussed on Him, and they can help us to have a sense of the wonder and majesty of God. I always think of this as one of the "magic moments" of the Mass. What a privilege it is for us to be in the company of the angels and the holy men and women who have gone before us into heaven. "Hosanna in the highest" echoes the joyful cries of the crowd as Jesus rode into Jerusalem. We can picture ourselves in that crowd and catch some of their excitement as we say, "Blessed is he who comes in the name of the Lord." Jesus came to Jerusalem in triumph, and very soon He will be coming to each one of us in Holy Communion.

There are four Eucharistic Prayers which we use regularly. In all of them you will find the same elements. We praise God our Father, we invoke the Holy Spirit, and we re-enact the Last Supper. Then follows the memorial prayer in which we make present the death, resurrection and ascension of Our Lord. Finally, we ask God's blessing on ourselves and the whole church, and both the living and the dead. We pray alongside Our Lady and the saints, and we offer all these prayers in the name of Jesus.

Each Eucharistic Prayer is addressed to the Father. This pleases Jesus because His chief concern when He came on earth as a man was to lead us back to the Father. When we begin this prayer let us be conscious of the Father and His love for us. He longs for us to be with Him one day in His heavenly home.

At the Consecration the priest says "Let your Spirit come upon these gifts....." The priest asks the Holy Spirit to come down on our offering of bread and wine so that through His power they can become the Body and Blood of Christ. This reminds us that we cannot take one step towards heaven without the help of the Holy Spirit. We ask Him to lead us through the rest of the Mass, keeping our attention focussed on what is happening.

From the Lord's Last Supper (Lk. 22:14-18) the priest says "Take this, all of you...." Now we come to the climax of the Mass. The priest re-tells the story of the Last Supper, and when he reaches the words "This is my Body" (Lk. 22:19) it is Christ who takes over. At this moment the bread is changed into the Risen Lord, the Body and Blood of Christ. The priest raises the host above his head, and you should look at it and make your own prayer of adoration and offering. Then the priest genuflects in adoration and you should bow your head. The priest repeats these gestures with the chalice, which now contains Christ's Precious Blood.

Why does this gesture have to be repeated over the wine, if Christ is truly present under the appearance of the bread? It symbolises the separation of His flesh and blood during His death. It is also the drink which Christ referred to when He said, "Unless you eat the flesh of the Son of Man and drink His blood you will have no life in you" (Jn. 6:53).

What prayer is Jesus saying to His Father? I think it could be summed up as, "Heavenly Father, I offer myself to you for all my brothers and sisters." Uniting yourself to what Christ is doing at that moment you could say the prayer, "Heavenly Father, I offer you your Son and myself." There is no greater gift you can give to the Father. You also have time to say the prayer you were probably taught when young, the prayer of St. Thomas, "My Lord and my God."

After the consecration the priest invites us to proclaim the mystery of our faith. It is a mystery of Christ's death, His resurrection and His second coming.

Part 5.1.6 (vii) – Holy Mass

PREPARATION FOR COMMUNION

We now come to the Memorial Prayer, in which we remember the life, death and resurrection of Christ, and we thank God for counting us worthy to be present at this celebration. We ask God to unite all of us present in His Holy Spirit. Now we remember the Church, our Pope, our own bishop and clergy, and all God's holy people. Here we are praying for the Church Militant, that is to say the Church here on earth. Next we pray for the Church Suffering, those who are in purgatory. We remember particularly our loved ones, and those who have no-one to pray for them. They are longing for our prayers to release them from purgatory so that they can enjoy God's presence in heaven. Then we remember the Church Triumphant, those who are now in heaven. This is the point at which we pray for ourselves, asking that we may share a place in heaven with Mary, the Mother of God, the Apostles, and all the saints. You might like to think about your own patron saint, the saint of the day, or the saint of the church.

Then in the final part of the prayer, "Through Him, with Him and in Him", we give praise to God our Father through Christ and in the unity of the Holy Spirit. This is our great prayer in praise of the Trinity. We give glory to God the Father by praying to Him through and with Jesus with the help of the Holy Spirit. The congregation's response to this is "Amen." This is called the Great Amen and so it should be said with more vigour than any of the other Amens in the Mass. It is our Yes to all that has gone before, our agreement with all that we have professed during this Mass. How firmly do we say this Amen? Very often the priest hears only a faint response, so make it as audible and joyful as you can.

Then we make our preparation for Communion with the "Our Father". When we begin our preparation for Holy Communion, what better way can we begin than by reciting the prayer that Jesus Himself taught us. It is made up of six petitions. The first three are concerned with God, and the next three with ourselves and our needs. Very often when we pray we put ourselves first, but Jesus teaches us to put God first and then ourselves. When He taught this prayer to His disciples He highlighted just one of the petitions, the one concerning forgiveness. In another part of the Gospel Jesus says that if we are at odds with our neighbour we must be reconciled with him or her before we can join in the Mass. So before we think of receiving Jesus in Holy Communion He wants us to be in union with each other.

Next, "Deliver us, Lord, from every evil...." this prayer is a very beautiful one and it can be said on many different occasions, not just at Mass. It sums up everything that we need, every day of our lives. First, we ask God to protect us from all evil. People experience evil in different ways. Famine and sickness are evils. Unemployment is an evil. We can feel threatened by evil when others wish us harm. Above all, when we think of evil we think of Satan, who is the father of all evil. Here and now, as we approach Communion, we ask God to keep Satan at bay. Satan doesn't like the thought of us being united with Jesus and with each other, and he will try to spoil the holiness of this occasion by distracting us, putting irreverent thoughts in our minds, or making us go to Holy Communion in a routine or careless way.

We ask God to give us peace at this present moment. Holy Communion is meant to be like a golden thread uniting us all, but when we look at our world we see so much unrest which is the result of greed and desire for power. We see a lack of peace in our families, in our parish communities and within ourselves. If we pray now for peace in our own hearts, then we may begin to achieve peace elsewhere.

We pray that God will keep us free from sin, because it is sin which separates us from Him and from each other. Sin is the worst of all evils, worse than any sickness. Some people would say that a disease like cancer is the most terrible thing that could happen to a person, but sin is destructive to the soul, and the soul is more important than the body. So we pray that through the Sacrament we are about to receive, that God will help us to avoid sin.

This prayer also asks God to protect us from anxiety. All kinds of worries and distractions fill our minds, and sometimes our worldly responsibilities can weigh us down. Anxiety which is channelled into sensible planning is useful, but worrying about problems which are beyond our control is pointless and can cause unhappiness or even illness. If only we put our trust in God, we could face life more calmly. That's why we pray now that God will help us to put aside our anxieties and concentrate on the beautiful gift He is about to give us.

We have placed all our needs in God's hands, and we conclude this prayer with joy and hope. We are waiting eagerly for Jesus to come to us, today in Holy Communion; but we remind ourselves also that at the end of the world He will come again, and we want to be ready for Him.

The phrase, "For the kingdom, the power and the glory are yours, now and forever" was not a part of our traditional liturgy, but was introduced into the Scottish Book of Common Prayer in 1637, and in Protestant worship it forms the last part of the Lord's Prayer. This prayer was inserted into the Mass when the English was introduced after the Second Vatican Council.

Part 5.1.6 (viii) – Holy Mass

CONCLUSION OF THE MASS

After the thanksgiving at Communion, we are at the final part of the Mass. The Mass concludes with a final prayer and dismissal.

Part 5.1.7 (i) – The Sacrament of Marriage

GOD CREATED MAN AND WOMAN

God created man and woman. He gave them the power to perpetuate their form of life. They do this through the intimate union of sexual intercourse. Into this body that they produce, God wondrously creates an immortal soul; sex is not something which is only good, it is something sacred and holy.

To assure the right use of the procreative power God founded the institution of marriage; the lifelong and irrevocable union of one man and one woman. God wanted parents not merely to give birth to their children, but lovingly to rear them and care for them in the structure of a family.

God not only instituted marriage for the increase of the human race, but also that man and woman should complete each other, draw strength from each other and contribute to one another's spiritual growth. God established this union of Adam and Eve in the Garden of Paradise. This uniqueness and permanence of marriage was strictly enforced by God throughout Biblical history, with two exceptions. After the Flood God permitted the Patriarchs such as Abraham and Jacob, to have more than one wife so that the earth might be more quickly repopulated. Later, after the Jews escaped from the slavery of Egypt, God permitted them to divorce and remarry on the grounds of proven adultery; although as Jesus pointed out to the Jews, it was only because of "hardness of their hearts" that God relaxed His strict law (Mt. 19:8).

With the coming of Jesus, these relaxations to the permanence of marriage ended. Up to the time of Christ, marriage, although a sacred union, was still only a civil contract between a man and a woman. Jesus made this contract into a sacrament. Matrimony is defined as "the sacrament by which a baptised man and a baptised woman bind themselves for life in a lawful marriage and receive the grace to discharge their duties". Jesus raised this union to the status of a sacrament. This union was God's instrument for the begetting, the rearing, the education, and the moral training of successive generations of human beings.

No matter how well couples get along, it is not easy for any two people to live together day in and day out, year after year, with their inescapable faults and personality defects, grating each other. No matter how selfless a couple may be, it is not easy for them to face the prospect of responsible parenthood, with all the sacrifices that entails. They will one day have to answer to God for the souls of the children He entrusted to them. Parents are meant to be saint makers. If there was ever a state that called for grace, this is it. Without guiding grace and strengthening grace, this would be a hopeless task.

When Jesus made marriage a sacrament, no one knows. Some think it may have been at the wedding feast of Cana. Others think it was when Jesus said to the Pharisees, "Have you not read that the Creator from the beginning made them male and female and that He said, 'This is why a man must leave father and mother, and cling to his wife, and the two become one body?' They are no longer two, therefore, but one body. So then, what God has united, man must not divide'. (Mt. 19: 4-7). The fact is that we just don't know the exact time Jesus made marriage a sacrament. What we do know is that it has been the constant and unbroken tradition of the Church, that Jesus raised this state to a sacrament.

A sacrament is as outward sign that confers an inner grace. In Matrimony, the outward sign is the giving of one baptised man's entire self to a baptised woman and vice versa. In other words the couple who are getting married are the ministers of the sacrament and not the priest. He is the official witness, representing Christ and Christ's Church. The priest's presence is normally essential; without him there is no sacrament and no marriage. But he does not confer the sacrament.

In rare cases a priest's presence is not required for the sacrament of Matrimony. If a baptised couple wish to marry, but it is impossible for them to reach a priest for thirty days or more, the Church legislates that they may exchange marital consent in the presence of two witnesses and it will be the sacrament of Matrimony. This could happen in missionary countries where they seldom see a priest. If one of the parties is in danger of dying, they are allowed to marry, and the thirty day clause does not hold.

The competent priest at a marriage is the parish priest in which the marriage takes place, or the bishop of the diocese, or a priest delegated by either. A Catholic who attempts to get married, whether to another Catholic or to a Non-Catholic, in a registry office is not married in the eyes of God. He or she commits a grave sin by going through such a ceremony. The couple will be living in habitual mortal sin as long as they continue to cohabit. Two non-Catholics who are married before a minister or in a registry office are truly married. If the two are unbaptised, theirs is a "natural" marriage, such as was marriage before Jesus instituted the sacrament of Matrimony. If both non-Catholics are baptised, however, their marriage is a sacrament.

Marriage is not a bed of roses. Husbands and wives have bad days. They may become discouraged under the pressure of acute domestic problems. They may be tempted to self-pity. Sometimes the awful feeling may arise that it was a mistake to get married. This is a good time to remember the grace of the sacrament they have received. Jesus did not promise that He would only be with them on their wedding day, but every day of their married life. We humans can be fickle and not keep our promises, but God is always faithful. His grace and help is always there when it is needed.

Marriage, like every sacrament gives two kinds of grace. First of all there is the increase in sanctifying grace, imparted at the very moment that the sacrament is received. As the newlywed couple leave the altar to the beautiful music they have chosen, their souls are spiritually stronger, spiritually more beautifully than when they came to the altar a few moments earlier. Of course it is presumed that they received this sacrament in a state of grace. A person who receives this sacrament in mortal sin, commits a sacrilege, a grave sin. The marriage would still be valid, but it would be a most unhappy beginning for what is designed to be a partnership with God. The grace of the sacrament would only work when the person in mortal sin had confessed their sins to God in confession.

Besides sanctifying grace, Matrimony gives its own special grace, its sacramental grace. This consists in a claim upon God for whatever actual graces the couple may need, through the years, to make a happy and successful marriage. For its full effectiveness this grace needs the co-operation of both partners to the marriage. The sacramental grace of Matrimony perfect the love of husband and wife. It elevates this love to a supernatural level which far surpasses mere mental and physical compatibility. It helps couples in their matrimonial state to achieve sainthood. This special grace of Matrimony also imparts conscientiousness in the begetting and rearing of children, and prudence in the innumerable problems consequent upon family life. It enables husband and wife to adjust to one another's shortcomings and to bear with one another's faults. This is only a little of what the grace of Matrimony will accomplish for those who, by their co-operation, give God a chance to show what He can do.

St. Paul wrote, "Husbands should love their wives just as Christ loved the Church" (Eph. 5:25). These words tell me that a Christian husband and wife should realise that Jesus was thinking of them as He suffered His Passion. They should be conscious that one of the things for which Christ died was the graces they would need in marriage.

Once a man and woman are completely united in a consummated Christian marriage, there is no power on earth, not even the Pope, who can dissolve the bond. "What therefore God has joined together, let no man put asunder" (Mt. 19:6). The Church does have the power, under very special circumstances, to dissolve a marriage that was not a sacramental marriage (for example, the marriage of two unbaptised persons when one of the parties has later been baptised), and to dissolve a sacramental marriage that has never been consummated. God, and so His Church, do not recognise divorce. The divorced person who remarries, and his or her new partner, are living in habitual adultery if the previous marriage was valid.

There are times when the unbreakableness of the marriage bond seems to result in a great hardship. I'm thinking of the case when say the husband suffers from Alzheimer's disease. The wife is left with several small children on her hands, yet she cannot remarry as long as her husband still lives. Or I'm thinking of a wife who is obliged, for the safety of herself and her children, to separate from a drunken and abusive husband. The children need a father, but she cannot remarry so long as her husband still lives. Then there is the case of a husband or wife who is deserted by a spouse who is a waster. The innocent partner is left to struggle single-handed in rearing the family or to live a solitary and lonely life. There can be no remarriage so long as the deserter lives. However, they can secure a separation agreement or civil divorce if it is necessary to protect themselves against a vicious or a deserting spouse. The civil divorce does not break the marriage bond. If such persons enter into a civil union with a new spouse, it means that they cut themselves off from God's sanctifying grace, but not entirely from God's love as they are still His children. They barter their eternal happiness for the sake of the few years of added comfort which their second "marriage" may bring. Even this comfort must be tainted by the knowledge that they have separated themselves from God.

We are tempted to ask, "Why is God so adamant against any breaking of the marriage bond? Why can't there be a dispensation in case of exceptional hardship?" There can be no exceptions if God's plan is to succeed. When a man and woman know that "this is for life", that they have to make a go of their marriage, then they are more likely to succeed. If adultery were grounds for severing the marriage bond with the right to remarry, or cruelty or desertion, then how easy it would be to provide the grounds. We have seen this in our own country, as our divorce-and-remarriage rate grows and swells. This is a case where God must hold the line firmly or God's cause is lost.

It is a case where an individual, an innocent deserted mother, for example, is sometimes called upon to suffer for the common good. If you say that the innocent should not have to suffer you are saying in effect that virtue should be practiced only when virtue is easy. By this principle there would never be martyrs who die for their faith. As for the deserted wife or lonely husband, God knows their problems better than anyone else. He gives the courage, strength and help which is needed, if given the chance. The abandoned children need a father, but God will be doubly a Father to them!

It needs to be said that with so many divorces taking place, a single person has to be very careful with whom they form relationships. Once they know that a person is divorced, no matter how much they feel attracted to that person, if they love God and their faith more, they will not enter into a relationship.

Some people take great care when choosing to buy a house or a car. When they do buy one, very few keep them for life. Do people take the same care in choosing a spouse, who cannot be changed, but who must be cherished for life? When a man trains to be a priest he can spend five, six and even seven intensive years before pronouncing his vow of chastity. A marriage vow is just as permanent, and just as binding as the vow of celibacy, yet a young man or woman will enter into marriage after a few months or even weeks of acquaintance, with a partner whose sole recommendation is one of physical attraction. When the physical attraction fades there is nothing but wrinkles and grey hairs and long dreary years ahead. Most dioceses lay down that engaged couples are to receive at least four instructions from their priest preparing them for their marriage. My first instruction is to tell them of all the horrible things I have seen in some marriages, and that it is far from a bed of roses. They can never say no one ever told us how hard the vocation of marriage is. On one occasion after my first talk, a man turned to his fiancé and said, "He's right, it's not going to work," and turning to me, he continued, "Father, you won't be seeing us again. You've saved a divorce!"

If you are choosing marriage as a vocation, it would be preferable to choose a practising Catholic. A husband and wife who cannot receive Holy Communion together, who cannot live by a shared set of moral principles, who cannot pray the same prayers together with their children, begin married life with a handicap.

Once a man and woman decide to marry, no matter how attracted they are to each other, even if they are engaged, they have no right to have sex with each other before they are married. It is now common in our modern society for unmarried couples to buy a house and live together. Because nearly everyone is doing it, that doesn't make it right. If nearly everyone committed murder, that doesn't make murder right. Some young people say that living together before marriage is a good thing because it helps them to get to know the person they will one day marry. I want to know how they get round the sin of fornication? Fornication is that which makes living together wrong. Marriage is a sacred step they must take. Besides statistics show that those who live together before marriage are more likely to divorce than those who kept themselves pure for each other.

When it comes to marriage it is not the parents but the son or daughter who will have to live with the spouse they choose, and it is the son or daughter who must make their own decision. But it is very wise for a young man or woman to talk the matter over of their intended spouse for life with their parents. At the age of forty or fifty parents can penetrate beneath the surface of a shallow charm and spot a phoney character much more accurately than a youth of twenty. Of course there are parents who think that no one is good enough for their son or daughter. But on the whole they would give good advice, and it is at least worth listening to them. They love their children and want them to make a good and wise decision. If parental bias does seem totally unreasonable, they can always turn to their priest or confessor. Prayer to the Holy Spirit for guidance must always be sought. Parents and young couples can be mistaken, but God cannot be mistaken. Asking God for enlightenment in the making of such a choice and listening to God's answer in occasional quiet moments of meditation before the tabernacle would seem to be elementary steps in any courtship.

I strongly recommend frequent Confession and Holy Communion as the best preparation for marriage. Even with the best of intentions, the close companionship of an engaged or steady-dating couple presents a danger to the virtue of chastity. The couple who seek a truly happy marriage will come to the altar secure in the knowledge that they have kept their desire for each other under the control of reason and grace. How wonderful and happy they will be when they are married and know with God's help they have managed to keep themselves pure for each other.

Prudent counsel, prayer and pre-marital purity, with a Catholic partner, are the foundation stones of a happy, lasting, and enriching marriage. When eventually they do marry their Nuptial Mass will be the icing on the cake.

Part 5.1.7 (ii) – The Sacrament of Marriage

NOT GOOD FOR MAN TO BE ALONE

There is a story told of Fr. Vincent McNabb who used to preach to the crowds at Hyde Park Corner. Unfortunately, a hostile woman would always stand right in front of his platform and whenever Fr. McNabb quoted scripture she would scream at him, "Chapter and verse, chapter and verse!" She got the nickname "Screaming Jenny". One day a man at the back of the crowd shouted, "You Catholic priests, why don't you get married?" Fr. McNabb didn't have to say a word; he just pointed down at Screaming Jenny!

That incident must have raised a smile in the audience, but of course it wasn't a serious attempt to put anyone off marriage. God instituted marriage for the mutual benefit of men and women. He created Adam, and gave him all the beauty of creation to enjoy and all the living creatures as his companions. But Adam was lonely. He wanted a companion who would be like himself, someone who could feel and think and understand as he did. God said, "It is not good that the man should be alone" (Gen. 2:18) and so He created Eve, the woman who would be his equal partner throughout life. He established a permanent union between Adam and Eve. By creating man and woman God gave them the power to perpetuate human life. They do this through the intimate union of sexual intercourse. Into the physical body that they produce, God wondrously creates an immortal soul. This is the first purpose of marriage. The second purpose is that the partners should give support and friendship to each other, sharing the joys and the hardships of life's journey. God intends that man and woman should complete each other, draw strength from each other and contribute to one another's spiritual growth.

Since God is the author of all things, including sex, and since all that He does is good, it follows that sex itself is good. Indeed, because of its close relationship with God, who is a partner to the reproductive act, sex is not merely something good, it is something sacred and holy. Married couples enjoy the great privilege of co-operating with God in His creative work.

To assure the right use of the procreative power God founded the institution of marriage: the lifelong and irrevocable union of one man and one woman. God wants parents not merely to give birth to their children, but lovingly to rear them and care for them. This is a task which both parents share and it calls for a long-term commitment. During this time the emotional bond between the husband and wife is growing stronger, so that long after the children have become independent the couple go on caring for each other.

As we have seen, God took pity on Adam's loneliness. If it is not good for man, or woman, to be alone, does this mean that everyone should get married? Not necessarily, although we tend to assume that this is so. No-one wants to be lonely and it can be tempting to rush into marriage with someone rather than be left "on the shelf". Young people are often under tremendous pressure to marry. Their friends are all getting engaged and they don't want to be the odd ones out. Their mothers are dropping hints about grandchildren. Society seems to be designed only with couples in mind; think of all those dating shows on television! .

Marriage is a vocation, and God does not call everyone to the married state. There are some people who devote their lives exclusively to working in a caring profession such as teaching, nursing, missionary work or even the religious life. They feel called to give their lives to their work rather than to marriage and family life. We call this the vocation of the single person.

There are others who think they would like to be married but are actually quite unsuitable candidates. They are too self-centred, too irresponsible, too unwilling to make a commitment. They may have a serious addiction such as gambling or alcoholism, or a sexual problem. They may have enjoyed a promiscuous life and be incapable of "forsaking all others" in order to maintain a faithful relationship with one partner. Such people should never consider entering into marriage, but unfortunately many do, with disastrous consequences. Worse still, some divorce and re-marry, bringing their personality disorder to a second disastrous marriage. How much happier they and their partners would have been if they had remained single.

Then there are people who long to be married, and who would quite possibly make good husbands or wives, but seem unable to find Mr. or Miss Right. Life seems hard and disappointing, but perhaps God has some other plan for them. Only by praying about it can they learn what God wants them to do. They may well find that He leads them into a situation, a way of life, which gives them great fulfilment. In the end, He knows what is best for their well-being and happiness. Perhaps we should remind ourselves that although marriage can be wonderful for those who are genuinely called to it, the single life can be wonderful, too.

We've looked at the reasons why God established marriage. In the next section we will examine how marriage evolved and what Jesus teaches us about it.

Part 5.1.7 (iii) – The Sacrament of Marriage

THREE THINGS THAT LAST

Marriage is a difficult vocation, there's no doubt about that. Cynics would say that the idea of lifelong marriage is totally unrealistic. Is marriage more difficult nowadays than it was for earlier generations? And what can be done to safeguard and support our Catholic marriages?

In previous generations, life was often hard. Men worked long hours, domestic chores for women were exhausting without the benefits of electrical appliances, and health care was rudimentary. Yet in terms of social interaction life was a lot easier. People knew what was expected of them and generally accepted their role in life, and in marriage, without too much dissatisfaction. Nowadays the choices and pressures experienced by young people, especially young women, are vastly different. This can lead to different expectations of marriage and therefore potential conflict.

Economic pressures can be a source of stress in marriage. The cost of property and living expenses often mean that both husband and wife work in paid employment roles. Sometimes, of course, peer pressure has a lot to do with it. They want to keep up with their friends, buying the latest gadgets or expensive holidays. But it's true to say that money is a frequent bone of contention, how it is earned and how it is spent.

A common problem in modern marriages is a lack of commitment by one or both parties. It's hard to blame them, for they have grown up in a throw-away, consumer society.

Nothing is built to last. Nothing is intended to be permanent. Jobs are not for life, only for short-term contracts. No wonder there is a feeling of insecurity. People expect their relationships to break down after a time, along with the electric kettle and the hair dryer. In this atmosphere it is difficult to trust another person with your lifelong wellbeing and happiness.

We have seen how important marriage and family are to our society and the upbringing and wellbeing of children. So what can we Catholics do to maximise the success of marriage and to make divorce less likely? Two important factors are choice and preparation. Parents are always anxious that their young sons and daughters should find "suitable" partners, or at least avoid the unsuitable ones! What constitutes a suitable partner? As we saw earlier, people with serious problems and personality disorders do not make good marriage partners. Do not think for one moment that by marrying someone you can change his or her character. A wedding ring won't turn a heavy drinker or compulsive gambler into a model husband. On the other hand, everyone has faults and there is no point in searching for Mr. or Miss Absolutely Perfect. You have to be ready to accept your partner's failings and be able to live with them comfortably.

Choose someone whose background, outlook on life, moral standards and expectations of married life closely match your own. This will make a harmonious marriage so much more likely. Having a Catholic partner will make your marriage stronger, but perhaps this is an ideal not available to everyone. It seems a pity there are so few Catholic clubs and societies nowadays, as they used to be great meeting places.

It should go without saying that no Catholic should become involved with a separated or divorced person. When you do meet someone you like very much, ask the opinion of your parents, family and friends. They may have some useful observations.

Marriage preparation, in the Catholic Church, usually lasts for up to six months. This is not merely red-tape, but an insurance against hasty and ill-advised marriages. It is an opportunity for the couple to get to know each other really well and the preparation programme involves talks on various marriage-related topics. These talks will help both of them to focus their minds on the realities of married life. Any areas of serious disagreement should be talked over now, not after their wedding.

Because the Church cares so much about families, Catholic couples should have the support and encouragement of their parish community. Just talking to other married couples can increase their confidence. Young parents can receive advice and reassurance from more experienced ones and practical help such as babysitting can be offered. I believe we should give lots of support to our Catholic families, as they are often the unsung heroes of the Church! We hear a lot about "failed" marriages but it's good to remember that there are many very successful ones. I know several elderly couples who have weathered all kinds of storms, troubles and disappointments during their lives, but they are still together, loving and caring for each other just as they promised to do on their wedding day.

What can husbands and wives do to maintain a happy marriage? St. Paul gives some good advice (1Cor. 13) True love is patient and kind, he says, never jealous or boastful. Love does not take offence and is not resentful. Loving couples are always ready to excuse, to trust, and to endure whatever comes. They grow and mature together, "putting away all childish things". A lifelong marriage is not an improbable dream, but a wonderful reality which, with God's help, can be achieved. St. Paul would tell you that in this shifting and uncertain world there are three things which last: faith, hope and love; "And the greatest of these is love" (1Cor. 13:13).

Part 5.1.7 (iv) – The Sacrament of Marriage

FOR BETTER OR FOR WORSE

When God made Adam and Eve for each other He intended that their relationship should be permanent. This was the pattern for marriage, a man and woman deliberately choosing an exclusive and lifelong partnership. There were times during Jewish history when Moses allowed divorce, in most cases to make life easier for the men. Women could be divorced for trivial reasons such as being a poor cook. But Jesus' teaching reinforced His Father's original intention. He reminded the Pharisees that God had made male and female so that "a man must leave father and mother, and cling to his wife, and the two become one body? They are no longer two, therefore, but one body. So then, what God has united, man must not divide" (Mt. 19:5-6). In this way Jesus restored equality between the sexes. Today, the Church still upholds that teaching.

Some gay couples want the Church to recognise their relationship and allow them to "marry". Same sex relationships can never be a marriage because as Jesus pointed out marriage is a union between a man and a woman. The Catholic Church permits individuals who are in a gay civil union to be blessed as individuals because they are children of God, but not the union itself.

God has good reasons for insisting that marriage be permanent. A stable marriage benefits the couple, the family and society. To recognise that this is true, we have only to look at the effects of divorce: the pain caused to the husband and wife, the distress and disturbance suffered by children, the anguish of grandparents and other relatives, the de-stabilising effect on the community in general. A happy family is one in which husband and wife are able to trust in each other's continuing presence and support and where children can be confident that both parents are going to stay with them.

Marriage may exist as a legal contract, but Jesus raised it to the status of a sacrament, which we call Matrimony. This means that man and wife are joined together not merely physically but also spiritually. A sacrament is an outward sign that confers an inner grace. In Matrimony, the outward sign is the giving of a baptised couple to each other. This is what makes the bond unbreakable. The priest's presence is essential, without him there would be no sacrament, but it is the couple who administer the sacrament to each other. There must also be present two witnesses to declare that this is a valid marriage.

Like every sacrament, Matrimony gives two kinds of grace. Sanctifying grace is a general grace which strengthens the couple spiritually. Sacramental grace is a specific spiritual gift which will help them to make a success of their marriage. It gives them encouragement in times of trouble, patience and wisdom in their dealings with each other and their children. This grace will remain with them all their lives. Of course, in order for these two types of grace to be effective, both partners must be in a state of grace when they receive the sacrament. This is why Confession is an essential part of the wedding preparations. Should a couple marry in mortal sin they are truly married but the sacramental grace will only be effective when the obstacle of mortal sin has been removed through Confession.

What about the wedding itself? It normally takes the form of a Nuptial Mass. God wants to give the couple all His graces and blessings to sustain them throughout their married life, and it is through the Mass that this will be achieved. As at the marriage at Cana, Jesus is an important guest whose presence will powerfully transform the lives of the couple. This is true even when one party is not a Catholic. Every couple has a right to benefit from the Nuptial Mass. It is also an opportunity to welcome the non-Catholic partner (and his or her family) and may well be an incentive to take part in the life of the Church.

It is the priest's role to ascertain that both parties understand the commitment they are about to make, and that both of them are entering into it willingly. He reminds them that they will have a responsibility to support and care for each other in all circumstances; "for richer, for poorer, in sickness and in health, for better or for worse." Their agreement is symbolised by the exchange of rings, representing the permanence of the union. At some weddings there is a candle ceremony. At the beginning of Mass the bride and groom each light a candle to represent themselves. Straight after their exchange of vows they blow out the two candles and light one large candle to signify that they are no longer two but one. The priest encourages them on each wedding anniversary to have a party and re-light their candle, remembering this happy moment. The Nuptial Mass ends with a Nuptial Blessing.

Part 5.1.7 (v) – The Sacrament of Marriage

TILL DEATH US DO PART

We have examined the reasons why marriage must be a lifelong bond, but there are still some Catholics who are confused about the Church's teaching on divorce and re-marriage. Some people are uncertain about their right to receive the Sacraments and others are puzzled by the idea of annulment. In this article I shall try to dispel a few misconceptions.

A civil divorce is easily obtainable nowadays and it may be hard to find a partner who hasn't already been married. Living in a "divorce culture" can make life difficult for Catholics. Priests are often approached by couples who wish to marry in Church but are not able to do so because one of them has a spouse still living. They are disappointed and sometimes resentful. The Church does not recognise divorce, even though it is legally permitted. A couple who decided to "re-marry" following a divorce would be deliberately embarking on an adulterous relationship.

Naturally, the Church wants to discourage such a decision, and it is a priest's duty to warn couples of the consequences. It is also a priest's duty to defend and support an existing marriage. Many marriages pass through difficult times and many couples have rows and disagreements. But if, as a result of these difficulties, the couple start to think about separating, then their parish priest has a vital role to play in mediating between them.

Since this marriage was blessed by the Church, it is important that the Church continues to be involved. When any couple experiences serious difficulties, they should turn first of all to their priest. Unfortunately, in most cases the first person they think of is a solicitor. At least the Church doesn't charge any fees! Mother Church feels for you in your difficulties, you will always be her children, and you must not feel abandoned or uncared for. Many marriages, I am sure, could have been saved if couples had turned to the Church for help.

A priest can talk to the couple, together and separately, listening and advising. He must use his best efforts to bring about a reconciliation between the husband and wife. He is in a unique position to help, especially if he knows the couple well and already has their trust and confidence.

Sometimes, sadly, all efforts to save the marriage fail. The couple, or perhaps one party, is determined to go ahead with a divorce. But what about God, the third partner in the marriage? Divorce affects the relationship between husband and wife and also their relationship with God. As we have seen, a couple who undergo a form of marriage following a divorce are committing adultery. For as long as the adulterous relationship exists the Catholic partner excludes himself (or herself) from Holy Communion. If such a couple decide to live together as brother and sister they are entitled to receive Communion, provided they do not cause scandal to others. If scandal does arise, they should go to a different parish where their circumstances are not known. A divorced person who remains single and celibate is still in full communion with the Church.

No matter what your circumstances are, you should not stop coming to Mass. You may break the sixth and ninth commandments, but there is also the third commandment, to keep the sabbath holy. The important thing is to keep telling God you love Him. He never stops loving you.

I even advise couples in these situations to approach the confessional and ask for a blessing. They tell the priest they are unable to receive absolution because of the life they are living, but in their own way they still love God and want to confess their sins. By doing this, should their circumstances change in the future, going to confession will not be such an ordeal.

There is another possible solution for Catholics who wish to re-marry, and that is annulment. This process is unique to the Catholic Church and much misunderstood by non-Catholics who often think of it as simply being divorce by another name. Many Catholics, too, are suspicious of annulment, especially when it involves high-profile Catholic celebrities! But it is not necessarily as easy as you might imagine. In order to obtain an annulment it must be proved that the original marriage was invalid, that is to say, no true marriage existed. The grounds for annulment are varied, restricted and often complicated. Each case has to be scrutinised carefully by a tribunal which will hear evidence from the couple and from witnesses. Obviously, the system is open to abuse and manipulation; witnesses may be "prompted", and personal memories may be unreliable. Nevertheless, only after a rigorous examination will an annulment be granted, allowing the parties to marry again.

Remember, no matter what happens, the Church will always be there for you.

Part 5.1.7 (vi) – The Sacrament of Marriage

CONTRACEPTION

Large families seem to be a thing of the past. Most couples have no more than two or three children, whereas in earlier years Catholics had larger families. How has this come about? Are couples less fertile today? Are they practising abstinence? Or are they using artificial contraceptives? I have heard it said that the majority of people do not realise they are committing a sin by using contraception, and do not understand God's teaching about contraception, or have decided to ignore it. In this article I would like to explain what the Church teaches and why.

Regulating the size of a family is extremely difficult and delicate. Yet it is a subject which couples need to discuss and agree on. My heart goes out to those many couples who want to observe God's law and are finding it a problem. I hope I can offer them some enlightenment, comfort and help.

Let me start by stating what the Church does not teach. The Church has never said that all couples are obliged to produce large families. The Church does not dictate the size of a family. She leaves that to the discretion of the couple. It is for them to bring into the world a reasonable sized family. In fact, there may be very good reasons for limiting the size of one's family. For example, it would be an act of cruelty to insist on a wife having more pregnancies than her health can permit. And it would be an act of selfish irresponsibility to bring into the world more children than you can afford to feed, clothe and educate. In such circumstances the use of birth control would be recommended. Of course, we have to be careful here. It is easy to mistake selfishness for responsibility. Many Western countries are suffering an imbalance of populations because of contraception. Nor would it normally be permissible for a fertile couple to decide to have no children at all. Still, the Church certainly does not teach that Catholic families should be large ones. But the Church tells us that, if and when we decide in all good conscience to restrict the size of the family, it must be by natural birth control. The use of artificial contraception is not permitted.

In 1967 Pope Paul VI in his encyclical Humanae Vitae taught that when a married couple make love they must leave open the possibility of the procreation of children. This was no new teaching. Sex is not simply something at our disposal. It is part of the sacredness of life itself. Any use of artificial contraception wholly separates pleasure from the fertility inherent in God's creation. Some people may wonder why the Church makes a distinction between natural and artificial birth control. If it is permissible, in principle, to limit the family then what is wrong with using condoms or pills? The evil of it is in saying "No" to the possibility of God creating a human person in an act which is inherently linked to that possibility. Natural birth control is not evil because the couple are still leaving open the possibility of a pregnancy arising and not impeding God.

If all this sounds far too difficult, take heart. Artificial contraception is not the only option available. An acceptable alternative is Natural Family Planning (NFP). The Church really has a responsibility to make this method more widely understood, in order to help couples to live a Catholic marriage. I would recommend to Catholic couples that they gain for themselves a level of knowledge about the NFP method so they can decide if this might help them in their married life.

How does NFP work, and what are its advantages? Nature has provided women with a highly effective built-in system of fertility regulation. NFP helps men and women to observe and record the signs of fertility and then to work in harmony with this natural cycle. By identifying the patterns of fertility a couple can choose to refrain from intercourse at the fertile times, in order to avoid pregnancy, or to use the fertile time if they want to achieve a pregnancy.

There are several advantages to the Natural Family Planning method. I have it on good authority from a woman who has run clinics, that NFP is extremely reliable. There are no dangerous physical side effects, as there are with the contraceptive pill. The method does not interfere in any way with the woman's natural cycle. A major benefit is the strengthening of the bond between the husband and wife. They share the decisions and take joint responsibility for their acts of love. With the use of artificial contraception it is all too easy to be selfish and pleasure-seeking, using the wife as a sex object. Such selfishness is much less likely when NFP is chosen. The husband learns to lovingly consider his wife, to the extent of abstaining from sexual intercourse at certain times. In this way the couple grow in respect and concern for each other. Of course, there will be occasions when abstinence at certain times will be difficult for both parties but the Church does not propose an impossible or inhuman teaching. Sexual love is not just a matter of human pleasure but involves bringing God-given passions and larger responsibilities into balance. All married couples have to do this don't they?

Any Catholic couple who want to know more about NFP and to learn to use the method correctly should ask their parish priest for a contact.

Non-Catholics often regard the Church's teaching on contraception as impractical, or as a needless burden imposed on married couples. I hope I have managed to convey the fact that the Catholic method of family planning is efficient, positive and beneficial to the development of happy Catholic marriages. It is so because it does not deny the facts of nature by artificial means and does not repudiate God, who is Lord of Nature. The continued casual use of artificial contraception is corrupting and leads to the 'Culture of Death' which the Holy Father Pope John Paul II spoke about.

Part 5.1.8 (i) – The Sacrament of the Anointing Of The Sick

ANNOINTING OF THE SICK

In the past Anointing of the Sick was referred to as Extreme Unction, meaning an anointing received at the very last moment of life. It also had a Latin name, Viaticum, meaning food for the final journey. The modern name, Anointing of the Sick, reflects more accurately the meaning and purpose of this Sacrament. It is not something to be received only at the point of death, but something that will give us strength when we are very sick and weak. It brings grace in the form of forgiveness of sins, peace of mind and, in some cases, restored physical health.

Who are entitled to receive this Sacrament? In a word those who are seriously sick. Let me give you a few examples. Supposing you are gravely ill and have to have an operation, you can ask the priest to administer the Sacrament of the Sick to you. If you have a chronic illness like heart trouble and are confined to bed, you can ask the priest to anoint you once a month. As well as individual anointing there are occasional Church services for all the seriously ill of the parish. These services are very rewarding not only to the sick themselves but also to their families and carers. There are also acute situations where a priest may be called to the Accident and Emergency Unit to visit a seriously injured Catholic, where he may administer the sacrament to them.

Reading the Gospels, we soon realise that an important part of Jesus' ministry was concerned with healing sick people. Sickness and death were not part of God's original plan for human life. As we saw in an earlier talk, they are the result of The Fall. They are not, as some of Jesus' contemporaries wrongly assumed, a punishment for the sick person's sin. Jesus came to restore and repair what was damaged, and part of this task involved healing of mind, body and soul. He also made it clear to His Apostles that this part of His ministry was to be continued by them. He gave them His authority and

His healing power with these words: "Whoever believes in me will perform the same works as I do myself, he will perform even greater works." (Jn. 14: 12). It is an amazing statement, and perhaps we have scarcely begun to channel this power.

We have evidence that the Sacrament of Anointing was used in the early Church. St. James's letter describes its form and its effects. "If one of you is ill, he should send for the elders of the church, and they must anoint him with oil in the name of the Lord and pray over him. The prayer of faith will save the sick man and the Lord will raise him up again; and if he has committed any sins, he will be forgiven" (Jas. 5:14-15).

It must be said that not all patients are going to be raised up again from their sick bed. We have to make a distinction between curing and healing. A physical cure may occur, but more often it is spiritual healing which takes place. We leave the sick person in God's hands. It may be His will that now is the time for their earthly life to come to an end. In such a case the power of the Sacrament of Anointing heals the soul, helping the person to accept and prepare for death. It forgives sin, takes away fear and gives the patient great peace. As an added bonus, this Sacrament can also give comfort to the patient's relatives, helping them to come to terms with what is happening.

The actual rite of anointing generally includes the elements mentioned by St. James: prayer, anointing with oil, and forgiveness. If the patient is conscious, the priest begins by inviting him or her to make their Confession privately. Immediately afterwards, the priest invites the family to join in the prayers of the Sacrament. If the person is unconscious the priest says the words of the penitential rite (which we use at the start of Mass) and if the patient is in a state of grace his or her sins will be forgiven. No priest would ever refuse to administer the Sacrament in these circumstances, even if the person was a notorious sinner or had lapsed for many years. Only God can know the disposition of a person's soul and so we trust in His understanding and mercy.

After the penitential rite there is a scripture reading followed by a short litany which ends with the laying on of hands with the words, "Give life and health to our brother/sister on whom we lay our hands in Your name."

In former years the priest would anoint all five senses, eyes, nose, ears, mouth, and hands and feet. Nowadays it has been simplified and only the forehead and the palms of the hands are anointed. Incidentally, if a priest is receiving the Sacrament, the backs of his hands are anointed; his palms were anointed when he was ordained. As the priest anoints the patient's forehead he says, "Through this holy anointing may the Lord in his love and mercy help you with the grace of the Holy Spirit." If the recipient can answer, he says, "Amen". When anointing the hands, the priest says, "May the Lord who frees you from sin, save you and raise you up." Again the recipient responds "Amen". If the sick person is conscious Holy Communion follows.

Part 5.1.8 (ii) – The Sacrament of the Anointing Of The Sick

A GOOD LIFE IS THE BEST PREPARATION FOR THE NEXT LIFE

There was a time when you went to hospital and you were asked what was your religious persuasion. Most Catholics were proud and happy to say that they were Catholics, hoping that while in hospital they would receive a visit from the Catholic Hospital Chaplain. This procedure can no longer be taken for granted in many of our hospitals today. Because of the very literal interpretation of the Data Protection legislation, many hospitals throughout the country no longer provide Hospital Chaplains with a list of Catholic patients in the hospital. Now that you are not asked your religious persuasion, if you say nothing about being a Catholic it's very likely you will not see a priest. That would be sad. Patients must now sign a consent form if they wish to receive a visit from the priest and it would appear that the onus is on the patient or relative, to request the consent form from the Ward Staff. Fortunately there are still a few hospitals that continue to provide the Hospital Chaplain with a list of Catholic patients. This could change if the powers that be decide not to allow them to do so. Catholics need to be aware of this, and if you are going to have a spell in hospital and you would like to be visited by the Hospital Chaplain, make sure your wishes are known when you enter hospital. If the hospital does not have a chaplain, inform your parish priest. In letting the hospital authorities know you are a Catholic you are witnessing to Christ. "If anyone declares himself for Me in the presence of men, I will declare myself for him in the presence of My Father in heaven" (Mt.10:32).

On a number of occasions people have come to me greatly distressed because for one reason or another, a relative has died without receiving the last rites. I've tried to comfort them by saying that the Sacraments of the Sick and Viaticum are most desirable but not essential. God is our loving Father and he calls us when the time is most propitious for us. The best preparation for a happy death is a good life. Worrying at this point is not going to change the situation. All people must do is to pray for their loved one and leave the repose of their soul in the hands of our loving Father. An excellent prayer to say for them when they are concerned about them is the prayer that Jesus gave St. Gertrude: "Heavenly Father, we offer you the most precious Blood of your divine Son Jesus, in union with all the Holy Masses being offered today, throughout the world for the Holy Souls in purgatory."

I find every now and then in my newsletter or from the pulpit I have to inform Catholics about preparations they need to make in their homes if the priest brings them the Sacrament of the Sick or Holy Communion. You would be surprised at the reception you sometimes get when you take Communion to the sick at home. There have been occasions when I have had to ask the person receiving Holy Communion if the television or radio could be switched off. Sometimes there is literally no spare spot on a table on which I can place the corporal on which rests the Host. Once I even had to ask if I could close the paper which displayed a Page Three girl!

When a priest is bringing Holy Communion to a home there should be provided a small table or a clean space where he can open the corporal on which he can place the pyx containing the Sacred Host. On the table there should be a small crucifix and at least one candle and a small bowl of water so that the priest can purify his fingers should this be necessary, and a small cloth or tissue paper for wiping his hands.

If you need to go to Confession please inform the priest before he administers either the Sacrament of the Sick or Holy Communion.

When a priest is called upon to administer the Sacrament of the Sick or Holy Communion in hospital he will draw the curtains around the sick persons' bed in order to give them some privacy. It is good to have the family members present to cluster round the bed. I have never been able to light candles in hospital because of the presence of oxygen and smoke detectors. It is rare to be able to clear a space for a corporal and a crucifix. Often the crucifix and the oil stock have to be placed on the bed clothes. The priest will hold the pyx. The priest should wear a purple miniature stole over his cassock, clerical suit or religious habit. He tries to get as close as he can to the patient. This is very important if the patient is unconscious. When the priest makes the Sign of the Cross, and those present copy him or not, he will get some idea just how staunch Catholics they are. It is very encouraging if they join in the responses with him.

We thank Jesus for giving us the Sacrament of the Sick which brings great comfort to the one who is ill, forgives sins and healing of mind and body.

Part 5.1.9 (i) – Holy Orders

THE SERVANTS OF CHRIST

The Sacrament of Holy Orders is the sacrament by which a man is consecrated to the priesthood. What is a priest? Why do we need priests? In Old Testament times, and also in pagan religions, a priest was regarded as a mediator who offered sacrifices to the deity on behalf of the people. In one sense we are all priests. St. Peter tells us that as followers of Christ we are "a chosen race, a royal priesthood, a people set apart to sing the praises of God." (1 Pet 2: 9). But a Catholic priest has particular duties, conferred on him by Christ Himself.

Christ is, of course, the only mediator between God and man, but He intended His Apostles to continue His work in the world and so He consecrated them for this purpose. The functions of a priest are to offer the sacrifice of the Mass, to administer the sacraments, to instruct the laity and to bless them in God's name. At the Last Supper Jesus instituted the Eucharist with the words "This is my body……this is my blood." He told the Apostles to "do this as a memorial of Me." (Lk. 22:19) With these words Jesus ordained His first priests. They were to do as He did, consecrating bread and wine, offering them to God the Father, and sharing Christ's body in Holy Communion, all of which we now know as the Mass.

Before that final meal with His Apostles Jesus washed their feet, telling them that they must follow His example. Their lives were to be dedicated to serving and caring for others, and we can read in the Acts of the Apostles how the early Church carried out these duties. A priest cares for his flock by bringing them the sacraments they need at various times in their lives: baptising the children, officiating at marriages, bringing Holy Communion to the sick and housebound, strengthening penitent sinners in Confession, attending the dying, conducting funerals and comforting the bereaved.

A bishop has the complete fullness of the priesthood with the power to confirm and to ordain priests, deacons and other bishops. Only a bishop can ordain a priest. He does this through laying on of hands and anointing the candidate with oil of chrism.

The rite of ordination to the priesthood is one of the oldest ceremonies in the Catholic Church. Some of the gestures practised today were performed in the first century. The rite of performing the ceremony of ordination of a deacon, priest or bishop always takes place between the reading of scripture and the Eucharistic liturgy. It begins with the bishop calling each candidate by name to which the candidate replies 'adsum' which means 'I am present'. The candidate makes a promise of chastity. Then the candidates prostrate on the floor of the sanctuary in a gesture of humility, recognising their unworthiness. While prostrate on the floor the litany of the saints is sung calling upon the saints to help them in their vocation. Then takes place one of the most important gestures, when the bishop lays his hands on the candidate. All the priests present will do the same. It is the moment when the Holy Spirit descends upon the candidate. Then follows the consecration prayer when the deacon become a priest. The bishop will then anoint the palms of the priest's hands, these hands will now be able to consecrate, changing the bread and wine into the body and blood of Christ. When the priest has been ordained all present will kiss the hands of the priest and receive his first blessing.

A priest must also be a teacher and missionary. When Jesus said to Peter (Jn. 21), "Feed my sheep," He gave him authority to hand on to others the teaching he had received, entire and unadulterated. He instructed the Apostles (Mt. 28:19) to "go and teach all nations" so that the Good News would be spread all over the world. And so a priest has a duty to preach and to instruct those in his care, whether he is a parish priest in Britain or a missionary in a distant country. Jesus also told His Apostles how they should approach the people to whom they were ministering. They were to give a blessing, "Peace to this house" (Lk. 10:5). A priest gives a blessing, "In the name of the Father and of the Son and of the Holy Spirit" at the beginning of Mass and again at the end as he dismisses the people. He will bless an individual, a home, a devotional object, even your dog and your car. The words are not an empty formula. The priest has the power to invoke God's blessing on all who ask for it.

It is obvious that the priest's power comes from Christ. He gave this power first to His Apostles at the Last Supper. His words, "Do this as a memorial of me" (Lk. 22:19) enabled them to do what He was doing, to change bread and wine into his body and blood and be of service to His flock. Those words were their ordination to the new priesthood. We can think of those Apostles as the first bishops. As the early Church grew and expanded more priests were needed and so the bishops handed on Christ's power to the next generation of priests. This is what we call the apostolic succession and it continues to the present day. It is wonderful to reflect that there is an unbroken chain between our own bishops and the men who walked with Christ.

Like the Apostles, today's priests must be called to the vocation of the priesthood. Then they will undergo several years of training and preparation. The trainee will study theoretical philosophy and theology, moral theology, biblical studies, Canon Law and such practical matters as the celebration of the liturgy, pastoral care, public speaking and catechesis. The first step is the diaconate. This enables the cleric to administer the Holy Eucharist, to baptise, conduct marriages and funerals and to preach. The next stage is ordination to the priesthood.

Recently with the shortage of vocations to the priesthood the Church has revived the permanent diaconate for married or single men. This came into being in the early Church when the Apostles found that they needed help with some of their priestly duties. This deacon does not become a priest but he can be a very valuable asset to a parish especially where there is an aged and sick priest. There must be many men who have the qualities necessary for being a deacon; the love of faith, a sense of service for the community, a desire to learn about the Scriptures and liturgy. If you feel called to this work why not approach your bishop through your parish priest.

Of course the final stage of Holy Orders is the ordination to the bishopric. One of his chief functions is to ordain men to the priesthood by the ceremony of prayer and the laying on of hands.

I began by asking why we need priests. If we agree that the Holy Mass is at the heart of our Catholic life, then we must have priests. No-one else is empowered to consecrate bread and wine into Christ's body and blood.

Part 5.1.9 (ii) – Holy Orders

THE RITE OF ORDINATION

The rite of ordination of a priest is such a beautiful ceremony that I have set out below the whole ceremonial procedure.

Calling of the Candidate
Deacon: Let the one to be ordained priest, please come forward.
(We shall call our candidate James. He is a Franciscan religious who's been studying for the priesthood.)
Br. James: Present.

Presentation of the Candidate
Provincial: Most Reverend Father, holy mother Church asks you to ordain this man, our brother, for service as a priest.
Archbishop: Do you judge him to be worthy?
Provincial: After inquiry among the people of Christ and upon recommendation of those concerned with his training, I testify that he has been found worthy.
Election by the Bishop & the Consent of the People
Archbishop: We rely on the help of the Lord God and our

Saviour Jesus Christ, and we choose this man, our brother, for priesthood in the presbyteral order.

All: Thanks be to God.

Homily & Instruction
A Chair is placed for Br. James

The Archbishop then addresses the candidate and the people on the duties of a priest.

Examination of the Candidate
The candidate stands before the Archbishop who questions him.

Archbishop: My son, before you proceed to the order of the presbyterate, declare before the people your intention to undertake this priestly office. Are you resolved with the help of the Holy Spirit, to discharge without fail, the office of the priesthood in the presbyteral order as a conscientious fellow worker with the bishops in caring for the Lord's flock?

Candidate: I am

Archbishop: Are you resolved to celebrate the mysteries of Christ faithfully and religiously as the Church has handed them down to us, for the glory of God and the sanctification of Christ's people?

Candidate: I am.

Archbishop: Are you resolved to exercise the ministry of the word worthily and wisely, preaching the Gospel and explaining the Catholic faith?

Candidate: I am.

Archbishop: Are you resolved to consecrate your life to God for the salvation of his people, and to unite yourself more closely every day to Christ the High Priest, who offered himself for us to the Father as a perfect sacrifice?

Candidate: I am, with the help of God.

Promise of Obedience
The candidate kneels before the Archbishop and places his joined hands between those of the Archbishop.

Archbishop: Do you promise respect and obedience to your Religious Superior?
Candidate: I do
Archbishop: May God who has begun the good work in you bring it to fulfilment.

Then follows the Litany of Saints which is sung.

Deacon: Let us stand

Then all stand and the Archbishop invites the people to pray.

Archbishop: My dear people, let us pray, that the all-powerful Father may pour out the gifts of heaven on this servant of his, whom he has chosen to be a priest.

The candidate prostrates himself in front of the altar. The cantors intone the litany, which invokes the mercy of God and the intercession of the saints.

Lord, have mercy on us. Lord, have mercy on us.
Christ, have mercy on us. Christ, have mercy on us.
Lord, have mercy on us. Lord, have mercy on us.
Christ, hear us. Christ, graciously hear us.
Mary and Joseph, Pray for us etc.etc.

The Archbishop alone prays: Hear us, Lord our God, and pour out upon this servant of yours the blessing of the Holy Spirit and the grace and power of the priesthood. In your sight we offer this man for ordination: support him with your unfailing love. We ask this through Christ our Lord
All: Amen

Laying on of Hands
This is the central part of the Rite. In silence, James kneels before the Archbishop who, with his hands extended on his head, prays over him. After this, all the concelebrating priests lay their hands upon the candidate and remain behind the

Archbishop on the sanctuary until the prayer of consecration is completed.

Prayer of Consecration
Archbishop: Come to our help, Lord, holy Father, almighty and eternal God; you are the source of every honour and dignity, of all progress and stability. You watch over the growing human family by your gift of wisdom and your pattern of order.

When you had appointed high priests to rule your people, you chose other men next to them in rank and dignity to be with them and to help them in his task; and so there grew up the ranks of priests and the offices of Levites, established by sacred rites. In the desert you extended the spirit of Moses to seventy wise men who helped him to rule the great company of his people. You shared among the sons of Aaron the fullness of their father's power to provide worthy priests in sufficient number for the increasing rites of sacrifice and worship. With the same loving care you gave companions to your Son's apostles to help in teaching the faith: they preached the Gospel to the whole world. Lord, grant also to us such fellow workers, for we are weak and our need is greater.

Almighty Father, grant to this servant of yours the dignity of the priesthood. Renew within him the Spirit of holiness. As a co-worker with the order of bishops may he be faithful to the ministry that he receives from you, Lord God, and be to others a model of right conduct. May he be faithful in working with the order of bishops, so that the Gospel may reach the ends of the earth, and the family of nations, made one in Christ, may become God's one, holy people. We ask this through our Lord Jesus Christ, your Son, who lives and reigns with you and the Holy Spirit, one God, forever and ever.
All: Amen

Archbishop sits.

Investiture with Stole and Chasuble

All sit.

After the prayer of consecration James stands and removes the stole he wore as a deacon and is vested in a priestly stole and chasuble.

Anointing of Hands
The Archbishop then anoints James' hands with the holy oil of chrism, as a sign of his participating in Christ's sacramental priesthood.

Archbishop: The Father anointed our Lord Jesus Christ through the power of the Holy Spirit. May Jesus preserve you to sanctify the Christian people and to offer sacrifice to God.

The Archbishop washes his hands.

Presentation of the Gifts
The candidate kneels before the Archbishop and is presented with the bread on a paten and wine in a chalice to be used in the celebration of the Eucharist.

Archbishop: Accept from the holy people of God the gifts to be offered to Him. Know what you are doing, and imitate the mystery you celebrate: model your life on the mystery of the Lord's cross.

Kiss of Peace
The Archbishop and other priests present give the sign of peace to the newly ordained priest.

That concludes the actual ordination ceremony.

Part 5.1.9 (iii) – Holy Orders

A DAY IN THE LIFE OF A PRIEST

In last week's talk we saw how important the priesthood is to the life of the Church. At present, in this country, we are experiencing a very acute shortage of priests. Should this worry us, and can we do anything about it? Perhaps we need some sort of recruitment drive, with a Kitchener-style poster of the Pope saying "Your Church needs you"! Let's start by looking at where we find our priests and what sort of people they are.

The priesthood is, of course, a vocation. If there are fewer priests today it does not mean than God has stopped calling. It suggests that young men have stopped listening. In my younger days, candidates for the priesthood often came from the ranks of the altar servers. Today, in my experience, there are fewer or indeed no altar servers, so this field of recruitment is dwindling or in many churches non-existent. Altar servers came from larger families which had strong Catholic values and a great love for the Church. Catholic schools would also give encouragement. But society in general seems to have become more materialistic, and young Catholic men are presented with commercially lucrative career choices. There is also the feeling that to be a priest is a waste of a life. I wonder how many Catholic parents and school career teachers encourage their sons and pupils to be priests. We priests also have a responsibility to act as role models. The vow of celibacy also has its challenges for young men who may want to marry.

What sort of people does God call to the priesthood? All sorts of people! They may not be conspicuously "holy", in fact they are probably very ordinary men, just like your son or your brother or the boy next door. Nowadays many of them are late vocations, men who have worked elsewhere before entering the priesthood. It has always been the tradition in the Church for only men to be candidates for the priesthood because when Christ ordained His first priests He chose His male apostles. He must have had a good reason for doing so.

A candidate for the priesthood must have a great love for Christ and the Church and must practise the faith. He should have a desire to help and encourage people and an ability to communicate the faith. He also needs to be of good health and average intelligence. A Catholic priest must also be prepared to live a celibate life. It is true that at certain times in Church history there were married clergy, but in the early years celibacy was observed and has certainly always been the ideal. There are good reasons for this. Celibacy is not a negative choice, a form of self-denial or an impossible sacrifice; rather, it has positive benefits for the priest's life. On a practical level, he can devote himself unreservedly to serving his parish and is free to move wherever his bishop may need him. He doesn't have to consider family responsibilities. On a spiritual level, he can be a living witness to the value of chastity. Especially in our modern world, which seems to promote self-indulgence and promiscuity, the celibate priest is a sign of hope for those who are trying to live a Christian life.

At present the Church makes an exception for married Anglican clergy who have left the Church of England and now wish to serve as Catholic priests. They are, almost without exception, older priests whose families have grown up and have less day-to-day family commitments therefore.
The life of a priest revolves around daily Mass, for that is his chief raison d'etre. First thing in the morning he will say private prayers, followed by the official morning prayer of the Church which is part of the Divine Office. This is followed by the Office of Readings and half an hour of meditation, often based on the readings of the day's Mass.

After Mass there is sure to be some administration work and letters to be written, bills to be paid, telephone calls to be made and doorbells to be answered. His next prayer session will be Midday Prayer, also part of the Divine Office. This takes only five minutes but it helps him to remember the Lord in the middle of his busy day.

In the afternoon, if he's sensible, he may briefly have a little nap. Then there is more work to do, such as preparing sermons for daily and Sunday Mass, writing the parish newsletter and doing some spiritual reading to improve his own spiritual life and to help others. He begins his evening by saying the Evening Prayer of the Church and his rosary. Then there are various parish commitments, such as parish visiting, parish council meetings, instruction for converts and marriage preparation courses for engaged couples.

After all this, there is time for some relaxation. Finally, he ends his day with the official Night Prayer of the Church.

I can't speak for other priests, but I find that there are a few priestly duties which are absolutely essential, and they happen to be the ones which give me the most job satisfaction. These are referred to in the next part of this Chapter.

Part 5.1.9 (iv) – Holy Orders

THE ATTRACTIONS OF THE PRIESTHOOD

The life of a priest is challenging and rewarding. There is ample scope for developing individual talents and, speaking personally, I find great fulfilment in the priesthood. Every priest has his own strengths and his own priorities. Some may excel at theological study, writing or broadcasting. Others may have a good rapport with the elderly or with children. Some are good organisers, some enjoy attending meetings. I'd like to describe what my vocation means to me and the aspects of priestly life which seem to me to be most important.

Obviously, for every priest the Mass is the most important event of the day. I feel very privileged to be able to say Mass and to share the Eucharist with my fellow-parishioners. I like to preach at every Mass, including weekday Masses, because I think people like to have a little spiritual thought to take away with them and ponder on during the day. This homily may be based on the readings for the Mass, or perhaps an incident from the life of a saint. This helps the priest to put his own personal stamp on the Mass.

Parish visiting is high on my list of priorities. It's hard work and time-consuming, but very worthwhile. Regular Mass-goers like to welcome their priest into their homes and it helps me to get to know them better. It is also a chance to visit the not-so-regular Mass attenders, the waverers and the lapsed who might otherwise feel forgotten. Visiting them demonstrates that the Church cares about them and that they do matter. In many cases it can be a means of welcoming them back to the practice of their faith. It would be a sad day when priests stop visiting their flock and lose the privilege they have of entering the homes of Catholics.

Let me tell you of a time I was giving a Mission in Glasgow. I aimed to knock on 100 doors. I had almost reached my target when I knocked on one door. The man who answered it looked surprised. I said, "May I come in?" He said, "You most certainly can." He ushered me in and told me where to sit. I looked above the mantelpiece and who should be looking down on me but a picture of King Billy!

One way of practising our faith is by sharing it with others. I really enjoy instructing people who are on a journey of exploration into the Catholic faith. I have great respect for the RCIA programme, but I find that there is no substitute for personal instruction, tailor-made to the individual person's needs. The course of instruction may last for a year or longer, making sure that each person can make a well-informed decision. It makes me very happy when they are finally received into the Church as fully-fledged "converts"!

I also take very seriously the preparation for marriage and baptism. This is particularly important where one partner in the marriage is a non-Catholic. It gives me the opportunity to talk about the Church's teaching on marriage and baptism, and to explain to parents and godparents the responsibilities they have towards their child. People tell me that this kind of preparation helps them to appreciate the Sacraments even more.

It gives me particular pleasure to welcome people to the Sacrament of Reconciliation. I know regular penitents who would not miss Confession because they know how much it helps them grow in their relationship with Christ. General absolution was introduced in an attempt to bring people back to the Sacraments, with the expectation that they would also go to private confession. Unfortunately, that didn't happen so general absolution has been withdrawn (except for grave and particular occasions), which means that individual confession is even more important. As with instruction, the personal and confidential relationship is vital. Availability for the Sacrament of Reconciliation is a great help to the penitent. It is important to advertise set times for Confession and for people to know that outside these times the priest will always be ready to hear their Confession and help them. Our Lord said that there is rejoicing in heaven when one sinner repents, and what a privilege it is for a priest to be able to bring Christ's forgiveness and peace to a troubled soul. The priest can listen to the penitent's troubles and anxieties, offer advice and then tell them, in Christ's name, that their sins are forgiven. That's job satisfaction!

In case you think a priest's life is all work and no play, let me assure you that relaxation is also a very important part of a priest's daily schedule. Like most people, I like to unwind by going for a walk, reading, watching television and crocheting or visiting family and friends. Some priests see the need of having a sabbatical to recharge their spiritual batteries. They may spend the time in study, prayer, lecturing and travelling. I know of priests who on their sabbatical work have been chaplains on a cruise ship, including myself! The Church in her wisdom allows priests to have regular holidays; 27 days in the Summer and the inside of the week at Christmas and Easter. If some men think we have it too easy, why not come and join us?

I hope this article may encourage a vocation to the priesthood.

Part 5.2 – The Four Marks of the Church

Part 5.2 (i)

THE CHURCH IS ONE AND HOLY

"We believe in one, holy, catholic and apostolic Church." When we recite this part of our Creed we are acknowledging four qualities or characteristics of the Church: it is one, it is holy, it is catholic and it is apostolic. These distinctive qualities are known as the "marks" of the Church. Looking at them more closely may help us to pray our Creed more confidently and meaningfully.

I was watching the Antiques Roadshow on TV recently and heard one of the experts explaining the use of hallmarks on silver objects. In many cases an item which appears to be silver is only an alloy, or silver-plated. The hallmarks are a guarantee that the object is truly silver. I started thinking about other everyday items which are marked. We might mark valuable possessions with an ultra-violet pen so that they can be identified in case of theft or loss. We micro-chip or freeze-mark our pets for similar reasons. So, marking is a way of identifying something we value and guaranteeing its authenticity. If this applies to our most treasured possessions, it also applies to our Church. The four marks are tests of genuineness. We can apply these tests to any church that claims to be Christian and we will find that while most of them have some of the marks only, the Catholic Church has all four.

First, we say that the Church is "one". This is in accordance with the wishes of our founder, Christ Himself. He told Peter,

"You are Peter and on this rock I shall build my Church" (Mt.16:18) He and He said, "There will be only one flock, and one shepherd" (Jn. 10:16). He requested, and indeed prayed, that His followers should be "one". It seems obvious, therefore, that He founded only one Church, not dozens of different sects each operating independently. In fact, divisions within the Church are contrary to Christ's wishes. The one true church, we believe, is the one built on Peter, the Catholic Church.

As we have seen previously, the Pope is the sign and focus of the Church's unity. Those who acknowledge his leadership share in the unity of purpose and of faith, as Christ intended. We are one in terms of doctrine, for we all believe the same things. We are one in moral teaching, for Catholics have the same code of behaviour. We are one in worship, for we all share in the Mass and the seven sacraments. If you travel to other parts of the world you will find local variations as regards music, prayers and rituals, but the Mass and the sacraments are constant. The Church has a duty to preach the Gospel and so the message must be consistent throughout the world.

Other churches lack this mark of oneness. There is internal discord because there are no agreed definitions of doctrine or morals or worship. There is no leader who speaks for them all. All Christians accept Baptism in some form, though their rituals may differ from ours. Not all administer the seven sacraments which Our Lord instituted. Individual members of the churches are left to decide these matters for themselves.

How can we say that our Church is holy? Surely it is made up of sinners! But the Church, St. Paul tells us, is the Body of Christ. He is the head and we are the limbs. Christ used another metaphor: "I am the vine, you are the branches" (Jn. 15:5). It seems reasonable, then, that we are sanctified, made holy, by our connection to Christ. We as individuals are far from perfect, but Christ promised that He would be with His Church until the end of time and this promise gives us hope.

Before ascending to heaven, Christ told His followers that He would send them a guide, comforter and friend. This is the Holy Spirit, who remains with the Church to steer it in the right direction. It is the Holy Spirit also who prompts us to do good. Because we are one body, any good acts we do will benefit the Church as a whole (just as our sinful actions will damage it).

The Church is holy because it inspires all the faithful, through the Mass, the sacraments and the Word of God, to lead holy lives. Through the influence of the Holy Spirit the Church has the power to produce men and women of exceptional holiness. These are the people we recognise as saints.

Are any of the other churches holy? No-one can limit the work of the Holy Spirit, who blows where He will, so we know that He works in some way within other church organisations. Baptised Christians have received the Holy Spirit and He is always with us even when He is not acknowledged or is rejected. I believe that in other churches there have been men and women of outstanding holiness who have died for their faith, such as the Protestant martyrs.

Part 5.2 (ii)

CATHOLIC AND APOSTOLIC

We have observed that our Church is one and holy. But it is not enough for the Church merely to exist in the world; in order to carry out Christ's wishes it must act in the world, too. Now we shall see that it is also catholic and apostolic.

Catholic means universal, all-embracing. Christ told His apostles to "go and teach all nations" (Mt. 18:19). His message was intended to reach every country in the world. This meant not only the few nations which were known to His contemporaries but also all those peoples yet to be discovered in other parts of the world. The Church was not to be a "church of Jerusalem" or a "church of Rome" or a "church of England", but a universal church in which everyone would find a home.

The Church must be all-inclusive, with no racial or class distinctions. As St. Paul says, when we become followers of Christ we no longer think of ourselves as "Jew or Greek, slave or free, male or female" (Gal. 4:28), but as members of Christ's body. At times this idea has given rise to accusations that Catholics are disloyal to their country. During the Reformation in Britain, for example, Catholics were condemned as traitors because their spiritual allegiance was to the Pope and not to the monarch. At that time it was considered more "patriotic" for an English man or woman to belong to the Church of England. Catholics were seen as a threat to the security of the realm, yet Catholics surely loved their country as deeply as anyone else. St. Thomas More exemplified this when he said, on the scaffold, "I die the king's good servant, but God's first."

In the past, one of the unifying elements of Catholic worship was the use of Latin. It was a universal language, a working language for all Christian clerics and understood by most educated people. If you had a Latin missal you could travel anywhere in the world and hear Mass in Latin. This contributed to a feeling of community with fellow Catholics everywhere. After Vatican II the Latin Mass was largely neglected, though that was not the intention of the Council, nor of the Pope. It seems to me a great pity that young people today have never heard a Latin Mass, and there are even young priests who cannot say the Mass in Latin. I hope it is not too late to revive this aspect of our liturgical tradition.

Nevertheless, there are many benefits in the use of the vernacular. Many people welcome the opportunity to worship in their own language and to hear the Word of God read to them in their mother tongue. If the church is to be all-embracing, it must make room for all languages and cultures and reach out to them in ways which are readily acceptable.

We say that the Church is apostolic because we can trace an unbroken link back to Peter and the other apostles. They, of course, were personally chosen by Christ. No other Christian church can claim to be founded directly by Christ. For example, the Wesleyans can't claim Christ founded their Church. It was John Wesley who was their founder. All Christian churches other than the Catholic Church are of human origin and came into existence either for political reasons or as a result of dissension from the teaching handed on by the apostles.

King Henry VIII was a staunch Catholic and in fact was honoured by the Pope with the title Fide Defensor (defender of the faith). But later, for personal and dynastic reasons, he severed this country's connection with the Pope and set himself up as head of the church in England (this title has been held by every succeeding monarch). He then dismissed those Catholic clergy who opposed him and appointed men who were sympathetic to his cause. They in turn began to ordain clergy without reference to Rome. Once that link with Rome had been broken, the church in England was no longer one and no longer apostolic. This opened the door to teaching not being of the Catholic Church.

In the following centuries the process of fragmentation continued. The Protestant church sub-divided into Methodists, Congregationalists, Baptists and so on. Their founders were no doubt devout, but they had little or no connection with the Catholic Church.

These are the four marks of the Catholic Church and the foundation of its authenticity.

Part 5.3 – Commandments of the Church

COMMANDMENTS OF THE CHURCH

"Oh no, not more commandments," I can hear you groan. As if the Ten were not enough, we have six commandments of the Church as well! Why are they necessary? I suppose you could say that the Ten Commandments cover the moral decisions we have to make and the ways in which we should relate to other members of society, whereas the Church's commandments cover the day-to-day practice of our faith. When Jesus established the Church He left the administrative details to Peter and the other Apostles. Therefore the commandments of the Church, unlike the Ten Commandments, can be changed if the Pope and bishops consider it necessary.

The first commandment is, "To keep Sundays and Holy Days of Obligation holy by attending Mass and resting from servile works." This reinforces in fact the third Commandment, to keep the Sabbath day holy, but it adds certain other days of the year which the Church thinks should be specially commemorated. At present in England and Wales these are Christmas Day, Epiphany, the Ascension, Corpus Christi, Saints Peter and Paul, the Assumption of Our Lady and All Saints. We keep these days holy because they remind us of the great events in Our Lord's life and the importance of Our Lady and the saints. Before the Reformation, these days would have been public holidays and it would have been easy enough to rest from work and to attend Mass. Nowadays it's more of a challenge for us. Most people have to work on weekdays and it may be awkward to get to Mass, but we should try our best to do so. Try to make it a special day at home, and talk to your children about the meaning of the feast day.

The second of the Church's commandments is, "To keep the appointed days of fasting and abstinence." Fasting days are days on which we eat only one meal and two snacks.

Abstinence means refraining from eating meat. Here is an example of the Church relaxing its laws. At one time, Catholics were expected to fast throughout Lent. Hence Pancake Day, when people would use up all their eggs and have a jolly good party, because they would be on short rations until Easter! Many people can remember having to abstain from meat every Friday. Nowadays we only fast on two days of the year, Ash Wednesday, being the beginning of Lent, and Good Friday, in memory of the sufferings of Our Lord. Every Friday is a day of abstinence. We are still expected to make some kind of sacrifice or do something extra for Our Lord on Fridays, but now the choice is left to the individual. You might decide to go to Mass, make the Stations of the Cross, say the Rosary if you do not say it every day, or do some act of charity. Also, am I right in thinking that many Catholics have forgotten that Friday is still a penitential day? Could we do a little more penance for the Lord?

The third Church commandment tells us we must go to Confession "when we are conscious of having sinned gravely". According to the Catechism of the Catholic Church 'each of the faithful is bound by an obligation faithfully to confess serious sins at least once a year.' I was always taught that if I offended God seriously I should try and get to Confession as soon as possible. If I let time pass without seeking Confession I would commit another grievous sin. It is like offending your mother grievously and not apologising immediately. How hurt she would be if you let several months go by. The Church in her wisdom sets a limit of one year as a guideline, otherwise we would let years go by before we made our peace with the Lord. Remember we are dealing with serious sins.

The fourth commandment is "To receive the Blessed Sacrament at least once a year, during the period from Ash Wednesday to Trinity Sunday."

Daily and frequent reception of Holy Communion was unheard of before St. Pius X who died in 1916. He was the Pope who promoted frequent Communion because he wanted the faithful to grow closer to the Lord in this Sacrament. The reason why the Church insists that we go to Communion once a year is because this is the very least she can do to make sure that we remain within the Catholic Church. How many people realise that this commandment is linked to the previous one? Most people seem to receive Holy Communion automatically every week, yet they are very rarely seen at Confession. They are losing the grace of this wonderful sacrament. Remember what St. John Paul II said, "If you do not go to confession once a month you are not taking your spiritual life seriously."

The fifth commandment of the Church is "To contribute to the support of our pastors". We priests need food, clothes and accommodation, just like everyone else! We also need to pay the bills for heating, lighting and repairing the church. The church building is at the heart of the parish, the place where we all come together to hear Mass, get married, baptise our children and bury our dead. Think carefully how much you can reasonably afford to give to your church each week, and if you are paying tax please use the gift aid scheme. But support of your pastor need not be restricted to financial contributions. You can support him by giving a little of your time to help with parish duties.

The sixth and final commandment forbids Catholics to "marry within certain degrees of kindred without dispensation." This commandment is intended to prevent closely related people from marrying, for the very good reason that children from such a marriage would be at high risk of physical or mental deformities. People who are related to each other, for example first cousins, are not allowed to marry.

We have already considered the importance of the Sacraments in previous sections of this book. The Commandments of the Church, referred to above, lay down only the minimum of what is expected of Catholics. This minimum is simply to try and help lapsed Catholics back into the habit of practicing their faith. To deepen our faith though and our relationship with God, we need the Sacraments of Confession and Holy Communion much more frequently, as previously discussed. What we have seen in the earlier sections of the book on the Sacraments, is to guide us in relation to the development of our faith and our relationship with God; this is fundamental to the progression of our spiritual journey to receive the reward He has waiting for us at the end of our earthly lives.

Part 5.4 – Sacramentals

SACRAMENTALS

Someone recently remarked that few people nowadays bless themselves with holy water when entering or leaving church. This could be either because they have lost the habit of using holy water or because they do not know the value of a sacramental.

I wonder how many Catholics know what a sacramental is. The word is very similar to "Sacrament", but whereas a Sacrament is instituted by Christ and gives grace, a "sacramental" is instituted by the Church and prepares us to receive grace. A sacramental helps us to keep God in mind.

Probably the best-known sacramental is holy water. It is ordinary water with some salt added to it. The priest blesses the water and salt, praying that it will bring health of soul and body to all who use it and keep Satan at a distance. He also prays that its use will bring peace to the person using it. In all churches this water can be obtained and used in homes. Dipping our fingers into the holy water font as we enter the church and making the sign of the cross reminds us of our baptism when water was poured on our forehead in the form of a cross.

The most popular sacramental used in Catholic homes is the crucifix. It is the symbol of Jesus' love for each one of us and as we look at it during the day it reminds us of the depth of that love. It can help us to feel sorry for our sins and it can help us to pray, even at times when we find prayer difficult. I have a beautiful olive wood crucifix which I bought in the Holy Land and it is one of my most treasured possessions. Other sacramental objects which are aids to piety might be rosary beads, candles, palms, medals, scapulars or holy pictures and statues. These objects have no intrinsic value; rosary beads worn as a fashion item, for example, are just beads linked together. But once such objects are blessed by a priest they are made holy and they become sacramentals. Where any such object is worn or broken, because it has been blessed, it should be disposed of with care rather than just being placed in a bin. For example, you may ask how do you dispose of a set of rosary beads or statue; you could bury them in your garden, and holy pictures can be burnt.

In order to be of benefit, of course, these sacramental objects must then be used. We use the rosary beads to help to meditate on the lives of Jesus and His Mother. Candles remind us of the presence of Christ, the light of the world. When we look at our medals, statues and pictures, contemplating what they represent, they can prompt us to raise our minds and hearts to God and the saints. It's rather like looking at a photograph of a loved one and keeping their memory alive.

One very specific sacramental action is the exorcism. This is a subject we hear very little about (apart from the Hollywood film version) because exorcisms are rarely performed. If a case of diabolical possession is suspected, the Church has to determine whether the person concerned is really possessed and not just mentally ill. An exorcist is a priest appointed by his bishop to ascertain whether there is a real case of diabolical possession.

Some sacramentals are objects, such as I have mentioned, but others are actions. Pilgrimages and processions are sacramentals, because their purpose is to honour Our Lord, Our Lady or one of the saints. Making the sign of the cross is sacramental and so is making the Stations of the Cross. When making the sign of the cross with your right hand, use your three fingers of your right hand, not just your index finger. This is to remind you of the three Persons of the Blessed Trinity who live in you. Another example would be a blessing given by a priest. The Church has numerous blessings for all sorts of occasions, circumstances and objects. It could be the blessing of a chalice or an altar dedicated for divine worship. Other blessings invoke God's protection upon a home, a sick person, a car or a field of crops. Priests can bless persons and pious objects because at ordination they had their hands blessed partly for this purpose.

Blessings are not exclusively the priest's prerogative; lay people may also give blessings, but these blessings are not sacramentals. A blessing is a prayer which asks God's favour or protection on behalf of the person or object being blessed. A parent can bless a child. It is a lovely custom for parents to bless their children at bedtime, asking God to keep them safe. It's also another reminder of baptism, when the priest invited the parents and godparents to make the sign of the cross on the baby's head. You can even bless your pets; they are God's creatures, too. A family (or an individual) may say grace before a meal, by which they thank God for their food and ask God's favour on those who cook and eat the food. Every blessing praises God and asks Him for some gift.

There are some people who suggest that the use of sacramentals and blessings is old-fashioned or superstitious. I disagree. Properly used, sacramentals can strengthen our faith and our spiritual life in general. They can also help to forge bonds within the Catholic community. If we are praying for each other and blessing each other, surely we must be growing in love for each other!

Part 5.5 – Indulgences

Part 5.5.1

HOW GOD INDULGES HIS CHILDREN

If there's one aspect of Catholic teaching that gives rise to confusion, misunderstanding and suspicion, it's the question of Indulgences. What does that word Indulgence mean? I'm sure that for some people it means giving themselves a special treat such as a box of chocolates or a glass of whisky. Those who realise that an Indulgence has something to do with religion are often suspicious of it. I know a convert who was taught at her Protestant school that Indulgences are just another superstitious Roman Catholic practice! So I'd better try to explain what Indulgences are, why we need them and how we can obtain them.

Let me begin with a little parable. Suppose one day you maliciously and deliberately throw a brick through a shopkeeper's window. Sometime later, you regret your action so you go to the shopkeeper, admit what you have done and apologise. The shopkeeper is, of course, angry about the damage you have done, but he recognises that your remorse is genuine so he accepts your apology and forgives you. But there still remains the matter of a broken window. Plate glass is very expensive and it will cost thousands of pounds to repair the shop front. The shopkeeper can perhaps claim some of the cost from his insurance company and pay the remainder himself, but in justice it is you who should pay for the replacement window since you are the person who broke it.

To show how sorry you are, you take on an extra job to pay for the window, but it's a real struggle for you. Meanwhile, your brother, seeing how sincerely you are trying to make amends, makes a donation towards the cost of the window. He is not obliged to help you pay off your debt, but he does it because he is in a position to do so, and because he loves you. That describes the effect of an Indulgence, which we can think of as being an amnesty or pardon.

When we commit sin it has consequences. Although God forgives us when we make a sincere confession there is still some degree of debt remaining. This is known as temporal punishment, which relates to venial sin. "Temporal" means that it will come to an end, either in this life or in Purgatory (eternal punishment would apply to mortal sins which are unrepented). The punishment is not God's vengeance but a natural consequence of sin. In the Sacrament of Reconciliation our guilt is removed and we receive from the priest a penance, but this may not be enough to settle our debt. The debt must be paid somehow, and we can try to obtain help through gaining an Indulgence.

Indulgences are not a substitute for Confession. In fact, an Indulgence only works once you have been to Confession and are in a state of grace. An Indulgence is obtained by drawing on what is called "the treasury of the Church". That doesn't mean the contents of the Vatican Bank, but the accumulated merits of Jesus and of all the saints and holy people who have gone before us. As we all form part of the Body of Christ, any good that is done by one member will benefit the whole Body. The granting of an Indulgence is part of the Church's role of "binding and loosing". We can see here the great mercy of God, for He offers us this blessing as a free and undeserved gift.

Indulgences have had a long and not always admirable history in the Church. In the early days, penances in Confession were a good deal heavier than we are used to today. Penitents would be asked to perform public acts of repentance such as almsgiving, going on a crusade or making a pilgrimage to a distant shrine or holy place. Such penances could take a very long time. Later, penitential practices were modified so that an act of devotion or a particular prayer would be equivalent to a journey of, say, 30 or 100 days. That's why you will sometimes see in old prayer books "100 days" or "300 days" attached to a prayer. It has nothing to do with the duration of punishment, but indicates the value of the prayer. Nowadays the conditions for gaining an Indulgence are clearly laid down, and I shall say more about them in my next section.

It has to be admitted that in the Middle Ages there were serious abuses of the Indulgence system. Indulgences were being sold, and some individuals were making a huge profit out of the business. This plainly contradicted the principle of God's mercy and was at odds with the teaching of the Church. Unfortunately, it became a source of scandal and division. The Church never promoted the sale of Indulgences, but perhaps it should have acted more quickly to eradicate the abuse.

Perhaps it is due to misuse or misunderstanding that Indulgences have become a little neglected. This is a pity, because I'm sure we need all the divine assistance we can get. The whole point of the Church giving us Indulgences is to make us realise the damage our sins do and the power within our hands of undoing that harm. An Indulgence brings us into contact with God's loving mercy.

Part 5.5.2

PAYING OUR DEBTS

Damage done by our sins can be reduced or repaired through Indulgences. A plenary Indulgence removes all the debt or punishment due in respect of forgiven sins. A partial Indulgence, as you might guess, removes part of it. We shall now consider how Indulgences work and what we can do to gain them.

The Church has always connected Indulgences with certain penitential practices or holy places. An example dear to my heart, as a Franciscan, is the "Portiuncula Indulgence" which was granted to St. Francis. One day, in October 1221,

Francis saw a vision in the tiny chapel of the Portiuncula. Our Lord and His Blessed Mother appeared to him, surrounded by a multitude of angels. Seeing this gathering, Francis fell prostrate and heard Our Lord say, "Francis, because of the zeal you and your brothers have shown for the salvation of souls you may ask some favour for them, for the glory of my name." Francis prayed that all who came to visit this chapel might receive pardon and indulgence for all their sins, if they had first confessed them to a priest. He was told to go to the Pope and ask him to grant this request. In August 1223 the indulgence was solemnly proclaimed at St Mary of the Angels in Assisi. Later, the indulgence was extended to all Franciscan churches and now it can be gained in any church.

By encouraging us to gain an Indulgence, the Church is actually helping us to live more holy lives because certain conditions must apply. Firstly, we must be free from mortal sin. Secondly, a "good work" must be performed. This good work could be almsgiving, a prayer or a visit to a Catholic Church or a visit to a holy place. The prayer must be one which has an Indulgence attached to it, and most of them are well-known. For example, reciting the Rosary, making the Stations of the Cross or saying the prayer before a crucifix ("Behold, O kind and most sweet Jesus") are all indulgenced prayers. Visiting a shrine or church which has been granted an Indulgence is another way of performing your good work. To obtain a partial Indulgence you need only perform the good work and say a prayer for the Pope's intentions.

A plenary Indulgence, as you might expect, has extra requirements. Usually this means that the good work must be accompanied by Confession and Holy Communion (on the same day as the good work, or within a week before or after) plus the prayer for the Pope's intentions. The Church also instructs that we must be "free from attachment to sin", which implies that we need to prepare ourselves very carefully. It is very hard to obtain a plenary Indulgence, but that should not discourage our efforts. At the very least, trying for a plenary

Indulgence keeps us in touch with the Sacraments, and there is always the possibility that we'll receive a partial Indulgence!

If we do the good work and say the appropriate prayers with the right spiritual disposition we allow ourselves to receive the benefit available through the Indulgence.   But there is even more good news. Not only can we obtain benefits for ourselves but also, as members of Christ's Body, we can obtain them for other people. We just need to perform the Indulgenced duties with the intention of helping a named person. The Indulgence can even be applied to the souls in Purgatory. This would be a great act of charity, for the Holy Souls have to pay off the debts of sin which they had not cleared during their time on earth. They can do nothing to help themselves, so they need help from us. Like having Masses said, this is something we can do for our deceased loved ones.

We have seen how an Indulgence can help us as individuals, but how can it affect the Church as a whole?   There are two major benefits. Firstly, Indulgences remind us of our dependence on Christ and on each other as members of His Body. The damage our sins have done, to ourselves and to our Christian community, cannot be remedied by our own powers alone; if it could, we would have no need of a Saviour. We recognise our weakness and call on the power of Christ which is at work in His Church.

Secondly, Indulgences can help us to develop the virtues of Faith, Hope and Charity. Faith develops through practice, and obviously if we are trying to meet the requirements of the Indulgence we must be practising piety, prayer and a love of the Sacraments. Indulgences encourage us to hope and trust in God, looking forward to our eventual reconciliation with Him. When we perform our Indulgenced good work and say the prescribed prayers we are making acts of charity. This is especially so whenever we apply the Indulgence to another person, living or dead.

Are you a Catholic who never uses Indulgenced prayers? If so, perhaps this will have aroused your interest.

Part 5.6 – The Papacy

Part 5.6.1

THE LEADER OF CHRIST'S FLOCK

When non-Catholics think about the doctrine and organisation of the Catholic Church, they often find that the idea of a Pope is a major stumbling-block. In this chapter I shall try to examine how and why the papacy was established and what a pope actually does.

Catholics believe that the Church today, under the Pope, is in unbroken continuity with St. Peter. Matthew's Gospel (Mt. 16: 17-19) recounts how, shortly before His death, Jesus examined the faith of His apostles. "Who do you say I am?" He asked them. It was Simon Peter who replied, "You are the Christ, Son of the living God." Jesus assured Peter that "it was not flesh and blood that revealed this to you but my Father in heaven." Faith and understanding had been given to Peter for a purpose and Jesus went on to explain what his mission would be. "You are Peter and on this rock I will build my Church."

Jesus was looking to the future, when He would no longer be with His followers in a physical form. He could not leave them like sheep without a shepherd; they and all future generations would need someone to guide them, to instruct them, to hand on to them the truths which Jesus Himself had taught, and to hold the Christian family in unity. That "someone" would act as Jesus' vicar, standing in His place on earth. The man He chose to hold this office was Peter.

The Gospel tells us that Jesus gave Peter the keys of the Kingdom of Heaven, saying, "Whatever you bind on earth shall be considered bound in heaven; whatever you loose on earth shall be considered loosed in heaven" (Mt. 16:19). This is evidence that Peter was given complete authority and responsibility for the spiritual wellbeing of the Christian Church.

It is a heavy responsibility and it has to be admitted that while some popes have been holy and saintly men, others have been notorious sinners. Nevertheless, their behaviour as individuals does not in any way weaken the papacy because Jesus promised that the Holy Spirit would remain with the Church always and protect the faithful flock from error. If a priest behaves badly in his personal life, he can still validly say Mass, consecrate the host and forgive the sins of others in the Sacrament of Confession. Similarly, if a pope lived badly he would be giving a poor example to others, but he could still exercise his papal function of teaching the faith. The faithful would not be harmed by his actions, for Jesus promised that nothing would destroy the Church, not even the scandalous behaviour of individual popes.

The same authority Jesus gave to Peter has been handed on to his successors. The Holy Spirit, who guides the Church, also guides the election of a new pope. When he is elected to the papacy, he chooses a new name for himself. From now on, he will be known to the world and to history by this new name, not by the one he was given at birth. The norms and procedures followed to elect him are public, but the actual twists and turns of the balloting are not. His electors, the cardinals, swear to reveal nothing of what happens in the conclave. The area of the Vatican in which they vote is closed until the voting is complete. This process of electing a pope has continued in more or less this way down through the centuries, and so we can say that there is an unbroken line of succession back to Peter and to Jesus.

There are some people who will object that we do not need a Pope. We have the Gospels, which we can read for ourselves, and nothing else is required. But let's consider for a moment how it would be if there were no Pope. That was the situation in Britain following the Reformation. At first, the Anglican church maintained a lot of Catholic doctrine and practice. It seemed that the Church of England was simply the Catholic Church without the Pope. But gradually everything began to change and disintegrate. Many aspects of Catholic teaching were abandoned and even outlawed, to the extent that it was no longer possible to regard the Anglican Church as being part of the universal Catholic Church. People began to make their own unguided decisions about spiritual matters. Individual interpretations of Scripture were encouraged and without a leader people went their separate ways. Soon the Church of England fragmented into several smaller groups, each with its own character and its own doctrine. The result was confusion and division, certainly not what Jesus wanted when He prayed "that they may all be one" (Jn. 18:21).

In our own times, there is a danger of what Pope Benedict XVI had called relativism, a point of view which claims that all religious beliefs are of equal value and no single one of them can claim to have the truth. People are searching for truth and certainty. Those who want to follow Christ need to know what the Church stands for and have confidence in its authority. It stands for Christ's truth, which can never be watered down or compromised. Is it likely that He would establish several churches, all offering different and conflicting messages? No, Christ founded one Church, with Peter to lead it, and He commanded His disciples to promote His teaching throughout the world. It is the Pope who is the guarantee and safeguard of that truth and he is the focus of unity for all Christians.

Part 5.6.2

STRENGTHENING THE FLOCK

We have considered the reasons why we need a pope. Jesus knew our need, and He gave us Peter and his successors to stand in His place as guide, teacher and unifier. Now we shall look at some of the ways in which the Pope exercises his mission today.

Jesus told Peter that he must "feed my sheep" (Jn. 21:17). How does the Pope carry out that instruction? Primarily, he gives them guidance on doctrine and morals. He is helped in this task by various Congregations. The Pope appoints these Congregations, each of which is supervised by a cardinal or bishop. There is a Congregation for the Liturgy, for example, a Congregation for the Doctrine of the Faith, a Congregation for Religious and so on. I think the most important of the Congregations is the one relating to the faith because this is where the orthodoxy of the Church is preserved. The Congregation collects and monitors the writings of theologians, moralists, historians and philosophers within the Church. It considers carefully whether the work of these writers is in accordance with the teaching of the Church or whether it is likely to mislead and teach falsehood. The Congregation may then advise and consult with the Pope. He acts on this information so that he can give clear instruction to the flock, for it is ultimately his responsibility to feed wholesome food to Christ's flock.

There are some tasks which are reserved to the Pope alone, for example the canonisation of saints. Again he relies on the evidence he receives from the body that collates information about these outstanding holy people. The Pope, too, is the only person who can convene an ecumenical council. There have been 22 Councils in the history of the Church.

It is natural that over many centuries the role of the pope has developed and changed in some details. Every pope has his own personal style and particular interests. Some people are puzzled by the idea of papal infallibility. This doctrine was made official in 1870 although the principle had always been generally understood and accepted. Infallible pronouncements of a pope today are rare. I can think of only three in the last 150 years, the Immaculate Conception, the Infallibility of the Pope and the Assumption of Our Lady into

Heaven. When we say that the Pope is infallible does it mean that he can never make a mistake? He can never make a mistake when he makes "from St Peter's chair" (ex cathedra) an official pronouncement about what we must believe and how we are to act.

There are those who will suggest that the Pope has too much power. The supreme authority is his alone, but he shares decision making with his bishops, who are the successors of the Apostles. The Pope himself is a bishop, the Bishop of Rome. Each bishop acts as "a mini-pope" in his own diocese and has considerable power over home territory, but he must be answerable to the Pope. Every five years a bishop is expected to visit the Pope and make a report of the progress of his diocese. The Second Vatican document on the Church says, "The infallibility promised to the Church resides also in the body of bishops when that body exercises supreme teaching authority with the successor of St. Peter." Notice it stresses that the bishops can only be infallible in conjunction with the Pope.

Jesus viewed power not as dominance but service. He said, "If anyone wants to be first, he must make himself last of all and servant of all (Mk.9:34). At the Last Supper He referred to Himself as Master and Teacher and yet as the one who serves and washes the feet of the Apostles. Pope Gregory the Great understood Jesus' meaning and called popes "the servant of the servants of God". The real power of the Pope is the opportunity to be of service to all people.

Service of all people is central to the Pope's role as Shepherd of Christ's flock. It is the duty of the Pope to take seriously Christ's words, "Other sheep I have which are not of this fold" (Jn.10:16). This is to strive to reunite the Christian family. The late Pope John Paul II liked to serve by going out to meet people of other nations. His presence in other countries was a strong Catholic witness, not only to Church members but to all the people he encountered. A pope can also be a powerful voice in diplomacy and world affairs. When he speaks out to support or condemn some course of action, the world has to listen, even if it doesn't always agree with him! John Paul, for example, is credited with having accelerated the end of Communist rule in Poland and helped the re-establishment of good relations between Church and state in Cuba.

In the last two hundred years God has blessed His Church with good and saintly Popes. We can show our loyalty to them and pray for them. Jesus' prayer for Peter was that he would be strengthened and that in turn he should strengthen his brethren. We would do well to follow the example of our saintly Capuchin Brother Padre Pio whose first prayer of the day was to pray for the Pope.

Chapter 6 – Prayer

Part 6.1

HOW TO BE HAPPY

If you want to be a really happy person, then it is essential that you are a person of prayer, which means being in love with God. There is so much to say on the subject of prayer. I would like to begin with a few thoughts that are true.

You are as good and big in God's eyes as your prayers. If you do not pray, how poor is your love for God.

Prayer is as important to your soul as breath is to your body. Stop breathing and you die. Stop praying and you will kill the life of God in your soul.

Prayer should change us to be more like God in the way we think and act. Very often when we pray we want to change God to think like we do and to do want we want.

The Penny Catechism definition for prayer is "the raising of the mind and heart to God". With your mind you think of God and with your heart you love God. In order to pray the two elements of thinking and loving God must be present together. You could be a theologian thinking about God all day, but if you are not loving Him there is no prayer.

How important it is to remember that in God's eyes you are unique. No one can say to God, "I love You" in the way you can. No one can pray the 'Our Father' as you can. That thought should encourage us to pray.

Obviously the best prayer we can offer to God has to be the Mass. When you pray the Mass and join your prayers with

Jesus, He unites your prayer with His and so it becomes perfect. In the Mass we pray in four different ways: We adore God (Adoration), we tell God we are sorry for our sins (Contrition), we thank Him for all His gifts (Thanksgiving), and finally, we ask Him for all our needs (Supplication). We remember this through the word ACTS.

If we want to know how to pray we have all we need to know in the Our Father. In another section of this chapter we shall look at the Our Father in greater detail.

Whenever we pray God is there. Each one of us has a hot line with God. If I want to get in touch with my Fr. Provincial, I could phone up the Friary where he lives only to be told he is away and if I phone in two days' time I should catch him. But if we want to get in touch with God, He is always there waiting for us to get in touch with Him. We all have a hot line to God.

When we pray to God we can be at ease. We don't need to put on any airs and graces. I remember when I was stationed in Uddingston near Glasgow I had to drive one of our priests to see Francis, the Bishop of Motherwell. He was a tall man, he must have been about six foot four inches. When I arrived at the Bishop's house I was asked to wait in his library. I started to look at the books on the shelves. Who should come into his library was the Bishop himself, this tall man towering over me. I was taken aback. In those days I had to remember that when you addressed a bishop you said, 'My Lord' and when you addressed an archbishop you said, 'Your Grace'. Within ten seconds I must have called him 'Your Grace', 'My Lord', 'Canon' and 'Father'. I remember that same evening when I was praying in our little chapel I knelt before the 'King of Kings' God Himself and yet I could be at ease and be myself.

When we pray we can be ourselves. There was once a family that always said their evening prayers before a statue of the Sacred Heart. Dad would always lead the prayers. This evening Mum led the prayers as Dad was in hospital. Mum ended the prayers by saying, "Dear Jesus, please make Daddy better and bring him home soon". At these words little Johnny ran to his bed and from underneath his pillow he took his toy pistol and pointed it to Jesus and said, "And if you don't make him better soon, I'll shoot you". Johnny was being himself. This was his desperate way of praying to the Lord. I'm sure Jesus was pleased with such a prayer.

When we fail to pray God is missing some of His praises from creation. We have all seen an orchestra performing. In it you see the violinists, viola players, trombonists, clarinets, at the back the drummer and standing beside him a man holding a triangle. All that is expected of the triangle player in the whole score of music is to strike his triangle once. The conductor waves his baton and the orchestra is playing beautifully. At last it comes to the moment when the triangle player has to strike his instrument. He is day dreaming gazing at the packed audience and thinking "we should get a bonus for this". The conductor with his baton even indicates that now he should strike his triangle, but to no avail. At the end of the performance, you and I may be full of praise for the orchestra. Ask the conductor what he thought. He will probably say, "You see that dreamer there. All he had to do was to strike his triangle once and he didn't. He ruined the whole performance". What God expects of us when we pray is so little but when we fail to pray He misses something of His praises.

Try to make prayer your first and last thought of the day. On awakening learn to say just two words, "Our Father". As you say it make it an act of love for our heavenly Father and place your whole day in His capable hands. If He can't look after you, nobody can. Let the last thought of your day be one of thanks for the way Our Heavenly Father has looked after us and also being sorry for where we have failed to live up to what God expects of us. Is there any better way to begin and end our day?

Part 6.2

PRAYING AIDS

St. Paul tells us that we cannot even say the name of Jesus without the help of the Holy Spirit. It is another way of his telling us that we cannot take the first step towards heaven without the help of the Holy Spirit. We are that helpless. So whenever we pray we should not use the word 'I' but 'we', that is the Holy Spirit and me. So whenever I pray to the Father I am not on my own, I always have a Companion and best Friend and He is the Holy Spirit.

Prayer involves two things, talking and listening. Some of us may be very good at talking to God, but do we listen to what God has to say to us. I'm sure there must be many a time as we are 'gibbering' on to God when He says to us, 'May I get a word in?' We can be certain that what God has to say to us is far more important than what we have to say to Him.

When I feel dry and find prayer hard I have several ways of trying to stir up some fervour in my heart. I think of God the Father loving me and putting His arms around me. I find this easy because I had a very loving father who loved to be hugged by his children. I also think of Jesus as my Brother, and I am happy just to be sitting next to Him. And of course, I like to think of the Holy Spirit who is always there urging me to go to the Father. Because He is God, the Spirit of love, I find that whenever I think of Him I am filled with joy and I can feel a glow of warmth. God blessed me with a very loving mother. I used to love hugging and kissing her. To me she was so beautiful. When I was a young boy, I couldn't believe that anyone could love me more than my parents. But when I discovered that Mary, the Mother of God, loved me more than they did I found it easy to approach her and ask her to help me to love her Son as she does. I can never thank God enough for giving us all a Guardian Angel. When I find prayer hard I ask my Guardian Angel to transport me to Heaven to join the rest of the Angels as they worship God saying 'Holy,

Holy, Holy'. Finally, I feel so fortunate in having several patron saints, Francis, my name in religion, Marcel Benjamin, my baptismal names, Joseph, my Confirmation name and Lawrence, the name I took at the age of fourteen when I joined the Secular Franciscan Order. I think how all these saints prayed to the Father and I ask them all in turn to help me to pray. I feel so sorry for those children whose parents fail to name them after a saint.

When it comes to prayers of petition I am helped by the story I heard about Alexander the Great. In his court he had a philosopher whom he greatly admired, but the man was as poor as a church mouse. Alexander would have loved to have showered him with gifts, but he didn't want to embarrass him. One day the philosopher was desperate. He couldn't make ends meet. He went to Alexander for help. Alexander was delighted. He told him to go to the Chancellor and ask for whatever he wanted. He asked for a good sum of money. The Chancellor said, "I can't give you that sum of money without the written authorisation of the Emperor. I shall ask him if I can give you that sum." When he did, Alexander said, "That man pays me a double compliment. Not only does he realise I am of great wealth, but that I am very lavish with my gifts." That is precisely how God wants us to treat Him when we ask for His gifts. They are there for the asking.

You cannot talk about prayer without saying something about distractions. These will always be there if we fill our mind with worldly things. When we realise we are distracted we should do all we can to banish them from our mind. At the beginning of our prayers we should ask our Guardian Angel to keep guard at the door of our mind and help us shut out distractions. Some distractions can be turned into prayer. If at prayer we are thinking about a particular person and realise this is a distraction we could pray for this person. If the distractions are about a meal we have to prepare, we could pray for the people who are going to partake of that meal. In this way we make an act of love for God and score a victory in His eyes. When we realise that we are distracted while trying to pray, it can be helpful to remind ourselves to try and pray from the heart rather than the mind, to put us back in communion with God as we pray. We should also be conscious that we are in the presence of the Almighty and Loving God and Father whenever we pray.

Of course we can pray anywhere, on a bus, in a shower, while ironing, in our bedroom, on the top of a mountain. The best of all places has to be in a Catholic Church which is God's home, where Jesus is present in the Eucharist. There we are surrounded by so many holy images which can help us to pray; the crucifix, statues and the Stations of the Cross.

Some people say that God never hears their prayers. God hears all prayers His way. So whenever we pray we should make our requests as He wills not as we want. He is a loving Father and He knows what is best for us.

In prayer we should be conscious that we are members of the Body of Christ. This means that the more prayerful person we are, the more we tone up the Body of Christ. When we don't pray we lessen the health of Christ's Body.

To conclude, ask the Holy Spirit to make all of us persons of prayer. Wouldn't it be marvellous if our ambition for the epitaph on our gravestone was "Here lies a person of prayer". To achieve that would be to fulfil God's ambition for you, because he wants us to love Him in return for all He has done for us.

Part 6.3 – The Lord's Prayer

Part 6.3.1

THE BEST OF ALL PRAYERS

If we want to know how to pray we need to look at Jesus. He gave us the model of all prayer when He taught us the Our

Father. Before we go any further we could ask ourselves a question, "Do I pray correctly?" When you pray to whom do you address your prayers? Is it always to Jesus? Jesus would be the first one to say, "I want you to direct your prayers not to Me, but to My heavenly Father. When I taught My Apostles to pray I did not teach them to say, 'Dear Jesus', but 'Our Father'". Jesus wants us to address our prayers to the Father and in His name. Did He not say, "You can ask the Father anything in My name and He will grant it to you"? Where does the Holy Spirit fit in? He is the one who motivates us. So to sum up how to pray correctly we should say we pray to the Father, through His Son and by the power of the Holy Spirit. In this way our prayers are Trinity centred and not just Christo-centric.

In this prayer Jesus teaches us to get our priorities correct. First we must be concerned with God our Father, honouring His name, willing His Kingdom to come and the doing of His will. Then, we must be concerned with our needs, our daily bread, forgiveness of our sins and strength in the face of temptation and deliverance from Satan.

How often when we pray we are only concerned about our own needs and forget to honour God. For example, when I awake on the day of a serious operation I have to undergo, my first thought and prayer would go something like this, "Lord, the dreaded day has come. I'm scared. Keep me calm. May the surgeon do a good job". That prayer is all about me. Surely if I really loved God and understood just who He is and how much He cares for and loves me, I would first love and adore Him and only then would I think about my needs. Jesus in teaching us the 'Our Father' wants us to give the first 50% of our prayers to His Father and then 50% to our own needs.

In fact you could say that this is how we do behave. Just supposing I was talking to a group of people who could not see the door behind them and the King was to enter. I'd stop speaking. My audience could see the surprise on my face and gradually turn their heads to see what made me stop speaking and what I was looking at. They too would be surprised. I'd say, "Yes, it's his Majesty the King". From that moment I would cease to exist. My audience would forget that I was talking to them and all their attention would be on his Majesty and quite rightly so, because of whom he is.

This is what Jesus is trying to tell us. If only you realise with whom you come into contact when you pray, namely God, your loving Father, then you are not going to be concerned about your own needs, but first give praise, honour and love to Him. Only when you have done this, will you think about your own world.

It is only when God is given His proper place that all other things fit into their proper place. Prayer must never be our attempt to bend the will of God to our desires. It must always be our attempt to submit our wills to the will of God.

The very first word 'Our' in the Our Father teaches us that this prayer is a social prayer. Nowhere in the Our Father will you find the words, I, me, my, mine. God is not any person's exclusive possession. He belongs to everyone.

The using the word 'Father' we understand something of the brotherhood and sisterhood of the human race; that no matter what race, colour or creed we belong to we are all children of God.

The very word that Jesus used for 'Father' must have come as a tremendous shock to the ears of His Apostles. The Jews did have a great love for God's name, so much so that even in their prayers out of reverence they would sometimes not even call Him by His name. The word Jesus used for 'Father' was 'Abba', which to their ears was equivalent to 'Daddy'. By this Jesus is indicating they were to be as at ease with our heavenly Father as a little child is with his daddy.

There is a story told of a Roman Emperor who was making a triumphal entry into Rome. The tall legionaries lined the streets to keep the cheering crowds in their places. The Empress, holding her son in her lap, sat on a special platform to watch the procession. Suddenly the little boy jumped from her lap, burrowed through the crowd, ducked under the legs of one of the legionaries and ran towards his father's chariot. The legionary stooped down and swung him in his arms. He said, "You can't do that boy. Don't you know who is in that chariot? He's the Emperor". The little lad smiled at him and said, "He may be your Emperor, but he's my Daddy". That is exactly the way in which a Christian should feel towards God. He may be God, but Jesus has told us that He is our Father.

To Jesus the word "Father" was so sacred that He never used it except among those who had grasped something of what it means. In Mark's Gospel Jesus calls God Father only six times and never outside the circle of His disciples. So we must only use the word 'Father' with reverence, adoration and wonder. There was one saint who could never say the prayer the 'Our Father' right through. He just said 'Our Father' and was lost in ecstasy. If only we could love our Father in heaven like that.

Part 6.3.2

HALLOWED BE THY NAME

The first petition of the Our Father is "Hallowed be thy Name". I used to wonder why Jesus made this the first petition. Surely the petition "Thy will be done" should have been first? Is there anything more important than doing God's Will? I think the reason why Jesus made "Hallowed be thy Name" the first petition was because He wanted to stress the importance of honouring God's Name. Of all the names that are used it is the name of God which is most abused. We witness this in conversation, on the radio, television, in the press, on football terraces, pubs and sadly in our own homes and on our lips. Jesus made the first petition the honouring of God's Name hoping that we would realise the importance of His name and that we would honour, love and revere it.

Although Jesus taught us to honour His Father's Name I'm sure we can conclude that He wants us to honour His own Name as well, since He is God, the Son of the Father. Devotion to the Holy Name of Jesus is a Franciscan devotion and its most prominent champion is a Franciscan St. Bernardine of Siena, who preached Missions and Retreats all over Italy to promote this devotion. Here is just a sample of how he preached about the Holy Name of Jesus. 'The Name of Jesus is the foundation of our faith and makes us children of God. Glorious Name! Beautiful Name! Name that tells of love and excellence. Through you we have forgiveness of our sins, victory over our enemies, healing in sickness, strength and joy as we suffer the trials of life.'

A name symbolises a person. Can there be any greater person than Jesus? So His name must be the greatest. He was given this Name by the Angel before His birth, a name which means Saviour.

How sad it is that particularly in Catholic countries the Names God and Jesus are not respected. Is it a question of familiarity breeding contempt? I remember when I visited Ireland for the first time and listened to five year-olds talking to each other. One girl used the word 'God' as an expletive. Obviously she did not know the gravity of her disrespect. She must have heard her elders speak like that and it was the most natural thing for her to do the same. I was quite shocked. St. Paul tells us that every knee should bow at the Name of Jesus, showing that the holy Name of Jesus demands our respect. Because we love Jesus, whenever we hear His Name used irreverently, it should be like thrusting a dagger through our heart, and we should be quick to make an act of love and reparation to the Name of Jesus. I thank the Holy Spirit for making me form the habit that whenever I hear God's name abused or misused I automatically say, "Sorry, Lord. I love You." You may like to try that in making reparation whenever you hear that God's or Jesus' name is being abused, including when people use the expression 'OMG'.

The Name of Jesus is our greatest weapon against the devil, for it is the Name above all names that he detests. The very Name of Jesus can be recited as a prayer and an act of love. It can give us strength in the face of temptation and release countless souls from purgatory. It is the Name Jesus tells us that works wonders with His Father. "Ask the Father anything in my Name and it will be given you" (Jn. 16:23). May the Name of Jesus be often on our lips in prayer and carried in our hearts with love.

In the seventies I knew a teenager who had a 'crush' on the pop star David Cassidy. Her mother took me into her teenager's bedroom. She must have had plastered on her walls, ceiling and cupboard every photograph that was ever taken of him. Whenever I met her I never said, "How's things, Jane?" I only had to say the name "David" and she'd look around as if she had heard sweet music. I met her about fifteen years later at the silver jubilee of my priesthood. I said to her, "How's David?" All she said was, "Who's he?" How quickly she had forgotten her star. Whenever I think of Jane I say to myself if only we could love and reverence and be aware of the Name of God as she once loved David Cassidy!

You could make a case that you can measure your love of God by the love and reverence you have for His Holy Name.

I notice one very good custom dying out among Catholics and that is to bow our head in reverence when we say or hear the name of Jesus. If we don't reverence His name in this way we could try to revive this beautiful custom. Every parent should look upon it as a great privilege to teach their little children this practice. It will be one I am sure they will never forget.

Part 6.3.3

THY KINGDOM COME, THY WILL BE DONE

The phrase 'Kingdom of God' is used a great deal in the New Testament. No phrase is used more often in prayer, in preaching and in Christian literature. So it is of primary importance that we know what it means.

The Kingdom of God was central to the message of Jesus. When Jesus began His public ministry He announced that He had come to preach the Good News of the Kingdom of God. (Mk. 1:14). In fact He described preaching the Kingdom of God as an obligation laid upon Him. "I must preach the Kingdom of God to other cities also, for this was I sent". (Lk. 4:43).

To understand the phrase 'Kingdom of God' we have to understand how the Jews prayed. They tended to say the same thing twice. First they would say something one way and then they would say it another way which repeated, amplified or explained the first. Many verses of the psalms show this parallelism. For example in Psalm 24 we read "Lord, make me know your ways. Lord, teach me your paths".

So if we want to understand the phrase 'Thy Kingdom come' we have to take two phrases together, 'Thy Kingdom come' and 'Thy will be done on earth as it is in heaven'. Here we see that the second petition explains, amplifies and defines the first petition giving us the perfect definition of the 'Kingdom of God', namely, "the 'Kingdom of God' is that society on earth where God's will is perfectly done as it is in heaven".

So to be in the Kingdom of God means we have to obey the will of God. If we are not doing the will of God then we cast ourselves outside God's Kingdom. So the Kingdom of God is not primarily about nations and countries. It has something to do with each one of us. It demands the submission of our wills, our hearts, our lives. To pray for the Kingdom of God means that we have to submit our wills entirely to the will of God. "Thy will be done" has to be the most important words in our lives.

We can say the words, "Thy will be done" in different ways. Firstly, in defeated resignation, knowing that God's will is too strong for us and that it is useless for us to oppose to Him. Secondly, in bitter resentment and smouldering anger, namely, why can't I have my way, why does God always have to have His way? Thirdly, we can say the words, "Thy will be done" in perfect love and trust, gladly and willingly for we know that God loves us very dearly and only wants the best for us.

It should be easy for a Christian to say these words for he can be sure of two things about God. Firstly, the wisdom of God, means that God is the expert in our life and His guidance will never lead us astray. Look at it in this light. If we want to make some alterations in our home, we call in a reputable builder. We tell him what we want. He comes to us with his plans and give us his advice. If we are sensible we say, "Look I'm no builder. You know what is best and I'll go along with you." Is there anyone wiser than God? Aren't we stupid when we act as though we know more than God? Secondly, we can be certain of the love of God for us. God has proved His love for us over and over again, in creating us, becoming man for us, dying on the cross for us, leaving Himself in the Holy Eucharist and preparing a home for us in heaven. Once we are sure of these two things, the wisdom and love of God, then we need never fear whatever happens to us or our loved ones. There is a story told of a Richard Cameron who died for his Protestant faith. His head and hands were cut off and taken to his father who was in Edinburgh prison. The moment his father saw them he took them in his hands, kissed them and said, "I know them, I know them. They are my son's, my own dear son's. Good is the will of God, who cannot wrong me or mine, but has made goodness and mercy follow us all our days". When a man can speak like that he must be certain of the wisdom and love of God in his life.

People often ask the question, "How do I get to know the will of God"? So often we discover the will of God through prayer. Jesus has taught us this. He spent so much time with His Father in prayer, not only because He loved Him, but also to be certain what His Father wanted Him to do. When through prayer we discover what God's will is for us we may find that it does not always bring us peace and tranquillity. This is because we are sinful and prone to evil and our will is often at odds with God's will. If we are sensible we will realise that God's will is our peace. Some people can't accept this for they say that Jesus came only to comfort us and not to disturb us. Jesus not only came to comfort the disturbed, but also to disturb the comfortable.

Is God's will always done? Sadly, God's will is not always done because we through our pride, greed and selfishness frustrate His will. God permits the evil we do, because He respects our free will, but He certainly does not will it.

God's will is often questioned by us. If God is in control of His universe why does He allow so much evil to take place in our world? God is so often blamed for evils for which He is not responsible. How can He be, for He cannot do anything evil. He can only do good. Where there is evil it can only be perpetrated by the devil or man.

Suffering will always remain a mystery for us, a mystery that we have to live with and not one we can solve. The cruel sufferings and death of Jesus can help us to appreciate this mystery. Why did Jesus who was innocent have to suffer and die? Did He really have to go to such lengths to save us? Surely, because He is God, any good He does has infinite value in His Father's eyes? We just don't know the answer. So because Christ suffered we have to be prepared to suffer as well.

The big question in your life and mine at this moment is, are we doing God's will perfectly and thus are members of His Kingdom?

Part 6.3.4

GIVE US THIS DAY OUR DAILY BREAD

Today we consider the petition of the Our Father, "Give us this day our daily bread." So far we have given God His due in the first three petitions. Now we consider the first petition concerning our needs.

In this petition Jesus teaches us to pray for the necessities of life just for this day, not the things we tend to ask God for; a win on the Lottery, a new home or car, a holiday in the sunshine. No, Jesus teaches us to pray for the basics in life, the necessities we need to survive, because He knows more than anyone that you can never satisfy greed and selfishness. The more we have, the more we want. We are never content.

I love that Aesop's fable about the dog who had a juicy piece of meat. He went to his hiding place where he could eat it in peace. First he had to cross a stream. As he was crossing, he looked into the clear water, and there he saw another dog like himself, with a large juicy hunk of meat. It looked so much larger and juicier than his own. He opened his jaws to grab at it. The meat within his jaws fell into the water and was swiftly washed away by the current. Only then did the dog realise he was looking at his own reflection. In trying to obtain what he hadn't got, he lost what he had. We behave like that dog, never content with what we have. As a result we are never happy. This is precisely why Jesus teaches us to pray, "Give us this day our daily bread."

The moment we realise that this petition is a simple petition for the needs of just today, there are several lessons to be learned.

It tells us that God cares for our bodies. Jesus showed us that. He spent so much time curing the sick and satisfying their physical hunger. Any teaching which belittles and despises the body is wrong. We can see what God thinks of our human bodies, when we remember that His Son took a body like ours and became man. Jesus came to bring complete salvation, salvation of body and soul.

This petition teaches us to live one day at a time and not to be anxious for the distant and unknown future. When Jesus taught His disciples to pray this petition, was He thinking about His ancestors in the wilderness who were hungry when His Father fed them with manna? They were to gather up only enough for their immediate need that day. If they gathered too much, or stored it away, it went hard and inedible. They had to be satisfied with enough for that day. This petition forbids anxious worry, which is so characteristic of the person who has not learned to trust.

This petition gives God His proper place. It admits that it is from God that we receive the food necessary to support life. No human person has ever created a seed, which will grow. The scientist can analyse a seed into its constituent elements, but no synthetic seed will ever grow without using things from God's creation, all living things come from God. Our food is the direct gift of God.

This petition very wisely reminds us of how prayer works. If a man prayed this prayer and then sat back and waited for bread to fall into his hands, he would certainly starve. Prayer and work go hand in hand. When we pray that prayer we must go to work and help to make our prayers come true. It is true that the living seed comes from God, but it is equally true that it is man's task to cultivate that seed.

There is a story told of a man who bought a beautiful mansion. It was in perfect condition, but the large garden was a jungle. How hard he worked to make it presentable. He cleared the stones, pulled up the weeds, dug up the brambles, fertilised the ground, until it produced the loveliest flowers and fresh vegetables. The grass on the lawns was lush and green and the rockery a picture to look at, ablaze with flowers and shrubs. One evening he was taking his friend around the garden. His friend said, "Isn't it wonderful what God can do with a piece of ground like this?" "Yes," said the man who had put it all that hard work, "but you should have seen this patch of land when God had it to Himself." God's bounty and man's toil must combine. Prayer, like faith, without works is dead. When we pray this petition we are recognising that without God we can do nothing, and that without our own effort and co-operation God can do nothing for us.

Notice Jesus did not teach us to say, "Give me my daily bread," but "Give us our daily bread". The problem of the world is not that there is not enough food to go round. There is enough and to spare. In America granaries overflow with wheat, and shiploads of wheat are thrown in the sea to steady the price of wheat. In Brazil they fire locomotives with blocks of surplus coffee. The problem is not that there is not enough of life's essentials; it is the sharing and distribution of them. This prayer teaches us never to be selfish. It is a prayer we can help to answer by giving to others who are less fortunate than we are. This prayer is not only a prayer that we may receive our daily bread; it is also a prayer that we may share our daily bread with those in need.

Finally, I think this prayer teaches us to pray daily for the Bread of life, the Holy Eucharist. Indirectly it teaches us to pray for a sufficiency of priests to say daily Masses in our churches, so that we can have Holy Communion every day, for without a priest this is impossible.

Part 6.3.5

FORGIVE US OUR TRESPASSES

"Forgive us our trespasses as we forgive those who trespass against us." Man hungers for food and so Jesus has taught us to pray, "Give us this day our daily bread." But there is also another hunger in us and that is the hunger to have our sins forgiven. And so Jesus has taught us to pray, "Forgive us our trespasses as we forgive those who trespass against us." We can only pray this petition when we have a sense of sin. One of the tragedies of today is that many of us have lost the sense of sin. There are so many people who believe they have no need of God. They have become so self-sufficient that they have made themselves God and so there is no need to ask forgiveness.

How fortunate we Catholics are in having the Sacrament of Reconciliation. How often we have sinned, been sorry for our sins and made a sincere confession and have come from the confessional so happy because we are absolutely certain that God through His priest has forgiven all our sins. I have known people of other faiths who wished that when they are sorry for their sins they had this same assurance we have.

You could claim that of the six petitions in the Our Father this is the hardest petition of all because of the terrible condition Jesus added to obtaining forgiveness, "as we forgive those who sin against us." Let me illustrate my point with a story.

I remember reading a book by Corrie ten Boom. She tells how she was in a concentration camp during the War with two of her relatives. She relates how cruelly they were treated. She survived but her relatives died in the camp. When the War was over she promised the Lord that she would travel the length and breadth of Germany and devote the rest of her life to preaching forgiveness for the Nazis. On one occasion she was speaking in a large hall and towards the end of her address she noticed in the audience the very guard who had ill-treated the three of them in the concentration camp. When she finished speaking, the guard came to the rostrum and said, "Fraulein, may I shake your hand?" For a moment she was petrified. Her hand stuck to her side and she could not lift it. There were feelings of anger and hate in her and the thought came to her, "How can I ever forgive this guard for what he had done to my loved ones?" She was covered in a cold sweat. Again she heard him say, "Fraulein, may I shake your hand?" She knew what God was asking of her and she responded to His Grace. She lifted her arm, shook his hand and said, "I forgive you."

How easy it is for us to say, "I love all peoples," but when we are slighted and hurt then it is much harder for us to say, "I love you." Jesus practised what He preached. He was captured, slapped across the face, spat upon, scourged, crowned with thorns, unjustly condemned to death and died the most cruel of deaths, and yet He loved His enemies and prayed for them, "Father forgive them, for they know not what they do."

Forgiveness was one thing Jesus never tired of preaching about. The rabbis taught that you must forgive your brother three times. One day Peter came to Jesus (Mt. 19:21-22) and said, "Lord, how often must I forgive my brother... as often as seven times?" Peter thought he was being generous, doubling the times mentioned by the rabbis and adding one for good measure. He expected to be warmly commended. But Jesus surprised him by saying "Not seven, I tell you, but seventy times seven." In other words you must place no limit on your forgiveness.

Then Jesus went on to tell the story of the servant who owed his master 10,000 talents; millions of pounds, an incredible debt he could never pay off. But it was this debt that was forgiven. When a fellow servant owed him 100 denarii, equivalent to £10, he showed no forgiveness, but had him thrown into prison till the debt was paid. The master was furious when he heard this. He said to the servant, "You wicked servant. I forgave you all your debt when you asked for mercy, should you not have shown the same mercy to your fellow servant as I showed mercy to you." He ordered that he and all his family should be thrown into prison until the debt was paid. Jesus added, and "so will my Heavenly Father treat you if brother does not forgive brother from his heart" (Mt. 19:23-35).

Notice the sums of money involved in this story. The contrast between the debts is staggering. When we offend God our debt is equivalent to millions of pounds, but when we offend one another it is equivalent to £10. The point Jesus is making is that nothing that others do to us can in any way compare with what we do to God. We must never forget that for our sins to be forgiven Jesus had to die on a cross. If God has acted so magnanimously in forgiving us, we too must forgive others or we can have no hope of forgiveness.

How unfair we are. We go to Confession and expect God to forgive us. What a shock we would get if one day when we went to Confession the priest said, "There is no forgiveness for you today." Wouldn't we be heartbroken?

If we are unforgiving to one another Jesus does not want to see us at Mass. Did He not say, "If you are at the altar and there remember that your brother has some ground of complaint to make against you, leave your gift lying there before the altar and go home, be reconciled with your brother first and then come back to offer your gift" (Mt. 5:23-24).

There is a story told about Our Lady. After she had buried her Son, she went to the Garden of Gethsemane to be alone with her thoughts. Suddenly she heard another woman sobbing. She turned and saw the silhouette of a woman. She recognised the woman and knew exactly what she was going through, because she too had lost her son that day. She went over to the woman, put her arms around her and tried to console her. The woman was none other than the mother of Judas Iscariot whose son had betrayed her Son. Since Mary had heard her Son pray, "Father, forgive them for they know not what they do" (Lk. 23:34), she was showing to Judas' mother the same compassion.

Remember the words of Jesus, "Blessed are the merciful, for they shall obtain mercy" (Mt. 5:7). And the words of St. James, "The merciful need have no fear of judgment" (James 2:13).

To forgive is a sign of a great person, but to forget is divine. God not only forgives, He forgets.

Jesus has the last word. We must never hate our enemies, but love them. When we tend to have hateful thoughts Jesus has the answer, "Pray for those who persecute you" (Mt. 6:44). We can hardly think bad of others and at the same time praying for their good.

Part 6.3.6

LEAD US NOT INTO TEMPTATION, BUT DELIVER US FROM EVIL

In the Bible when the word 'tempt' is used we do not understand it as God trying to seduce a person into sin, but to test his strength, his loyalty and his ability for service. We read about how God tempted Abraham to sacrifice his son. God did not want to tempt him to sin, but to test Abraham's loyalty and obedience. Again we read that Jesus was led by the Holy Spirit into the wilderness to be tempted by the devil. The Holy Spirit would hardly be a partner attempting to lead Jesus to sin.

Temptation is not designed to make us fall but to make us stronger and better persons. We may fail the test, but we were not meant to. We were meant to emerge stronger and finer people. If metal is to be used in a great engineering project, it is tested at stresses and strains far beyond those which it is ever likely to bear. So too a person is tested before God uses him or her in His service.

Where do temptations come from? They come from outside ourselves. There are people whose influence on us is bad things. A person should be very careful in his choice of friends and of the society in which he moves.

Temptations can come from those who love us. Even Jesus said, "A man's foes shall be those of his own household." (Mt. 10.36). Jesus' friends thought He was throwing away His life and tried to stop His work. Just think what the world would have lost if they had had their way!

Some temptations come from inside ourselves. We all have a weak spot. It could be anger, lust, pride, sloth etc. If we don't control it, it could be the ruin of us.

Temptation can also come from our strongest point. History is full of the stories of castles which were taken just at the point when the defenders thought them so strong that no guard was necessary. Nothing gives temptation its chance more than over-confidence.

Now let us see how we can assemble our defences against temptation. There is the simple defence of self-respect. Many a man has been urged to take a profitable, but dishonest course of action. He is told no one will ever know. A person can escape many things, but he cannot escape his conscience. He must live with his memories and if he has lost his self-respect, he has lost a lot.

Tradition can help to combat temptation. We should never take our traditions and heritage lightly, especially when we know that it may have taken generations to build up. We belong to a family, a school, a church, a religious order, a country. What we do affects to what we belong.

Those whom we love can help us to overcome temptation. A poor man was once being enticed by his neighbour to be involved in a shady deal. He was told the job was easy and it would bring quick money and it was no more dishonest that the things that are done every day by respectable people. He would be a fool to throw away a chance like this. The poor man listened. At that moment, his wife whom he loved, entered the room and asked him to hold their baby while she went to the shops. As he looked into the eyes of his innocent child cradled in his arms, that was enough. He told his neighbour to go, he wanted no part in such dishonesty. A man may be willing to pay the price of sin, if that price only affects himself, but when sin will break the heart of someone else he loves, he just can't succumb to temptation.

Finally, in the face of temptation we should remember that Jesus is always standing beside us. He is not just a figure in a book, but our Brother and Saviour.

"Deliver us from evil" should read "deliver us from the Evil One". In the Bible evil is not an abstract force but an active, personal power in opposition to God. The Evil One is Satan. Satan stands for everything that is anti-God and anti-man. We must never underestimate the power of Satan. He has been around a very long time and has much experience, but he will never overcome God. Knowledge of this fact is our strength.

I love C.S. Lewis's story of the three apprentice devils. It was their final exam before they could roam the world to tempt people and bring them to hell. They had just one question to answer, "What tactics will you use to bring men and women rushing headlong into hell?" The first one said, "I'll tell them there is no hell." "Don't be stupid," cried Satan, "every man has a conscience and he knows there will be a day of reckoning, that there is a hell. You've failed." The next one said, "I'll tell them there is no God." "Will you never learn," said Satan in disgust, "although we hate the Bible, we have to accept what it says, "That only the fool says in his heart there is no God." You too have failed." Finally, he asked the third apprentice. Very confidently this little devil said, "I'll tell them they have plenty of time." "Marvellous, marvellous, " said Satan, "do that and you'll have them rushing into hell." Yes, Satan is very subtle and we must never underestimate his skill.

Have you ever considered how beautifully Jesus has put together the second half of the Our Father. When we think of bread, we think of God the Father who provides for us. When we think of forgiveness of sin, we think of Jesus who died to save us from our sins. When we think of help in time of temptation we think of the Holy Spirit who is always there to help us.

Again, when we think of bread for today we think of the present. When we think of forgiveness we think of the past. When we think of temptation we think of the future. Jesus has taught us to bring the whole of time, past, present and future before the whole of the throne of God, Father, Son and Holy Spirit. Only God could teach us such a beautiful and comprehensive prayer.

The 'Our Father' is without doubt the model and best of all prayers and we thank Jesus for teaching it to us.

Part 6.4 – The Rosary

THE ROSARY

There was a time when I found the recitation of the Rosary very hard. My mind would be flooded with distractions. I made an effort to try and meditate on each decade, but I found after having the first decade announced my mind would wander. Very often the next thing I heard was the recitation of the Hail Holy Queen. In fact I had hardly thought of the mysteries at all! What was I to do to pray the Rosary better? The only thing was to write down the story behind each mystery and divide each decade into ten thoughts. I did this for the Joyful, Sorrowful, Glorious and Luminous Mysteries.

I found it hard to hold a picture of each mystery for the space of about three minutes in my mind as I was meditating on the decade. So I decided to write the story of each mystery and divide them into ten sections, each section for the recitation of a Hail Mary. In doing this I found it cut out distractions.

I have heard people say, "Why not meditate on the words of such beautiful prayers as the Our Father, Hail Mary and Glory be?" I think this would definitely make the Rosary a very laborious devotion. We would lose the whole point of the Rosary meditating on the events that took place in the lives of Jesus and Mary. Besides we could challenge anyone to say even one Our Father without a distraction. There is a delightful story told of one saint who, while riding on his horse in the countryside, met a weary traveller. He dismounted and challenged him. "If you can recite the Our Father without a distraction, my horse is yours." The weary traveller was ready for the challenge. He said, "I could do that easily." He joined his hands, closed his eyes and slowly and deliberately began saying the Our Father. Half way through, he opened his eyes and he saw the beautifully carved leather saddle. He said, "Do I get the saddle as well?" Even with the incentive of a horse, the traveller was unable to say the Our Father without a distraction. How could we possibly get through all the prayers of the whole Rosary without distractions?

Our blessed Mother has appeared at Lourdes and Fatima and other parts of the world asking us to pray the Rosary daily for peace in the world and for the conversion of sinners. The Rosary is based on meditation on the events that took place in the lives of Jesus and Mary. If you want to strengthen your love of Jesus and Mary praying the Rosary is a very good way. Just as Jesus has said, "If you love Me you will keep My Commandments" (Jn. 14:15) so, too Mary could say: if you love me, do as I request and pray the Rosary every day for my intentions. If we do not pray the Rosary as Mary, our Mother has asked. Could she say that we do not love her as she would like us to?

The Rosary is a powerful prayer. When it was recited before the Battle of Lepanto the Christian troops vanquished the Turks. It saved Europe being overrun by the Turks.

Our saintly Brother Padre Pio gave me the incentive to pray the Rosary daily. One day he was asked by his Guardian how many Rosaries he had recited that day. He replied, "I would prefer not to tell you, but since you are my Guardian, and you have asked me I can tell you I have said thirty five Rosaries today." That is enough to tell me there must be something wonderful in this devotion. If a mystic like him should daily desire to say this prayer over and over again, how much more I should love saying this prayer. For St. Padre Pio, the Rosary was his weapon against the devil. We should all use the Rosary as a means to holiness.

There is a story which helped me make a promise to Our Lady to say her Rosary every day. During the time of the Reformation people were expected to attend the newly established church every Sunday. If you didn't, you could be fined one shilling, which in those days was a lot of money. If you were a priest and you were caught exercising your priesthood, you were a traitor and could be hung, drawn and quartered. With that as a backdrop, I want you to picture on a fine sunny day an old man making his way through the woods. He hadn't slept in a bed or had a hot meal for three days. All he could think of was rest and refreshment. Suddenly he saw above the trees a wisp of smoke. "Good", he thought, "there must be a home there where I can beg for some food." He quickened his pace. When he arrived at the house he knocked on the front door. He heard the shuffle of little feet. A girl of twelve opened the door. Before he could speak she said, "Come, quickly. My granddad, he's dying!" The girl ran up the stairs and he tried to follow her as quickly as he could. A door at the top of the stairs was ajar. He peered through and saw the girl bending over her granddad in bed. The old man stood beside the bed and felt the dying man's pulse. It was weak and irregular. The old man said to the girl, "Would you be so kind as to make me a sandwich and a drink." Obediently she left the room. The grandfather opened his eyes and in a very weak voice said, "Who are you?" He explained how he had come to be at his bedside. The visitor said, "You know, my friend, you are very ill." "Oh don't worry; I am not going to die" the sick man replied. "I have been at the bedside of many a man who have died and I can tell you that you are going to die" said the visitor. "I tell you I am not going to die" the sick man protested. "What makes you so convinced that you are not going to die?" asked the visitor. "When I was fifteen I struck up a bargain with Our Lady. I told her, if I said her Rosary every day she would have a priest at my side to see me on my way to Heaven. I have been true to my side of the bargain. I have said her Rosary every day. I know Our Lady will be true to her side of the bargain. There is no priest here and so I am not going to die." the sick man said. "O yes, my friend, you are going to die. For some reason Our Lady must have brought me to your side. I am a priest" the visitor said. He then opened his coat and revealed a crucifix and a stole, being the sign of a priest, which he wore around his neck. He then heard the old man's Confession and he died in the arms of the priest.

When I heard that story I too made that bargain with Our Lady. May I recommend you to say the Rosary every day for Mary's intentions, peace in the world and for the conversion of sinners and ask her to provide for you at the moment of your death, to have a priest by your side to see you on your way to Heaven.

My book "Praying the Rosary without distractions" will help you to recite the Rosary, with a description of the key events of the lives of Jesus and Mary in it. It can be purchased online from Amazon.

Part 6.5 – The Stations of the Cross

THE STATIONS OF THE CROSS

The Stations of the Cross depict 14 events in the Passion of Jesus Christ, beginning with Jesus being condemned to death and ending with His body being laid in a tomb. In this devotion we witness Jesus' ultimate expression of His love when He shed the last drop of His blood for us.

After that barbarous scourging and crowning with thorns, Jesus carried that heavy cross to Calvary. He was physically broken yet He mustered up enough energy, with the help of Simon of Cyrene, to carry that heavy cross to Calvary.

Jesus told one saint that the greatest physical pain He experienced on this journey was when the rough wood of the cross rubbed against the bone in His shoulder. It was also a constant ache as He hung on the cross. We shall never understand how Jesus endured being nailed to His cross and hang on it for three hours. It must have seemed like an eternity.

Surely the greatest spiritual pain He experienced was when He thought His loving Father had forsaken Him and He cried out, "My God, My God, why have you deserted Me?" (Mt. 27:46). On this journey His faithful mother also accompanied Him all the way to Calvary. It was on the cross that Jesus gave away His last treasure, His Mother Mary. From the cross Jesus said to His Mother, "Woman, this is your son" and then turning to John, His beloved disciple, He said, "This is your Mother." (Jn.19:26-27). In saying those words to John, He was giving Mary to all of us as our mother.

The pious practice of praying the Stations of the Cross originated in medieval Europe when pilgrims were unable to visit the Holy Land, so instead they "visited" these Holy places through prayer.

St. Francis of Assisi loved Jesus his Master so much that he wanted to imitate Him as closely as he could. It was he who gave us the first crib in the town of Greccio. He had real life figures for his crib. We have him to thank for all the cribs that are erected in our Churches and homes at Christmas time. He also had a great devotion to the suffering Christ. Before he died he prayed, "Lord Jesus, let me experience in my body just some of the pain you endured on Calvary." His prayer was answered when Jesus gave him the stigmata, the very wounds that He bore on Calvary. Because of this it was his brothers who initiated the devotion of the Stations of the Cross to the Church. They popularised the devotion throughout the world.

Today, you'll find the Stations of the Cross on the walls in almost every Catholic Church, and they are particularly prayed on Lenten Fridays, but also available throughout the year for meditation and reflection. The Stations are the final journey of Jesus to Calvary. The Church is inviting us to re-live that journey with Him; this helps us appreciate the enormity of the self-sacrifice our Lord Jesus Christ made for us as the Saviour for all who believe in Him.

You may like to buy from me my book on the Stations of the Cross, "Were You There". It's available from Fr Francis Maple, Franciscan Friary, 15 Cuppin Street, Chester CH1 2BN or you can email me at brfrancis19@gmail.com I have written 21 versions of this devotion, which are contained within the book. They begin with Jesus leading us round the stations, then His Mother Mary, St. Peter, St John, Mary Magdalene, the Repentant Thief, the Centurion, Barabbas, and others.

Chapter 7 – Our Final End

Part 7.1

MATTERS OF LIFE AND DEATH

I want to consider a topic which affects us all, but is something we often try to avoid thinking about, namely death. What does the Church tell us about death? How do we prepare for it and cope with it when it comes? And what happens after death?

Atheists will say that human life comes to an end with physical death. Our bodies are buried or cremated and that is the end of the matter. But Christians believe that there is much more to look forward to. As St. Paul says, "If our hope has been for this life only we are the most unfortunate of people. But Christ has been raised from the dead and.....all men will be brought to life in Christ" (1 Cor. 15.). We are spirit as well as body and our souls will live on. It's difficult for us to comprehend this mystery, but our souls, the essence of our being, are immortal and somehow we shall continue to exist for all eternity. As the Preface of the Requiem Mass says, 'life is changed, not ended'.

Naturally, we are anxious about the conditions in which we are going to exist in eternity. Two factors will be decisive: the mercy and justice of God and the way we have lived our earthly lives. God wants us to live with Him in heaven. That is the destination He always intended for us and so He will help us to get there. Christ, through His Death and Resurrection, has made it possible for us to achieve that goal, but ultimately the choice is ours. God does not "send" anyone to heaven or to hell against their will, nor will anyone arrive there by accident. Wherever we find ourselves it will have involved a deliberate course of action on our part.

No Christian should ever fear death because Jesus has taught us that we have a loving Father in Heaven who has prepared a home for us where we can hope to live with Him and all our loved ones. There is nothing sad or morbid about that.

The Church has always encouraged us to pray for a "happy death", and that our death would not be sudden and unprovided. That doesn't necessarily mean dying with a smile on your face, but dying in love with God and our neighbour in a peaceful and dignified manner, confidently placing our future in God's hands. The late Saint John Paul II was a great example of this. When he was aware that he was dying he summoned all his friends, staff and cardinals and said a loving farewell to them. But death does not always give advance warning. It may arrive suddenly and violently, when we least expect it. There is no time for prayers or farewells. If death can come "like a thief in the night" (1 Thess. 5:2) it seems reasonable that we should try to be ready. No matter how old or young we are we can prepare for death, and the best preparation is an effort to live a good life. To die well we must live well, and if we are truly doing our best then the idea of death will hold no fear for us.

You can compare every life to a tree. If a tree is pointing in a certain direction very likely when it dies it will fall in that direction. If our lives are always pointing Godwards, we can hope that when we die we shall fall into His loving arms.

Some people are anxious about the physical aspect of death, for themselves or a relative. If they have a deteriorating condition, will death be unbearably painful and distressing? There have been tragic cases where people have resorted to euthanasia in order to end the suffering of a loved one. Because God is our loving Father and we are His children, He will never test us beyond what we can endure, and He has given medical staff the skills to alleviate severe pain. He has also given us a wonderful saint to help us in our last hours: St. Joseph, patron of the dying, who will give us comfort and courage. How fortunate was Joseph. He died in the loving arms of Jesus, his adopted Son and his loving wife Mary. We can therefore leave the timing of death in God's hands.

We can also prepare for death in practical ways. Most sensible people make a will, describing how their property is to be dealt with and making provision for their families. But we can also leave instructions for our funeral arrangements, detailing the hymns and readings we want and where we wish to be buried or cremated. Every Catholic is entitled to a Requiem Mass and there is no reason to settle for anything less. You might also like to leave instructions with your family for a Mass to be said for you on the anniversary of your birthday or your death.

For the bereaved, the greatest pain of death must be separation from a person they love. How painful it must be for parents to lose a child. How hard it must be for a husband or wife who has enjoyed a long and happy marriage and now faces life without their partner. The future looks bleak, empty and lonely. Grieving is a natural process and we all need to go through it in our own way and in our own time. If you are grieving, don't let anyone tell you to "pull yourself together". Life does go on, but it is going to be very different without that important person. You need support, patience, love and companionship from your Catholic community so that you can begin to turn your life in a new direction.

Our Blessed Lady, who witnessed the death of her own Son, is a great source of strength to those who mourn. Faith in the resurrection gives bereaved Catholics hope for the future. We know that we will see our loved ones again and be happy in their company. Meanwhile we continue to love them and pray for them and to have annual Masses said for them.

We recall the prayer which Jesus gave to Saint Gertrude for the release of the souls in Purgatory. Jesus told her that whenever this prayer is recited He would release many souls into heaven. The prayer is: Eternal Father, I offer you the most precious blood of your divine Son Jesus in union with all the holy Masses being offered up today throughout the world for the holy souls in Purgatory.

Thinking of my own death I asked the Holy Spirit to help me write a prayer which I could recite constantly to keep me close to God and get me to Heaven. The prayer is: Heavenly Father with the help of your Holy Spirit may I lead the best life I can today and when I die please don't send me to Purgatory but may I fall into your loving arms, and on the day of my death may I hear Your Son say to me "I promise you this very day you will be with me in paradise" (Lk. 23:43).

Part 7.2

PURGATORY

What is purgatory? Purgatory is a place or state of suffering inhabited by the souls of sinners who are expiating their sins before going to Heaven. The basis of our belief in Purgatory is scriptural. In the Book of Maccabees (2 Macc. 12:40-46), Judas Maccabeus had noticed that his soldiers that had fallen in a battle had around their necks some idol charms which made him believe that they had not put their full trust in the one true living God. So he ordered a collection to be taken so that sacrifices may be offered in expiation for their infidelity, and he concluded with the words "it is a holy and wholesome thought to pray for the dead that they may be released from their sins".

The unbearable pain that souls in Purgatory suffer is the fact that at this moment they are not able to see the face of God and possess Him. All their yearning is to be with God in Heaven and at this moment it is impossible. They have to wait patiently until all the temporal punishment due from their sins has been wiped away. They are completely helpless and need the mercy of God, the prayers of Our Lady and the saints and our prayers to help them. But we know that they can help us by their prayers. This is the link that is present between those in Heaven, us on earth and the Holy Souls in Purgatory. One thing we can be certain of is that if we, by our prayers and sacrifices, have helped holy souls to get to Heaven when we find ourselves in Purgatory they will be the first ones praying for us and helping us to get to Heaven.

St. Therese of Lisieux who is a doctor of the church has her own view of Purgatory. She maintains that one does not need to go to Purgatory. While still only a novice, she spoke to Sister Maria Philomena, who believed in the impossibility of going to Heaven without first passing through Purgatory. Therese's response was, "You do not have enough trust. You have too much fear before the good God. I can assure you that He is grieved over this. You should not fear Purgatory because of the suffering there, but should instead ask God to take you straight to Heaven. As soon as you try to please Him in everything and have an unshakable trust He purifies you every moment in His love and He lets no sin remain. It is then you can be sure that you will not have to go to Purgatory."

She maintained that we *offend* God if we do not trust Him enough to take us to Heaven as soon as we die. When she found out that her novices talked occasionally that they would probably have to expect to be in Purgatory, she corrected them saying, "Oh! How you grieve me! You do a great injury to God in believing you're going to Purgatory. When we love, we can't go there."

Now, this is a development of the doctrine of Purgatory, but only for those who don't know God, who are not childlike, who don't trust. It is so correct to see things this way. It is true that God will judge us at one point, but He is always and first our Father Who suffers when He has to punish His child and sees him suffering. The child should do His will just out of love, and not to avoid punishment. This really means that God does not want Purgatory! He allows His children to suffer, but only as if He had to look away.

Once St. Therese had a confrontation regarding this topic with Sr. Marie Febronia, who was sub-prioress. She heard that Sr. Therese encouraged her novices to believe that they could go straight to Heaven. She did not like this as she considered this kind of confidence presumptuous, and thus she reproached Sr Therese. Therese tried lovingly and calmly to explain to Sr. Febronia her point of view but with no success as she clung to her belief. For Therese God was more Father than Judge, and she concluded by saying, "My sister, if you look for the justice of God you will get it. The soul will receive from God exactly what she desires."

Soon after this Sr. Marie Febronia died. Three months after her death Sr. Therese had a dream which she related to her Mother Prioress, "Sr. Febronia came to me last night and asked that we should pray for her. She is in Purgatory, *surely* because she had trusted too little in the mercy of the good Lord." Sr. Febronia told her, "You were right. I am now delivered up to the full justice of God but it is my fault. If I had listened to you I would not be here now."

St. Therese also tells us that there are many people who refuse the mercy of God when He offers it. On knowing this she said to the Lord, "If they do not want Your mercy, give it to me. I want it." She maintains that this also helps her to bypass Purgatory. We too can ask God for His mercy which others refuse to accept.

St Gertrude had a tremendous devotion to the holy souls in Purgatory. She said to the Lord, "I want you to give all merits due to me to the holy souls in Purgatory. When she was dying

Satan appeared to her and said "You foolish woman, your hands are empty. What can you offer to God? You have given all your merits to the holy souls in Purgatory". At that moment Jesus appeared and said "Be gone Satan. I myself have come to take Gertrude to Heaven". At one point in her life Jesus taught Gertrude this payer: "Eternal Father I offer you the most precious blood of your divine Son Jesus in union with all the holy Masses being offered today throughout the world for the holy souls in Purgatory". Jesus told her that whenever this prayer is recited, He would release countless souls from Purgatory. This has certainly motivated me in my own ministry to say this prayer many times every day.

Part 7.3

HEAVEN AND HELL

These are my musings of what I think of Heaven. The great St. Paul attempts to tell us what Heaven is like. These are his words. "Eye has not seen, nor ear heard, neither has it entered into the heart of man what things God has prepared for those who love Him" (1 Cor. 2:9). This is Paul's way of telling us about the eternal bliss of Heaven. What God has prepared for us has to be the best, beyond our wildest imagination. Our first meeting with God in Heaven will be mind boggling. I think our meeting with God will be an eternal 'Wow!'

Heaven is a place of eternal peace, joy, and the presence of the divine. Heaven is the ultimate dwelling place of God and the final destination for the righteous after death. Those who reach Heaven are promised direct communion with God, experiencing His love and glory without any barriers. It will be a place of eternal life, free from suffering, pain, and death. Jesus speaks of preparing a place for His followers in heaven (Jn. 14:2-3), often interpreted as having individual dwelling places or "mansions".

Although Heaven will never end, it will just go on and on, we shall never be bored. Even after trillions and trillions of years we will just be beginning to plumb the depths of God's wisdom, knowledge and love. What bliss we shall experience of being loved by Father, Son and Holy Spirit! I just can't wait to be hugged by Mary, our Blessed Mother. All those holy men and women, whom we admired in life and whom we call saints, will be our fellow companions in Heaven. I just can't wait to share their life stories. I know I shall have to apologise to my patron, St. Francis of Assisi for not living up to the high standards of love and poverty that he set for me. I shall realise then just how much he loved the Lord Jesus and me.

My parents were very saintly people and I have no doubt they are in Heaven. How wonderful it will be to be welcomed by them into Heaven. I have thanked God many times a day for the wonderful parents He gave me. But the thought of meeting them again will be wonderful. What happiness it will be to be hugged by them in Heaven. I am looking forward to meeting all my relatives going right back to Adam and Eve. There will be so much I shall learn about their lives, and I will want to thank them for all they did to make me the person I am today, because of their many sacrifices and the example of their lives.

Surely the number of people in Heaven will be countless and we shall have the opportunity of getting to know each one and sharing our experiences.

After describing all this bliss, how foolish would it be for anyone not to spend every moment of their lives on earth loving God and our neighbour so that we attempt to gain entry into Heaven? The sufferings and the pains we endure upon earth will be infinitesimally small compared to the eternal joy we shall possess in Heaven.

I ardently want to get to Heaven and not miss out on what God has prepared for me. I once asked the Holy Spirit to help me write a prayer that I can say daily to keep me close to God and get me to Heaven, and this is the prayers I wrote: "Heavenly Father, with the help of Your Holy Spirit, may I lead the best life I can today. When I die please don't send me to Purgatory, I want to fall straight into Your loving arms and on the day of my death may I hear Your Son say to me, "I promise you this very day you will be with Me in paradise."

These are now my musings about Hell. It is the home of Satan and his angels. These are the ones who rebelled against God in Heaven, saying 'I will not serve'. Hell is a place where there is no love, only hatred. It is no good saying, "If my companion on earth goes to Hell I shall have at least one person who will love me." In Hell you will hate your companion and he will hate you. Hell is a place or state of eternal punishment and suffering for the wicked after death.

Of course the greatest pain of Hell is the knowledge that God is the only One who can make you happy but you have foolishly rejected Him and made it impossible for you to live with Him. Hell is a place of eternal torment and separation from God for those who die in a state of sin without repentance. It is often described as a fiery abyss where souls suffer in perpetuity. This concept is derived from various passages in the Bible, such as the Book of Revelations, which speaks of a "lake of fire," and the Gospels, where Jesus refers to "Gehenna" as a place of punishment.

The terrible thing about Hell is the fact that it is eternal. If you knew that after a trillion years it would end and then followed the bliss of Heaven, it would make Hell bearable. I can remember my mother describing the duration of Hell. She said in Hell there is a clock which says, "Forever and ever".

Our faith teaches us that Hell exists and none of us know how many go there. I don't like those references in the gospel when Jesus says the road to Heaven is narrow and only few take it. Jesus said of Judas, "It were better if that man had never been born" (Mt. 26:24). Is it because Jesus saw Judas sending himself to Hell?

It was never the will of God that anyone should be in Hell. God prepared Heaven to be the home of everyone but our evil lives have prepared Hell as our home. God sends no one to Hell. Those in Hell have sent themselves there. How evil and stupid they must be to do that. If we die in enmity with God and our neighbour we send ourselves to Hell.

What utter ingratitude it is to Jesus for us to go to Hell. He left His home in Heaven to become man like us, die the cruellest of all deaths to save us, and by our sinful lives throw such love back in His face and say "I don't care and I don't love You." If that is our attitude we deserve the eternal fires of Hell. The greatest regret of everyone in Hell is the fact that they did not love Jesus in return. May that never happen to any of us.

Why has Mary our Mother appeared in so many places in our world? It is to encourage us to love her Son and live as He has asked us to do and save us from going to Hell. She taught us at Fatima to say this prayer at the end of every decade of her Rosary, "O Jesus, save us from the fires of Hell and lead all souls to Heaven especially those who are in most need of Your mercy". It breaks her heart if she was to lose any one of her children.

I don't want any of us to lose out of going to Heaven and so every day I earnestly pray, "Heavenly Father, do not consider what we truly deserve but forgive us our sins and lead us all to Heaven there to be happy with You forever."

Part 7.4

AND NOW THE END IS NEAR

I want to consider the end of our physical life and what comes after that. We can define death, theologically, as the moment when the soul leaves the body. But what comes next? "Since men only die once, and after that comes judgement". (Heb. 9:27) In fact, there will be two judgements, one called the Particular Judgement, which we each undergo as individuals, and a final one called the General Judgement, when all that had seemed strange and hidden is at last revealed.

The Church tells us that our Particular Judgement happens at the very moment of death. We do not know what form the judgement will take, but it has been suggested that it is a moment of self-revelation. God illuminates the soul in such a way that we can now see ourselves as God sees us. We recognise the good, -and the bad, -that we have done during our entire lifetime. We therefore know what our destination will be, and what we deserve. From this moment there can be no turning back; this is real food for thought for us now in how we choose to live our lives hereafter.

God's judgement is perfect justice, because He alone is in possession of all the facts about our lives. We cannot judge each other, in fact Jesus warns us not to do so (Mt. 7:1), because we do not see the full picture as God does. Human judgement can be faulty and biased. God knows our circumstances, our weaknesses, our motives, our trials and our hearts. He knows the opportunities and graces we have been offered and whether we took advantage of them. That is why He can judge us in absolute fairness. Were we given particular talents or advantages in life, and if so did we use them correctly? From those who have received much, Jesus tells us, much will be expected (Lk. 12:48). Were we compassionate and forbearing with the faults of other people? Again, Jesus says, "Blessed are the merciful, they shall obtain mercy". (Mt. 5:7)

After the Particular Judgement we shall find ourselves in a place of punishment or reward. You may wonder why there needs to be a second or General Judgement later on. We are told in the Book of Revelations that this will happen at the end of the world, when God winds up the world as we know it. Then our bodies will rise either into glory or damnation. They will now be reunited with our souls.

What will our risen bodies be like? We can only suppose that they will be like the risen body of Christ. They will be perfect, that is to say, all deformities will disappear. They will never suffer anymore from hunger or thirst or pain. Jesus appears to cause us a slight problem when He ate the fish after the resurrection, but He did this to let the apostles know that He had a real body and He was not just a spirit. Our resurrected bodies will be able to travel faster than the speed of light and pass through solid objects. Otherwise our bodies will essentially be the same as the ones we had on earth. What properties the damned bodies will have we just don't know since we have no experience of them.

I think the purpose of this final or General Judgement is to explain some of the things which formerly seemed so obscure and incomprehensible to us. Jesus says, "For everything that is now covered will be uncovered, and everything now hidden will be made clear" (Mt. 10: 26). How often during our lives have we wondered, "How can God allow that to happen?" We may have felt disappointed on some occasions, thinking that God hasn't answered our prayers. Now, at the final judgement, we shall understand how all the pieces fit together into God's great plan.

The General Judgement will give justice to all those who have been falsely accused during their lifetime. There are many of them. Just think of all those who have been put to death, wrongly imprisoned or reputations ruined for crimes they never committed. It is only now we shall realise the heartache these innocent people endured in their lives. The truth in all these things will be revealed. Also the truth will be told about those who appeared to be the pillars of the church or society and were not.

We shall see how our own lives affected other people, and how their actions influenced our lives. We shall understand how God was guiding us and helping us, even when we did not respond to His help. Many mysteries will be explained and many questions answered. No doubt there will be a few surprises, too!

After all this we may presume God will create the new heaven and the new earth. Perhaps this is why we will still need our bodies.

Part 7.5

A NEW HEAVEN AND EARTH?

We have considered what happens to our souls after death, but what about our bodies? We profess in the Apostles' Creed our belief in "the resurrection of the body", yet it seems that even in St. Paul's time this idea puzzled people. "Someone may ask," he says, 'How are dead people raised and what sort of body do they have?" (1 Cor. 15: 35 et seq). Paul answers the query by comparing a plant with its seed. "The thing you sow is not what is going to come." Imagine a daffodil, for example; you sow a small brown bulb and what comes up is a lovely yellow flower. "It is the same with the resurrection of the dead," Paul goes on. "The thing that is sown is perishable but what is raised is imperishable and glorious. And when this mortal nature has put on immortality then death is swallowed up in victory". God will raise our bodies and transform them, far more fundamentally than the daffodil bulb.

Flesh and blood, being perishable, cannot enter God's kingdom. It follows that the bodies we inhabit during our life on earth will have to undergo some kind of change. When our bodies are reunited with our souls they will be recognisably our own bodies but at the same time profoundly altered. They will be incorruptible, no longer subject to decay or suffering. They will be able to pass through solid objects, as Christ did in His risen body. They will be able to move rapidly at the speed of thought.

Our belief in the resurrection of the body is based on Jesus' words to Martha, "I am the Resurrection. If anyone believes in Me, even though he dies he will live." (Jn. 11:25). St. Paul supports this teaching when he says, "Christ in fact has been raised from the dead, the first fruits of all who have fallen asleep." (1 Cor. 15:20). So if we believe in Christ and we try to live good Christian lives we too shall enjoy the resurrection of the body.

The next question which arises is why we should need our bodies and I think there are two possible explanations. First, our human bodies were created by God and He will not destroy what He has made. We know what God thinks of our bodies because when He wanted to redeem us He chose to do this by assuming a human body like our own. It is fitting, too, that our bodies should be raised because during our life on earth they are the temples of the Holy Spirit and He wants us to keep our individual bodies for all eternity, but He changes them into a condition even more wonderful and perfect.

Secondly, as I suggested previously, we may need our bodies in order to inhabit the "new earth" which has been prophesied. As we saw at the very beginning of this series, God's creation was originally perfect. He looked at all He had made and "saw that it was very good". The "Fall" of Adam and Eve had a catastrophic effect not only on mankind but on the whole of creation. All this must be restored, through Christ, so that "everything in the heavens and everything on earth will be brought together under Christ, as head." (Eph 1:10) Like the human race, creation will be "set free from its bondage to decay" (Rom. 8:20) and the world will be restored to the way God made it and intended it to be.

"We have new heavens and a new earth to look forward to, the dwelling place of holiness" (II Peter 3:13). Why should heaven, already perfect, need to be renewed? This is a question which is impossible to answer. The Catechism of the Church tells us that at the end of time, when the Kingdom of

God comes in its fullness, the universe will be renewed. God will prepare a new dwelling place for humankind, a world of harmony, justice and happiness. He will dwell amongst us. Nature itself will be restored to harmony, the lion lying down with the lamb. Perhaps this earth we know now will not be totally destroyed at the end of time but will be re-fashioned into a perfect place and we, in our resurrected bodies, will live in it. Is this partly what we pray for when we say, "Thy kingdom come, on earth as it is in heaven?"

The papal encyclical Gaudium et Spes suggests that we should make every effort to care for and develop this world in which we live. If, indeed, the earth is our future dwelling place then there is all the more reason for us to take care of our environment and protect it from harm. Our efforts, though they may be imperfect, will ultimately be perfected by God.

Jesus once said to His Apostles, "I still have many things to say to you, but they will be too much for you now (Jn.16:12). Has our Heavenly Father treated us in the same way when He has not revealed all about the end of the world? Perhaps it would be too much for us to take in now. Or like a parent I'm sure you will agree He has kept a good many surprises for us. We can only speculate about what the future holds for us.

In the meantime we pray "In your mercy keep us free from sin and protect us from all anxiety as we wait in joyful hope for the coming of Our Saviour Jesus Christ."

Part 7.6

CONCLUSION - REMAIN IN CHRIST'S LOVE

We are now reaching the end of this book on the Catholic faith, and I hope it has been helpful. We have covered a lot of ground together, with a good deal of information and much food for thought. How can we put this into practice? What does it all mean for a Catholic living in Britain in the 21st Century?

Being a Christian has never been easy. Christ Himself said that if we want to follow Him we must take up our cross and carry it every day of our lives. In the 1st Century this might have been literally true, for Christians were often tortured and put to death on account of their faith. During the Reformation Catholics were again persecuted and martyred. Today, thank God, we are no longer in physical danger; but there are dangers and pressures of a different kind.

First, I think there are economic pressures on families today. In former times, a man could earn enough to keep his family without needing both husband and wife to have to go to work. Now, the relationship between income and the cost of living has changed. It seems that in many cases both partners need to be breadwinners in order to pay the mortgage and all the household bills. This can have a detrimental effect on family life. We could, of course, question whether a particular lifestyle is strictly necessary, or whether a simpler one would be more desirable, but that is a decision for individual families. The situation is common to many people in today's society, and Catholics can be all too easily get caught up in the scramble for promotion and the desire for possessions.

Secondly, we Catholics are conscious of being a minority in our society. We are often regarded as rather strange people, even derided as old-fashioned and inflexible. People with whom we work may mock us and our Church, and this can affect our confidence. We may find our Catholic values being undermined in various subtle ways. Churchgoing in general has declined and new habits have been established. If friends and neighbours are enjoying outings at the weekends, and invite us along, it can be very difficult to insist on going to Mass first. It must be particularly hard to persuade children that Mass is more important than a game of football with their friends. Again, when people around us are living together outside marriage, or getting divorced and re-married, it takes a lot of courage to speak up for Catholic teaching and to give the right message to our children.

So, how can a Catholic survive in today's world? Only by staying close to Christ and to His Church. Christ is the way, the truth and the life and He has promised to be with us until the end of time, so whatever problems we face we do not have to cope with them alone. Christ founded His Church to be the means of our salvation and through the ministry of the Church He gives Himself to us in the Sacraments. To maintain our spiritual strength we need to develop a great devotion to the Holy Eucharist and a habit of regular confession. Sunday Mass is a "must", even though it may mean sacrificing a bit of that precious leisure time. Might it be possible to attend a weekday Mass as well? Those who work all week or have children to care for may consider this idea to be impossible for them, because there is simply no time to fit in a morning Mass. Many parishes do not cater for those parishioners who work all day. But what about an evening Mass? If there isn't an evening Mass in your parish, ask your priest if he would consider having one occasionally. He might be pleasantly surprised at the attendance!

The Church is Christ's visible Body and as members of it we need to support and comfort each other. Some parts of the Body may be strong, others weaker, and we should try to be encouraging. The Church must be a place where everyone finds welcome and fellowship. "If you love me," Jesus said, "keep my commandments" (Jn. 14:15). He condensed the Ten Commandments into two, love of God and love of neighbour. This is the challenge He sets us, and we remember that "neighbour" may include those very people who ridicule our faith or are downright hostile towards us.

The final weapon in our armory is (as someone else has said) "education, education, education". If we want to strengthen our faith and defend it confidently we need to learn as much about it as we can. There are plenty of good Catholic books, newspapers, magazines and online sources to help our understanding. This will make our Catholic life more meaningful and our Catholic devotions will not be merely a chore or duty but something we truly love and cherish. We'll also have more confidence, as parents and teachers, in handing on the gift of faith to the next generation.

There is great joy in being a Catholic, and when we remember that Christ is always with us we need never be downhearted.

Ref: 020824/87210/257VM

Printed in Great Britain
by Amazon

55651361R00145